D0900075

KATHERINE MANSFIELD AND HER CONFESSIONAL STORIES

KATHERINE MANSFIELD AND HER CONFESSIONAL STORIES

C. A. Hankin

St. Martin's Press New York

 For information, write:
St. Martin's Press, Inc., 175 Fifth Avenue, New York, NY 10010
Printed in Hong Kong
First published in the United States of America in 1983

ISBN 0-312-45095-8

Library of Congress Cataloging in Publication Data

Hankin, C. A.
Katherine Mansfield and her confessional stories.

Includes bibliographical references.
1. Mansfield, Katherine, 1888–1923—Biography—Character. 2. Mansfield, Katherine, 1888–1923—Criticism and interpretation. 3. Confession in literature. 4. Authors, New Zealand—20th century. Biography. I. Title.

PR9639.3.M258Z68 1982 823′.912 [B] 81-21340
ISBN 0-312-45095-8 AACR2

To those teachers and friends from North America
whose generous encouragement made this book possible
Professors Frederick Crews, Henry Nash Smith,
John Garrett and the late Charles T. Samuels

Contents

PART IV 1918–1923

Preface

The special quality of Katherine Mansfield's writing has kept her work before the public ever since her premature death in 1923. Yet there is a sense in which the nature of her achievement has resisted definition. Different generations of admirers have read her stories, but remained puzzled by their significance. Critics have discussed her inimitable prose, have analysed her technique, and have averred that Katherine Mansfield helped change the direction of the short story in English. Two new biographies have been published. The question that remains unanswered is why a modest body of work, written by a relatively young woman, should continue to fascinate readers of all ages and nationalities.

In 1923 Conrad Aiken offered his opinion as to what distinguished Katherine Mansfield from her contemporaries. 'Far more identifiably than most modern writers,' he said, '[she] used the short story as the medium for undisguised confession. . . . She was at her best when a theme, a scene, a character, most closely and intricately invited her own unclouded confession.'[1] He was right. Greatly influenced in her girlhood by the French diarist Marie Bashkirtseff, Katherine Mansfield belongs in a long line of confessional writers stretching from Rousseau to Proust. Her achievement was to carry the confessional tradition forward into the twentieth century, examining the inner life in a manner which places her among the major psychological writers of her age. Confession, albeit under the guise of fiction, was an inseparable part of Katherine Mansfield's lifelong quest for psychological understanding. Relentlessly, she probed her own conflict-ridden personality, the personalities of her parents – and, by extension, human nature.

Quite deliberately, she wove her stories around her own emotional experiences. Emotion, she once wrote, is what makes a work of art a unity. 'Without emotion, writing is dead; it becomes a record instead of a revelation, for the sense of revelation comes from that emotional reaction which the artist felt, and was impelled to communicate.'[2] Invariably, the revelation which is at the heart of Katherine Mansfield's best stories is psychological. She was impelled to explore and communicate, with remarkable honesty, the unconscious as well as the conscious determinants of human behaviour. Like Freud and D. H. Lawrence, she turned for information about the unconscious mind to her own mind. Even as she used her own dreams and disappointments as the raw material of fiction, however, she employed all the resources of art to disguise, distance and shape her themes. In the process, she created a great variety of characters whose emotions with astonishing skill she examined under the microscope of her art.

Because Katherine Mansfield's unique contribution to twentieth-century literature has not been fully understood, the present study takes as its subject the psychological bases of her stories. Her experiments in the fictional representation of human personality are, I believe, as important in their own way as those of her more celebrated contemporaries: Joyce, Lawrence, and Virginia Woolf. Virginia Woolf possibly knew this when she wrote after her friend's death, 'Katherine's my rival no longer. More generously, I felt, but though I can do this better than she could, where is she, who could do what I can't. . . . And I was jealous of her writing – the only writing I have ever been jealous of.'[3]

In her quest for understanding, Katherine Mansfield again and again looked back to her own beginnings. It was as if only there she could find the clue to her true identity. She was still wondering in 1920: 'Is it not possible that the rage for confession, autobiography, especially for memories of earliest childhood, is explained by our persistent yet mysterious belief in a self which is continuous and permanent?'[4] This study follows her own line of enquiry by starting at the beginning and examining her earliest writing – and emotional reactions. Her youthful stories and poems throw light both on the meaning of her mature fiction, and on the development of her artistic technique. As Murry noted long ago, it is hard to separate Katherine Mansfield's art from her life. Paralleling a discussion of individual stories, therefore, is an account of the emotional experiences they in some way reflect. At the end of her life, what

Katherine Mansfield wanted more than anything else (except health) was to be understood. It seems fitting that an attempt to penetrate the psychological meanings of her stories should also be an attempt to understand the woman who had the courage to write them.

University of Canterbury
New Zealand

C.A.H.

Acknowledgements

I owe a debt of gratitude to Professor F. C. Crews of the University of California at Berkeley, who inspired this study and continued to offer advice and encouragement; and to Professor J. C. Garrett of the University of Canterbury, Christchurch, New Zealand, who helped with his encouragement and valuable checking of the typescript. Other people who generously assisted me are the late Mrs Maude Morris (and her daughter, Susan Graham), Mrs Margaret Scott and Mrs Julian Vinogradoff. I am also grateful to the reference librarians at the University of Canterbury for their assistance, and to the typists and others who gave practical help.

I am indebted to the University of California at Berkeley for the Advanced Graduate Travelling Fellowship which first enabled me to undertake research on Katherine Mansfield's unpublished papers, and to the University of Canterbury for generous research assistance. The Alexander Turnbull Library in Wellington, the Humanities Research Center at the University of Texas at Austin, and the British Museum kindly allowed me to use material in their possession.

Permission to quote from the unpublished letters of Katherine Mansfield and John Middleton Murry has been granted by the Society of Authors on behalf of the Estates of Katherine Mansfield and John Middleton Murry.

PART I

1888–1908

1 Childhood Fantasies

The thoughts and emotions of Katherine Mansfield were dominated by memories of her childhood to an extraordinary degree. Childhood and the continuance of childlike attitudes in the behaviour of adults are themes which echo and re-echo through her writing. In a notebook she fancifully outlined, towards the end of her life, two contrasting versions of the life and death of the little girl who might have been herself.[1] There was first of all the nice, chubby, conventional little girl:

> Once upon a time there was a nice, sweet, chubby little girl. . . . She had never heard of the verb 'to think' and as to 'reason', why it was Greek to her. At last she became so adorably chubby, so ridiculously light-hearted, that she fell down the stairs, and they made her a heavenly funeral, and the most warming little grave you can imagine. And even the undertaker said . . . 'Well, she *was* a dear!'

Then there was the nasty, thin, unconventional little girl:

> And once upon a time there was a nasty, thoughtful, thin little girl. . . . She babbled solely of the verb 'to think' and as to 'reason', it was life to her. At last she became so disgustingly thin, so preposterously wretched, that she fell up the stairs, and they threw her into the darkest, moistest little hole you can imagine. And even the undertaker said . . . 'Well, she *was* a horror!'

That Katherine Mansfield should construct such diametrically opposite portraits of herself as a child is strangely appropriate. Ever since her death arguments have raged about whether she enjoyed a conventionally happy childhood, or whether she was indeed the misfit she describes in her youthful, thinly disguised self-portraits: a rebellious girl, misunderstood and unloved by her family. Her sisters in particular insist that the childhood of all the Beauchamp girls was especially fortunate and happy. Outwardly, the facts seem to verify this. Kathleen Beauchamp was born into a prosperous and socially prominent Wellington family. She had the emotional security of companionship in addition to the security of material comfort. There were two older sisters and a younger brother and sister to play with; her Aunt Belle and her maternal grandmother lived with the family. Not far away were her Aunt and Uncle Waters and their two boys. And there were plenty of opportunities for social outings with friends and neighbours.

Katherine Mansfield's mature stories about her New Zealand upbringing, stories such as 'At the Bay', 'Her First Ball' and 'The Garden Party', support the view of some early critics, as well as the assertion of family members, that she returned so often to the theme of childhood precisely because her own had been so nearly idyllic. Yet her youthful attempts at fiction, generally ignored by commentators because of their artistic inferiority, present a very different picture – a picture as different as that of the two little girls whom Katherine so playfully (or so bitterly) sketched at the end of her life. The inescapable fact is that such early stories as 'How Pearl Button Was Kidnapped', 'New Dresses', 'The Child-Who-Was-Tired' and 'The Little Girl' portray children who are far from happy; and even such later works as 'Prelude', 'A Suburban Fairy Tale', 'Sun and Moon', 'Sixpence' and 'The Doll's House' convey a child's unhappiness or ill-defined anxiety.

At least two people who knew Kathleen Beauchamp as a girl did not see her as a conventionally happy child. The late Tom Mills, a journalist whose opinion of Kathleen's abilities as a writer was sought by her father, once commented,

> Her father confessed to me that he scarcely remembered Katherine Mansfield as a child – too much absorbed in building up the business of Ballantyne and Co. . . . always an L.S.D. man. . . . Katherine once told me that her family took not the slightest notice of her – too busy occupied social climbing. . . . In the latter days of her girlhood Mother took enough interest to read her literary exercises and hear her cello playing. . . . Here is the psychology of the Beauchamp family:

> Father absorbed in making money, mother a social climber, daughters training themselves for the highest station in life aimed at. Only son a nice lad and only natural character in the family, loved by all – the hope and heir of Father.[2]

Margaret Woodhouse, who knew Kathleen at school in London, has recorded,

> She would talk to me for hours about her life (in New Zealand) the wonderful scenery and different flowers, and often of her mother whom she loved very devotedly. But she had bitter resentment against her father and disliked her two 'smart' elder sisters whom she despised and who were quite antipathetic to her. The little brother was too young then to interest her much except as a charming child. I think she liked to nurture her sense of misfortune and evil destiny.[3]

That sense of evil destiny seems to have begun very early in Kathleen Beauchamp's life. Her youthful poems and stories, prefiguring her later writing, abound with expressions of loneliness, alienation and a longing for love – love at almost any cost. Whatever her family actually thought of her, Kathleen imaginatively felt herself to be an unloved, even unwanted child. Outwardly comfortable her life might have been; but the evidence of her writing suggests that inwardly she was acutely disturbed. Katherine Mansfield's biographers generally agree that there were some grounds for her sense of emotional deprivation. She was the third child born in four years to a mother whose fragile health made child-bearing an almost insupportable burden. Consciously the mother may have rejected her new baby when, only a few weeks after the birth, she accompanied her husband on a long sea-voyage to England. Kathleen's grandmother took over responsibility for the infant, loving and nursing it as she did all the other Beauchamp children. But two years later another, sickly, baby arrived and Kathleen had to take second place. Although the new baby lived only three months, the appearance of a rival for grandmother's love made a lasting impression on the child. 'All day, all night grandmother's arms were full', remembered Katherine Mansfield as an adult. 'I had no lap to climb into. . . . All belonged to Gwen.'[4] The birth of two subsequent children made Kathleen the middle one in the family. Her sense of being left out, as she grew up, compounded her sense of being displaced. That displacement she wrote about when she was twenty-one in a poem called 'The Grandmother'.[5] Grandmother is walking under the cherry tree and holding 'Little Brother' in her arms:

He was fast asleep,
But his mouth moved as if he were kissing.
'Beautiful!' said the Grandmother, nodding and smiling,
But my lips quivered,
And looking into her kind face
I wanted to be in the place of Little Brother,
To put my arms round her neck
And kiss the two tears that shone in her eyes.

Katherine Mansfield's juvenilia reveal that already, as a young girl, she had begun expressing her feelings in writing. The poems and stories that survive from her childhood cannot be said to have literary merit; but they do cast valuable light on her development as a writer. To survey the whole spectrum of her writing, from the stories produced in childhood to the later, great stories *about* that childhood, is to see that artistic self-expression was always indissolubly bound up with her emotional life.

By the time she was fourteen, the writing of poetry seems to have offered the lonely girl one kind of substitute for the love she felt denied: in imagination, at least, she could conjure up the attention she craved. The idea of death and illness was particularly attractive, as 'To a Little Child'[6] indicates:

Would I could die as thou
Hast done this day
In childish faith and love
Be ta'en away
Rest, my little one
Flowers on your breast
Safe in the cold earth's arms
Ever at rest.

'Childish faith and love' are doomed to disappointment, the young writer says. It is better to die than to live without love. Something of her own inner grief is expressed in this open death wish, as well as Kathleen's awareness that sickness brought its own rewards. Sickness made her ailing mother even more cherished by those around her; and it had given baby Gwen (before she died) sole possession of the loved grandmother.

Another childhood poem, 'In the Darkness', expresses Kathleen's fantasy that if only she were sufficiently ill she, too, might secure the grandmother's undivided care:

I am sitting in the darkness
And the whole house is still
But I feel your presence
Since I've been ill. . . .

Granny darling, then I want you
For I know you understand
And I yearn for your presence
And to feel you clasp my hand. . . .

And I thought and thought about you
Would you sorrow? Would you care?
When you heard that I was blind
And was left to linger here?

There is a note of melodrama in the sing-song lines, typical of the self-pitying child who imagines herself able, through illness, to blackmail inattentive parents. But there is also a suggestion of very real despair in the yearning for a supportive mother. These sad little poems were written when Kathleen, along with her sisters, was *en route* to boarding school in England. The girl who chronically felt undervalued probably regarded the separation as yet another betrayal. In imagination, her 'you'll be sorry when I'm gone' fantasy was a way of symbolically punishing her parents, of expressing hostility towards them as well as of soliciting love.

At school in England, far away from home and her beloved grandmother, Kathleen continued to seek comfort in the private world of fantasies. The stories she wrote at school exhibit the self-pity and sentimentality which pervade her poetry of the same period. But it is significant that the most interesting of her early attempts at fiction are not the conventional little pieces, such as 'Your Birthday' and 'One Day', in which she tries to write about other people and the ordinary, outside world. Even as a child, Kathleen was most original when she modelled her heroine upon herself and attempted to convey her own inchoate inner life. In form as well as expression, these stories which reflect her innermost feelings are extended fantasies. Through fantasy, she was attempting to create and possess at will what she wanted most: a tender, all-loving mother. The endings of these pieces show, however, that when the young writer tried to reconcile her wishes with the demands of reality, she experienced almost unsuperable emotional and artistic difficulties.

'His Ideal',[7] written when Kathleen was fifteen and revised a year later, is the first extant piece of writing in which a beautiful elusive woman plays a central role. The woman, plainly a surrogate mother, only appears to the nameless hero when he is ill. 'He was but a child when he first saw her, such a wee child, and, ah, so ill, so very ill', the story opens. The narrative continues with a description of the ideal 'magical' figure:

> She was tall, and wore a long white robe, that shimmered like the moonbeams. Her white throat was bare. . . . She leant over him with a face full of tenderness and pity. And he, not knowing, ah! the poor little child, not knowing, stretched out his arms for her to take him up, and soothe him, and hold him to her breast. He was so tired, so very very tired!!

But, as in the poem 'To a Little Child', 'childish faith and love' are doomed to disappointment; and the first part of the story concludes with the magical figure shrinking back and vanishing.

The second part continues with a description of the growing child which might almost be Kathleen recording the effects of fantasy-living upon her own personality: 'He grew unlike other children. He did not play, or laugh, but sat apart, and in silence, always thinking of her, always longing for her.' When as a young man he becomes seriously ill, the lady in white reappears. After this second visit 'he grew more silent, more reserved, living quite by himself. He had indeed seen her, but she had not taken him, although he has longed to go. She had shaken her head, and vanished as before.'

The third and final episode of the story is the one Kathleen considered important enough to rewrite. In the original version the youth became an old man who yearned:

> Ah, for one sight of her. Then the thought flashed across his brain – why not go to the river and fling himself in its depths, and see her again, for always and for ever. And he gave one hoarse cry and then, ah, he saw her again. She stretched out her arms . . . and clasped him to her heart. She held him in her arms as she would a little child, but as her arms touched him he felt all his sorrows, his tears, and his bitterness fade away into the past, become buried with the past. Then he looked up at her: 'Take me with you,' he moaned, 'take me with you.' She looked at him and smiled and clasping him more tightly . . . she took him . . . and her name was Death.

This first version of the story thus ends with the hero attaining his desire through a virtual act of suicide. There is a kind of emotional logic to such a conclusion since the magical woman has only been available to him through illness. Even then he has merely glimpsed her. In life (or in reality) gratification of his longing to find permanent shelter in her arms is impossible, partly because she represents the mother. Through a condensation of meaning, however, the beautiful mother-figure becomes Death personified; the grown-up child can return to the mother, become one with her, only in death.

Kathleen's revision of the story shows that she was not entirely happy with the idea of fulfilment through death. 'Pity him, the old lonely man', she now wrote. 'And as he stood by the bank, a terrible fear rose in his heart. He felt he was going to die. Here alone, all in his terrible loneliness. He could not bear it. He must struggle, he must live. But he felt his strength leave him, and sank to the ground.' As before, the lady appears and takes him. The significance of the alteration is that the hero now no longer *wants* to die; his passive dependence is suddenly transformed into an active struggle to live. Here, at the very end, the author's uncertain attempt to reconcile fantasy with reality has introduced an element of conflict. In the sudden reversal of the hero's desires that this conflict causes, we can detect an incipient glimpse of self-knowledge shared by both character and creator.

For the school magazine a year later Kathleen Beauchamp wrote a story far more emotionally complex which she called 'Die Einsame' ('The Lonely One').[8] A beautiful woman is again central to the fantasy; but this time it is from the woman's point of view that the story is told. The complexity of the work derives in part from the fact that Kathleen has now identified herself with the lady of her dreams: the heroine is at once a magical figure with magical powers – and the fictional representative of the very real author. To a much greater extent than in 'His Ideal', Kathleen's own conflicts and fears are expressed deviously, in symbolism; only if we perceive that the story conveys psychological states which were not fully understood by the author is its meaning comprehensible. But the most important development in this particular fantasy, in view of the stories to be written later on by Katherine Mansfield, is the way in which concrete shape is given to the author's sense of living in two different worlds, one magical and the other real.

The heroine of 'Die Einsame' is depicted as suffering from an acute sense of isolation, and, perhaps in consequence of that, leading a double life. 'All alone she was', the story begins. 'All alone with her soul.' Being 'all alone with her soul' carries the hint of a dual personality: this inner division is further suggested by her inhabiting two distinct worlds of night and day, seashore and forest. The daytime, which the lady spends with the flowers and birds in the forest, seems to symbolise reality. But this is overshadowed in importance by night-time and the lady's night self, or 'soul'. All night the lady wanders by the ocean singing 'with a passionate longing, a wild, mad entreaty . . . the tears streaming down her face':

All, all alone, God, yes, all alone,
No one at all, God, I pray and moan.
Take me, Father, I cannot stay;
God, my God, can'st hear me pray?
All, all alone, God, yes, all alone,
No one to hear me cry and moan.

The night seems to represent the unreal world of dream and fantasy, the realm of the unconscious mind. And the lady's song seems to reflect her unfulfilled desires, the repression of which is conveyed by the complete change that occurs in daytime: 'Thus she would sing all through the night, and when the dawn began to come, she would hasten back to her cottage. Her feet scarce seemed to touch the grass, and there was no trace of her past agony in her face.'

The repression of her desires is apparently the cause of the lady's inner conflict. When she is no longer able to maintain a distinction between unconscious and conscious, between fantasy and reality, she loses her magical omipotence, and the central crisis of the story occurs:

> One night. . . . She felt that all was coming to an end. . . . How weak and exhausted she was as she stole home! . . . The sun sank lower and lower . . . then a sudden fear smote her heart. She feared the silence and the darkness and the forest. Could she reach her cottage before the sun went down?

The heroine's sudden fear of the darkness indicates that the world of dream has become menacing. In the second part of the story, she is depicted as being drawn, fascinated, towards the sea. This appears to be a desperate attempt to break out of her isolation, but it is also a confusion of fantasy with reality which ends in a virtual act of suicide.

There is a remarkable similarity between the ending of this story and that of 'His Ideal'. In both pieces, death is the only solution the author can devise for the dilemma of her central character and in both pieces water is the agent of death. This is revealing, because in these stories, as in the later writing of Katherine Mansfield, there is a close symbolic association between river or sea and the idea of a nurturing mother. Although no mother-figure is actually present in 'Die Einsame', the images of 'boat' and 'moonshine' carry feminine overtones. Thus the appearance of a boat 'fashioned of moonshine' seems to represent symbolically the arrival of a kindly mother come to rescue the heroine. It is the presence of a male 'Figure' on the boat which gives this increasingly dreamlike story a curious turn. The Figure appears to be the materialisation of an earlier participant in the psychic drama being enacted: the omnipotent 'Father' to whom the lady has so often cried out. At first, with 'his arms outstretched, and his lips smiling', he looks beneficent. He proves to be treacherous. For, having lured the heroine away from the comparative safety of the land, he sails away and leaves her to drown. It is as if, by excluding her from the partnership of mother and father, he has brought about her destruction.

'My Potplants',[9] written in 1904, when she was sixteen, is more obviously a revelation of Kathleen's feelings about her parents. The story is a kind of family romance, a fantasy form typical of childhood, in which the real but unsatisfactory parents are replaced by substitutes more in keeping with the child's deepest wishes. As in 'His Ideal' and 'Die Einsame', there is a beautiful woman, a lonely, misunderstood central character, and a final conflict between wish-fulfilment and reality which only death can resolve. But this is a far more self-conscious piece of writing; in it the author introduces herself as the first-person narrator and speaks in a manner which is openly confessional. Katherine Mansfield frequently used memory as the basis of her fiction. In 'My Potplants' memory is used to introduce – and emotionally to distance – the nameless narrator's feelings about an earlier period in her life.

As she gazes at some primrose potplants, the narrator recalls a house she had lived in as a child – a house which seemed to have human characteristics:

> That old house has an extraordinary fascination for me, I always thought of it, as a species of ogre who controlled all our garden and our meadows and our woods. May I go and play in the hayfield today, I used to say, and gaze up timidly at its stern, unblinking face, and it never failed to give me an answer. The great thing about it that puzzled me, was that it never closed its eyes. Poor tired old house, I once remarked, perhaps if I was to lie you down on your back, you could shut your eyes and go for a nice long nap. The day we left that old house, after my father died, all the blinds were down. I stared up at it. The old house had at last fallen asleep, yet its worn weather beaten face seemed to gaze up at me sorrowfully and gently.

In suggesting that the ogre-like house with its stern unblinking face 'lie down . . . and go for a nice long nap', the narrator seems to be displacing a guilty wish for her father's death onto the house in which he lived. The imaginative identity of the two is confirmed – and her wish is depicted as fulfilled – when her father's death coalesces with a sense that the house has 'at last fallen asleep'. Having disposed of her father in this indirect manner, the narrator despatches the rest of her family with: 'My mother died when I was very young, and I had no brothers or sisters'. The way is now clear for her to conjure up and dwell lovingly upon a beautiful surrogate mother who appears out of the woods:

> Someone was coming towards me. . . . It was a woman, dressed in a white soft gown. . . . My heart beat fast, and I felt the colour rush to my face. I never dreamed of her as an ordinary living woman. I thought her a fairy, or a Goddess of the Wood. . . . Then I stretched out my arm and plucked at her dress. She looked at me, startled. O you little child, she said, is this your wood? Why are you here all alone? My nerves were so unstrung I could do nothing, say nothing, but I hid my face in her dress and sobbed wildly, madly. In a moment she was down beside me. She took me on her lap and brushed my thick heavy hair from my hot face and kissed me, and begged me to tell her what was the matter. Nothing, nothing, but they don't understand me, I answered. Who? little one? Nurse and the servants at home. But what about Mother and Father? she answered. Until that moment it had never dawned on me how utterly without people I was. I realised it then, and cried the more. Little by little, I told her all that my life had been. She listened in silence, but at last she said, would you like me to come here every day and talk to you, and be your friend? Yes, yes, I cried. Well, I will, she answered, and now run home. Be good, and you will be happy. I went home slowly, wonderingly. That night as I knelt at my window with the starlit sky above me, I cried, God, God, I love the beautiful white angel you have sent me. All through the summer days we lived together, she and I. I told her all my stories of my flowers and my trees, and she sang to me and read to me and talked to me. All my life seemed to begin anew in a wonderful beautiful way. In all I did, her hand seemed to lead me.

The relationship of the narrator with this desirable but ultimately elusive woman is at the emotional centre of the story. During their idyllic summer together, the narrator enjoys a sense of fulfilment which she experiences as a kind of rebirth. Her physical reactions to the lady imply that her companion is more than just a surrogate mother. In the lady's own loving response to the lonely girl, there is an indication that she combines the roles of protectress and soulmate, mother and lover.

Invariably, Kathleen Beauchamp was unable to bring her fantasy of union with a beautiful woman to a satisfying conclusion when, at the end of her story, she was faced with the need to achieve some kind of reconciliation between dream and reality. In the early part of 'My Potplants' there is a suggestion that the lady of the woods is really a tall lily, brought to life. At the end, the narrator, as if preparing for a sudden return from the world of dream, herself casts doubt upon the lady's reality: 'Are you the Queen of the snow, I whispered, or one of my white white lilies?' Since the question cannot be answered without a more profound self-examination than she is prepared to undertake, the piece closes abruptly:

> Stop! Why do I sit here and dream of all that is past, long past. Life is before. I must step in the ranks and fight with the rest of the world. Fight until Death shall come and hold me close, so close so close, that I cannot breathe, that I cannot move, that I cannot cry. Then ah! then he shall fling me down in the tall sweet bracken of our woods and I shall lie there dead quite dead . . . and wait and wait till she comes to me once again.

The resolution to live and fight in the real world, and the simultaneous conviction that a highly eroticised death will bring fulfilment, is evidently a dangerous attempt to establish a truce between the warring elements of the author's personality: dangerous because she now wishes for death in real life instead of in the context of dream. From the psychological point of view this is understandable: the inadmissable nature of her fantasies, especially the barely concealed wish for the death of her parents, would evoke a need for absolution through punishment. Perhaps because she was dealing more openly with conflict-ridden material in this piece, Kathleen Beauchamp seems to be groping towards some concept of form, some framework at the beginning and end of the narrative which would contain and enclose her fantasies. The need for an artistic framework explains the function of the primroses, which introduce the memory of other flowers, such as the lily. As if mindful of this, and of the death of her dream, the author adds a final line: 'Ah! my poor little primroses in the blue dish, they have withered and died.'

2 The Pains of Adolescence

Kathleen Beauchamp's sense of inhabiting two separate worlds, the world of dream and the world of reality, she depicted haltingly but clearly in 'Die Einsame' and 'My Potplants'. Writing from school in 1903, she spoke almost openly to her cousin, Sylvia Payne,[1] of what was, in effect, her dual personality:

> I like you much more than any other girl I have met in England and I seem to see less of you. We just stand upon the threshold of each other's heart and never get right in. What I mean by 'heart' is just this. My heart is a place where everything I love (whether it be in imagination or in truth) has a free entrance. It is where I store my memories, all my happiness and my sorrow and there is a large compartment in it labelled '*Dreams*'. There are many many people that I like very much but they generally view my public rooms, and they call me false, and mad, and changeable. I would not show them what I was really like for worlds. They would think me madder, I suppose.

In singling out her cousin as a confidante, Kathleen was seeking a friend who would play in real life the role assigned to the lovely lady of her dreams. Kathleen's letter indicates that she felt most truly herself, most at home, in the world of her private fantasies or dreams. Her real self – her 'heart' – must be hidden from the general gaze because she feared the censure of those who, not understanding, called her 'false, and mad, and changeable'. All the same, she needed someone who would know both sides of her personality and accept her as she really was. And so Kathleen tried to explain herself to Sylvia, to win Sylvia's heart so that she could pour out her innermost feelings to her cousin, if not to others. The need was all the more urgent because already Kathleen felt driven to put on a mask in public and play the role that seemed expected. 'Don't think I mean half I look and say to other people', she later admitted to Sylvia. 'I cannot think why I so seldom am myself. I think I rather hug myself to myself, too much.'

Kathleen's role-playing in public was a defence which would protect her vulnerable, inner self from exposure and condemnation. The problem was that while her inner life with its important compartment labelled 'Dreams' had to be carefully guarded, this same inner life she felt a great compulsion to confess. 'Misunderstood',[2] one of her schoolgirl stories, reveals Kathleen in the act of discovering that a real solution to her dilemma lay in artistic self-expression. Art was a perfect outlet for the feelings: it was a means of confessing the fantasies harboured by the hidden self; it was also a means of obtaining forgiveness, acceptance and even approval of these fantasies. Under the cloak of fiction, moreover, she could be both known and not known.

'Misunderstood' contains the familiar motifs of the sick child, the parentless child and the parent surrogate. But, whereas in 'My Potplants' Kathleen had been at pains to divest herself of parents, the child heroine in 'Misunderstood' resolutely denies all knowledge of parents or home. Even more important, the fantasy centres not on a longed-for mother surrogate whose permanent embrace might be secured only in death, but on a surrogate father with whom a positive relationship might be established. 'One of the most beautiful and also one of the most eccentric children who had ever entered the Hospital', the protagonist of the story is set apart from those around her. She 'would sit hour by hour moving her right hand up and down as though wielding a bow, and singing a weird indescribable accompaniment'. One afternoon, as 'the little musician' is singing and playing in her cot, a patron of the hospital, an 'intensely musical' bachelor, stops and listens to her:

> When the last note had died away, Lord Hunter, strangely excited, spoke to the nurse. Who was she? Her name? Her age? . . . then the old man leant over the child. 'It was very sad', he said. 'Where did you learn that?' The little one looked up and seeing his kindly old face and sympathetic eyes she said, 'I didn't learn it, I just thought it'.

'Misunderstood' marks a clear step forward in Kathleen Beauchamp's handling of her emotional and artistic problems. For the first time, she is able to imagine a central character modelled upon herself who is not obsessed with the need for love. This heroine, by declaring that she is without home or parents, is spared the anxiety-ridden task of divesting herself of unsatisfactory parents before replacing them with better ones. She is free to take on an identity of her own, to become her own creator, as it were. The real source of the heroine's freedom is her possession of artistic genius. The power to create in others 'a sense of awe and wonder' gives her a degree of control over fate; it also brings the recognition of a kindly and powerful surrogate father. Kathleen, in asserting so affirmatively the value of artistic ability, seems to have replaced her obsessive desire for mother-love with a healthier wish for the approbation of her father. Healthier, because in contrast to the fantasy of union with a mother-figure, which necessarily entailed death, the dream of recognition by a father-figure was life-sustaining. Since she had found a solution which was viable in life as well as in day-dream, then, the author at the end of this story forgot her heroine's sickness and allowed her to live.

It was no accident that Kathleen Beauchamp chose a musician as the central figure in 'Misunderstood'. At the age of thirteen she had met and conceived a romantic passion for Arnold Trowell, a New Zealand child musical prodigy who was sent to study in Europe. For the next few years he remained to her a symbol of escape from irksome reality into the magical world of art and freedom. Even so, Kathleen's fantasies involving beautiful women suggest that, as an adolescent, her emotional intensity was directed more towards relationships with her own sex. Biographers indicate that, in spite of a tendency to withdraw from the crowd, Kathleen was not backward about selecting a few girls upon whom to bestow her special friendship. Ruth Mantz records that when Kathleen was ten she singled out a Canadian girl, Marion Ruddick, and later Maata, a half-caste Maori princess. At Queen's College there was a close friendship with Vere Bartrick-Baker, or 'Mimi' as Kathleen called her. Miss Mantz quotes Mimi as recalling, 'Katherine Mansfield and I had long discussions over Tolstoi, Maeterlinck, Ibsen in the lower corridor. We came an hour early for them, and were suspected of immorality.'[3] There was also Sylvia Payne, who probably did not entirely reciprocate her cousin's affection. Kathleen wrote to her in 1906, 'I have always wanted us to be friends – and we never seem to pass a certain point – once a term – perhaps – I feel "Sylvia and I really know each other now", and next time we meet – the feeling is gone.' The intensity of Kathleen's feelings may have kept her cousin aloof; but it had the opposite effect upon another Queen's College schoolfriend, Ida Baker. With Ida perhaps more than with any other, Kathleen Beauchamp could display herself in all the variety of her moods and remain secure in the knowledge that she would be loved, not criticised. Ida it was who in real life filled the roles of devoted mother, confidante, and loving companion. When Kathleen symbolically adopted a new identity with the pseudonym 'Katherine Mansfield', Ida followed suit and chose the name 'Lesley Moore'.

Kathleen's schooldays came to an end and her parents journeyed to England to escort their daughters home. At first Kathleen did not seem unhappy about her imminent return to New Zealand. To Sylvia Payne she wrote:

> A great change has come into my life since I saw you last. Father is greatly opposed to my wish to be a professional 'cellist or to take up the 'cello to any great extent – so my hope for a musical career is absolutely gone . . . but I suppose it is no earthly use warring over the Inevitable – so in the future I shall give *all* my time to writing. There are so many opportunities for a girl in New Zealand. She has so much time and quiet. . . . Do you love solitude as I do – especially if I am in a writing mood – and will you do so – to – write I mean in the future. . . . I am so keen upon all women having a *definite* future – are not you? The idea of sitting still and waiting for a husband is absolutely revolting – and it really is the attitude of many girls. . . .
>
> It made me rather smile to read of you wishing you could create your fate. O how many times I have felt just the same. I just long for power over circumstances. . . .
>
> Would you not like to try all sorts of lives – one is so very small – but that is the satisfaction of writing – one can impersonate so many people.

For all Kathleen's apparent acceptance of a return to New Zealand, the seeds of family conflict are evident in her letter. Determined now to be a writer, Kathleen in her Pateresque desire to 'try all sorts of lives' could hardly be satisfied in her own country. Nor, at home with her family, would there be much chance to create her own fate, or to exercise 'power over circumstances'. In fact, during the intervening months she became convinced that she must remain in England. And when her father emphatically refused to consider such a proposition her resentment against him grew. As her dislike of him increased she wrote the last of her schoolgirl fantasy pieces and gave vent to a new fear.

'Les Deux Étrangères',[4] written shortly before the family left England, depicts a small girl called Fifi very sick in bed. Nursed lovingly by her mother in the daytime, Fifi is frightened of the whispering dark. One night, after she has confused the words of a hymn in her evening prayers – 'Jesus was that Father mild, Mary was his little child' – and begged Jesus's forgiveness for such an enormous offence, she is visited by two figures: 'One tall and dark – wrapped in a great flowing cloak with a grass cutter in his hand (she knew it was a grass cutter because Daddy had one in the summer) and the other – very small and pale – with little wings wrapping him round. . . .' The tall figure spoke in a deep voice:

> 'We have come a long journey in the dark and are very very tired. We have searched through all the rooms – but you are the smallest and you have the largest bed. Will you make room for one of us to sleep with you tonight?'
>
> Fifi looked at him meditatively. 'You are too big', she said, shaking her head, 'but the little one . . .' 'Oh' cried the sombre figure, 'I would fold you round in my great mantle – it is so soft and restful – and you would lie quite still – forget you had ever felt pain – and fall asleep.'
>
> Fifi considered. 'The little one is so cold', she said. 'You are really too big for my little bed.'
>
> 'I would carry you in my strong arms – and show you wondrous things' cried the tall figure, advancing nearer. 'But you might hurt me with your grass cutter', and her tears fell fast. 'I am so sorry to be nasty', she sobbed, 'but please, dear dark man, go away – I would like the little baby one.'

So he folded his great mantle round him and strode softly from the room. . . .

The child's sickness and the appearance of a dreamlike figure recall Kathleen's earlier writing. A notable difference is that the figure is not a desirable woman with whom the protagonist seeks union but a man, from whose physical closeness she shrinks. As in 'Die Einsame', the male figure seems to offer comfort to the heroine; but in this story she is not deceived. Perceiving his offer to be a source of danger, she rejects it fearfully. Since the figure's request is to share the little girl's bed, and since her fear is that he might hurt her with his 'grass cutter', it is likely that the threat she senses is a sexual one. The earlier references to 'Jesus . . . that Father mild' and to her father's ownership of a grass cutter imply, moreover, that the figure represents her father.

Kathleen's feelings about her father were complicated by the fact that she had reached the stage of being physically aware of the opposite sex. Before leaving England, she had visited Arnold Trowell in Brussels and her old passion for him, born out of admiration, had been rekindled. But, as her notebooks indicate, she knew only too well that her infatuation was not reciprocated. Possibly Arnold's rejection of her as a mate coalesced in her mind with a corresponding rejection by her father. For, at the very time when she was turning towards her father for the love and understanding she had formerly craved from her mother, he chose not to support, but to obstruct, her plans. Kathleen's one hope of attaining emotional independence, as she had intuitively expressed it in 'Misunderstood', was to achieve success as an artist. Yet Harold Beauchamp, instead of showing sympathetic appreciation as the fictional Lord Hunter had done, at first offered only resistance. What the symbolism of 'Les Deux Étrangères' suggests is that paternal domination was becoming inseparable in Kathleen's mind from sexual domination, and that she was beginning to associate sexual relations with pain.

The hostility Kathleen now felt towards men she put into words in the course of the long voyage back to New Zealand. Recorded in her journal are angry feelings towards her father that mount to a crescendo of almost paranoic hate and physical revulsion:

> They [her parents] are worse than I had even expected. They are prying and curious, they are watchful and catlike and they

> discuss only food. They quarrel between themselves in a hopelessly vulgar fashion. My Father spoke of my returning as damned rot, said look here, he wouldn't have me fooling around in dark corners with fellows. His hands, covered with long sandy hair, are absolutely evil hands. A physically revolted feeling seizes me. He wants me to sit near. He watches me at meals, eats in the most abjectly, blatantly vulgar manner that is describable. . . . He is constantly suspicious, constantly overbearingly tyrannous . . . I cannot be alone or in the company of women for five minutes – he is there, eager, fearful, attempting to appear unconcerned, pulling at his long drooping red-grey moustache with his hairy hands. Ugh!

Deliberately defiant, Kathleen vented her feelings in at least one shipboard romance: 'It is not one man or woman that a musician desires – it is the whole octave of the sex', she wrote in her journal, 'And R. is my latest. . . . When I am with him a preposterous desire seizes me, I want to be badly hurt by him. I should like to be strangled by his firm hands.' As her father's 'evil hands' had particularly revolted her, one can surmise that the masochistic fantasy of being strangled might well have derived from childhood memories – or fantasies – of receiving punishment from her father; punishment which was at once a source of pain and gratification. The reverse side to these fantasies of being hurt by the male sex was a desire to inflict suffering. Thinking about 'R.' in connection with a forthcoming ball, Kathleen wrote in her journal, 'I shall fight for what I want, yet I don't definitely [know] what that is. I want to upset him, stir in him strange depths. He has seen so much, it would be such a conquest.'

But there could be no such conquest of her father as Kathleen had planned for 'R.'. Her ambivalent feelings towards the most dominant male figure in her life were expressed instead, in a barely disguised wish for his death. Conveyed only obliquely in 'My Potplants', this wish became the specific subject of a notebook fragment entitled 'Juliet Delacours'.[5] It is Juliet Delacours' fourth birthday and she is playing with a chocolate-filled china teapot beside her father, who lies stretched out in an invalid's chair. 'To make him better', she offers him the china teapot to hold, but it falls to the ground: he is dead. The most startling aspect of this piece is Kathleen's depiction of the child's last encounter with her father: 'She was loathe to kiss the white face from upon the little bed. For a moment she shrank back frightened – but then leaned forward – and so they lay, a little space, warm cheek against cold cheek – and the lilies smothering both.' Once he is dead and powerless to hurt her, Kathleen can imagine the affectionate embrace of father and daughter. The love which now replaces hostility can be the more openly expressed because death itself effectively masks any incestuous overtones. Indeed, there is a sense in which Juliet's sharing of her father's funeral flowers symbolises her sharing in his death. This is significant because in the fantasies involving a beautiful woman, union or the fulfilment of the central characters' wishes could only occur in the context of death.

The idea of death as fulfilment, first enunciated in the schoolgirl poems, was apparently losing none of its attraction for Kathleen Beauchamp. Indeed, her writing indicates that as she matured it came to represent psychological states of increasing complexity. At about the same time as she was imagining her father's death, for example, Kathleen was also indulging in fantasies in which physical suffering was openly experienced as pleasurable. In one fragment the heroine ponders her own nature: 'I like riding down this road with the sun hurting me', she mused. 'I'll love anything that really comes fiercely – it makes me feel so "fighting", and that's what I like.' Yet another piece depicts 'Kathie', who 'wished that there were great thorns on the bushes to tear her hands. "I want a big physical sensation", she said, and then she ran back to her room and looked at herself in the long glass. The same Kathie as long ago – but yet not the same.'

As psychologists have often observed, there seems to be a connection between fantasies involving another's death and fantasies of one's own suffering. It is as if the mind unconsciously punishes hostile wishes, especially against family members, as though they were actual deeds. Attempting to ease its burden of imagined guilt, the psyche may turn destructively against itself with fantasies of suicide. Katherine Mansfield was to indulge in just such a fantasy in 1915, after her brother's death.

'What You Please', a story fragment written in 1906, strangely anticipates that unhappy set of circumstances. Without bothering to change the names of herself, her brother and sister, Kathleen carries to an extreme the idea of her own physical suffering.

The piece opens with the heroine, Kathie, wallowing melodramatically in self-pity after an accident:

> And another night was over, and another day came. Kathie lay still and watched the light creep into her room, slowly and mournfully. . . . Suddenly she buried her face in the pillows. 'O God, O God, O God' she cried, and then 'No, you damned old hypocrite, I won't shout at you.' She laughed suddenly. 'Dear Mr Death, would you kindly send round a sheet this morning as there is a large parcel awaiting your convenience.' Then she lay with her face towards the window, and cried – hopelessly, madly. Long shudders passed through her. She grew icy cold – only her left hand under its bandages seemed to burn into her like a white hot iron. 'I shall go mad, mad, mad' she moaned. 'Here me somebody. Is the whole place dead? Listen – damn you all – I'm ruined – and there the devils lie in their beds and dream and say "Never mind dear, you can always *write*." O the simpering brainless idiots. I shall commit suicide.'

The heroine's recollection of the accident reveals that, at the request of her little brother, Leslie, she lighted a firecracker, which exploded, blowing off all the fingers on her left hand. The injury does not affect her writing hand, however, and the vigour of the piece conveys the impression that the young author derived considerable satisfaction from thus visualising the maiming. Suffering has increased Kathie's narcissistic sense of importance: 'Then she looked at her reflection in the mirror above. A long thin face, lines of suffering deeply engraved by the Artist Pain, an extraordinary pallor in her cheeks and lips. "That is Kathie" she said hoarsely.' Suffering has also made her the centre of attention amongst her own family. For when Kathie recovers sufficiently to ask for a newspaper, 'Mother, almost unbelieving, rushed into the girls' room and told them, and the three of them clung together and then went in to see her.'

The fact that the injury was unwittingly caused by her brother, one of the two males in the family, and that the narrative breaks off with the heroine making furtive plans to attend a concert which features a musician resembling Arnold Trowell, seems to link the fantasy with Kathleen's reaction to being hurt by the men in her life. By directing her aggressive wishes against herself, she achieves a degree of compensation: the imagined injury is a punishment for her own destructive impulses, and as such it relieves the burden of guilt; more satisfyingly, the concept of herself as the victim of another's violence places the author in a position of moral superiority. It is as if in fantasy the tables have been turned, with the objects of her anger becoming themselves the guilty ones. In this situation, righteous indignation can be enjoyed to the full.

3 'Juliet': an Autobiographical Experiment

The emotional turmoil of Kathleen Beauchamp's adolescence is best indicated in the disjointed fragments of a would-be autobiographical novel, 'Juliet'.[1] Begun in May 1906 when she was seventeen and left unfinished, 'Juliet' consists of twenty sections of varying length covering about twenty printed pages. Here Kathleen sought to assemble the conflicting threads of her life; but it is indicative of her confusion that she was not able to impart any coherence to the disconnected episodes. Although 'Juliet' eddies around the relationship of the heroine and the musician David, the emotional preoccupations of the work are very much those of the author's earlier writing. That she was still deeply divided between the unreal world of her fantasies and the real world is evident from the opening section, where Juliet is depicted brushing her hair in front of a mirror and admiring her reflection. Out of harmony with her family, Juliet has established an intimacy with her own mirror face:

> Since her very early days she had cultivated the habit of conversing . . . with the Mirror face. Her childhood had been lonely, the dream-face her only confidante. . . . Juliet was the odd man out of the family – the ugly duckling. She had lived in a world of her own, created her own people, read anything and everything which came to hand, was possessed with a violent temper, and completely lacked placidity.

The characterisation of Juliet as a dreamer who 'lived in a world of her own' is reminiscent of the letter in which Kathleen wrote about the 'large compartment labelled "*Dreams*" ' kept concealed from most people. But when she shows Juliet selecting her own 'mirror face' as a confidante, she is near to depicting a well-known psychological phenomenon in which the mirror face becomes a kind of alter ego, or double, that provides a reassuring substitute for the approving glances of a loved person. In choosing her own mirror face as a confidante, then, Kathleen was in part trying to shed her dependence upon such friends as Sylvia Payne as well as upon the mother who was unavailable. Unconsciously she appears to have understood this, for the account of the mirror face in 'Juliet' is followed by an unflattering description of her parents:

> The Mother was a slight pale little woman. She had been delicate and ailing before her marriage and she never could forget it. Margaret and she looked after the babies – and Mr Wilberforce, a tall grey bearded man, with prominent blue eyes, large ungainly hands, and inclining to stoutness. He was a general merchant, director of several companies, chairman of several societies, thoroughly commonplace and commercial.

The self-confessed 'ugly duckling' of a family that had no time for her, Juliet compensates by believing that 'it was always, would always be the third who was the favourite of the Gods. The fairy tales that she devoured voraciously during her childhood helped to stimulate the thought.' When Juliet does emerge from her private world of fantasy, it is only to act a part, to pretend to conform while inwardly feeling hostile. Accordingly, the heroine is depicted as going to a party where 'for two hours she played as vigorously as the rest of them, inwardly rebelling and very satisfied when the clock pointed to five minutes to ten'. Like her creator, Juliet watches and makes fantasies not only about herself but also about other people. Indeed, Kathleen Beauchamp could almost have been describing the genesis of her own creative impulse when she depicts how, while her parents were entertaining, Juliet 'curled herself up in a corner of the sofa and watched the people with amusement and interest. She liked to listen to little pieces of conversation, create her idea of their lives'.

Fantasy can be a retreat from life, but when reordered as fiction it can also be a means of containing or defusing emotional conflicts. Deeply wounded by Arnold Trowell's lack of romantic interest in her, Kathleen cast him as a central character (named David) in 'Juliet' and proceeded to arrange and rearrange in her own mind the past and future course of their relationship. Her description of their first meeting suggests that Arnold was now less a real person than a figment of her imagination. For David, talking loftily of 'the Music of the Spheres' with a 'face full of compassion and yet joy', bears a remarkable resemblance to the other worldly figures of the fantasy pieces. Like those figures, he appears to combine the roles of kindly and compassionate parent, companion, soul-mate and now, it is hinted, of lover. The meeting with such a person has a transforming effect upon the heroine's life: at home that night, 'sleep was impossible. The whole world had changed, and he was coming again tomorrow night, and she should hear him play.' Her isolation bridged by one who appears to share her world, Juliet gains new confidence and security. Out on the hills the next day

> vague thoughts swept through her – of the Future, of her leaving this little island and going so far away, of all that she knew and loved, all that she wished to be. 'O I wish I was a poet' she cried, spreading out her arms. 'I wish I could interpret this atmosphere, this influence. . . . I am so strong' she said, 'and the strong are never hurt. It is always the weak who are pained.'

Most of the remaining sections deal with Juliet some four years later, struggling to create 'Art' in a semi-bohemian London environment; and they show how very tenuous in fact her strength and confidence are. Without David now, or any other powerful supporting figure, Juliet, like the protagonists of earlier fantasy pieces, instinctively seeks escape in oblivion or death. 'Juliet stumbled up the stairs', begins one brief episode:

> The room was flooded in the cold light of the moon. . . . A long shudder went through her and she fell heavily on to the floor. She was conscious as she lay there. Why didn't I strike my head on the fender, she thought. I'm not hurt a bit. I shall have to get up again and then it will be day. . . . A wheel began to go round and round and round in her head . . . and she fell.

In a later episode, Juliet's weakness is examined more fully and connected explicitly with the loss of David from her life:

> An extraordinary weakness stole over her. She was dying softly, softly, like the day. . . . 'O – O,' she said, 'How weak I am. How I ought to be full of strength, and rejoicing all the day'. . . . A great wave of bitter sweeping memories broke over her and drowned all else. Where was he now? What was he doing? . . . Nothing was known. She shook from head to foot with pain and anger with herself. . . . Would she never be strong enough to stand absolutely alone?

This passage ends with David miraculously appearing. In later episodes Kathleen Beauchamp was more honest with herself; but, predictably, she could imagine no possible alternative to his affection except death. Death was one way of negating unpleasant reality. It also served the purposes of illness in the earlier works, where the fantasy of near-death was a demand for love and an attempt to punish those who had rejected and hurt her.

Since the rejection suffered by Juliet is, in a sense, a sexual one, Kathleen has her heroine die of a sexually inflicted injury. By a kind of displacement, however, it is not David but his friend Rudolf whose seduction indirectly kills her. When Juliet visits David, but finds only Rudolf at home, she has a premonition of danger: 'for some inexplicable reason she felt afraid of him. . . . She could not trust herself to speak to him. He is a fiend, she thought – a perfect fiend. How can he look at me like that?' But, fascinated, Juliet allows herself to be drawn into conversation, and, as Rudolf plays *Tannhäuser* on the piano, he charges her with being inhibited by convention:

> 'Live this life, Juliet. Did Chopin fear to satisfy the cravings of his nature, his natural desires? . . . His face was mad with passion, white with desire. 'Leave me alone' said Juliet. She raised her eyes to his face, and his expression caused her to suddenly cease struggling and look up at him dumbly, her lips parted, terror in her eyes. 'You adorable creature' whispered Rudolf, his face close to hers. 'You adorable creature – you shall not go now . . .' She felt the room sway and heave. She felt that she was going to faint. 'Rudolf, Rudolf', she said, and Rudolf's answer was 'At last.'

The aftermath of this scene is that Juliet becomes pregnant–

and dies. Dwelling on her heroine's death with Victorian sentimentality, the young author portrays Juliet's friends David and Pearl (who have now married) lamenting at the bedside:

> Out of the dark two voices came. 'It cannot be long now.' 'But it is for the best. If she *had* lived, what could have happened?' 'I begin to believe there must be a merciful God.' 'I, too.' She opened her eyes, and saw the two beside her. 'Ought I to join your hands and say bless you?' she whispered. Suddenly she raised herself. 'O – o – I want to live' she screamed. But Death put his hand over her mouth.

What makes Juliet's death more than mere melodrama is its psychological significance. Repeated in the essential details of the narrative is the central fantasy of 'His Ideal' and 'Die Einsame': a loved but elusive figure, who has at least some of the characteristics of a tender and supportive parent, cannot or will not respond to the heroine's insistent demands for reciprocal love. As almost a direct consequence, the heroine dies. In one sense, then, the death is another version of the childish fantasies, 'You'll be sorry when I'm dead', and 'See, you have killed me and you'll be punished.' The presence of the two mourners at Juliet's deathbed seems to confirm this. David and Pearl have replaced the rejecting parents, and condemnation of their wayward child's behaviour is implicit in the whisper: 'But it is for the best.' That Kathleen's alter ego does not really want to die is revealed by her final scream, 'O – o – I want to live'. Indeed, it is the heroine's cry to be rescued when she realises that she has carried the game too far, as it were, that links this conclusion so decisively with the conflict-ridden endings of 'His Ideal' and 'Die Einsame'.

The death of Juliet suggests a child's fantasy of punishing parent-figures. There is also a sense in which death represents the heroine's self-punishment for her not altogether unwilling participation in an illicit sexual relationship. The sequence of events in the narrative implies an association in the author's mind between sexuality, violence and death; and another section of the 'Juliet' manuscript confirms such an interpretation. Juliet, now living with her friend Pearl, is in a 'mood'. To Pearl's query, 'You feel sexual', she responds, 'Horribly – and in need of a physical shock or violence. Perhaps a good smacking would be beneficial.'

The sequences of 'Juliet' are disjointed because Kathleen Beauchamp was testing out in fictional form the various courses of action open to her if she were to gain her dearest wish and live in London. The heroine's acknowledged dependency makes emotional support essential: 'I say I am independent – I am utterly dependent. I say I am masculine – no-one could be more feminine. I say I am complete – I am hopelessly incomplete', Juliet admits to herself. But there is an alternative to the unobtainable relationship with David, and to the death which follows his rejection: a marriage-like arrangement with Pearl. Two separate episodes explore this idea. In one, Juliet, rebelling against 'the Suitable Appropriate Existence' with her family, writes to Pearl,

> Pearl I am coming. Understand I answer now for good and for all . . . I don't know why I have hesitated so long. . . . What has held me back from coming has been I think, principally, the thought that we are not to be together for a week or a month or a year even but for all times. It is rather immense and requires consideration.

Another section depicts the two girls reviewing the advantages of their life together:

> 'Our friendship is unique' said Vere [Pearl]. . . . 'Nothing could separate us, Juliet. All the comforts of matrimony with none of its encumbrances, hein?' 'My word yes! As it is we are both individuals. We both ask from the other personal privacy, and we can be silent for hours when the desire seizes us.' 'Think of a man always with you. A woman cannot be wholly natural with a man – there is always a feeling that she must take care that she doesn't let him go.' 'A perpetual strain' . . . 'Ugh' said Juliet. . . . 'I loathe the very principle of matrimony. It must end in failure, and it is death to a woman's personality.'

It would appear that Juliet's principal reason for preferring a relationship with Pearl to one with a man is relief from the 'perpetual strain' which is associated with rejection anxiety. But a number of sections devoted to her obsession with David indicates that the solution offered by Pearl is by no means the simple answer. For one thing, Juliet's very preoccupation with throwing off her parents' conventional attitudes shows that the influence of this family background is still strong. Rebel though she might against 'the Suitable Appropriate Existence, the days full of perpetual Society functions, the hours full of clothes discussions, the waste of life', Juliet cannot disregard with emotional impunity the moral codes inherent in such a way of life. Rudolf detects this; and in the scene leading up to his seduction of Juliet seems to put her own doubts into words. As he analyses her conflicting attraction to, and fear of, the bohemian way of life, Rudolf seems virtually the personification of one side of her ambivalent nature:

> You are too conventional. . . . Yes you are more conventional than a child from a convent school. Also you never allow your feelings to run away with you. . . . It is the heritage from your parents. . . . You have fought against it, but voilà there it is, always conquering you. You are afraid of everything, and you suspect everybody. . . . Live this life, Juliet. . . . Why do you dwarf your nature, spoil your life? If you were a man you would be a teetotaller, and then a Revivalist.

Seen in psychological terms, the puritanical attitudes which Rudolf accuses Juliet of inheriting from her parents can only make more acute her sense of inner division. For the price of flouting sexual convention – whether with a man or with a woman – is such guilt and self-accusation as would, by a kind of grim logic, make death seem the only way out. But, as Kathleen's earlier writing indicates, death was also a means of returning to the arms of a loving mother. In 'Juliet' she found a curious solution, both to the problem of the protagonist who is torn between the attractions of life and death, and to that of the heroine who seeks the affection of both man and woman. For in one brief section she writes, 'David and Pearl were married as soon as [they] reasonably could be after Juliet's death, and a year and a half later, when a girl child was born, they both decided she should be christened after "poor Juliet".' Thus in fantasy, the complex of relationships has come full circle: Juliet has been symbolically reborn as the daughter of the two she loved the most. David, who first gave her the compassionate understanding she might have expected from a father, has become her father; and Pearl, who bestowed the attentions of a mother, is made to assume her mother's role.

In terms of its emotional preoccupations, 'Juliet' is a bridge between the writing of the adolescent Kathleen Beauchamp and that of the adult Katherine Mansfield. An unhappy or unsatisfactory relationship between male and female, such as that experienced by Juliet with David, is central to a great many of the mature stories: the theme appears in the *German Pension* collection and in such diverse works as 'The Woman at the Store', 'Prelude', 'Bliss', 'Je Ne Parle Pas Français', 'Mr Reginald Peacock's Day' and 'The Man Without a Temperament'. The association of sexuality with violence also recurs, both in comparatively early stories such as 'Frau Brechenmacher Attends a Wedding', 'At Lehmann's' and 'The Woman at the Store', and in the later 'Prelude', in which Linda Burnell fears her husband's physical advances. Childbirth kills Juliet: it is feared and hated by Sabina in 'At Lehmann's', by the woman in 'The Woman at the Store', by Linda Burnell in 'Prelude' and 'At the Bay'. The emotional alternative of a close relationship between two women, which is put forward in the episode centring on Juliet and Pearl, appears in altered form in 'Bains Turcs' and 'Bliss'; while the inability of the heroine 'to stand absolutely alone' is depicted in numerous stories, including 'The Little Governess' and 'Psychology'.

4 Forbidden Love

At home in New Zealand in 1907, Kathleen was out of harmony with her family and without the soulmate who, as 'Juliet' indicates, was so essential to her well-being. 'It is a nightmare', she wrote to Sylvia Payne. 'Life here is impossible – I can't see how it can drag on – I have nobody – and nobody cares to know me. . . .' For comfort in her unhappiness Kathleen turned (as she did again and again in later life) to memories and dreams, to recollections of a happier period. One letter to Sylvia reveals her trying, as if by an act of will, to summon up the affection that she found absent in her immediate environment.

> I must tell you . . . that I love you far more than I loved you in England. . . . I dreamed that I came back to visit College . . . I asked for you . . . and then I saw you standing by the window in the waiting room – My dear – I felt I must run and put my arms round you and just say 'Sylvia' but you nodded and then walked away – and I did not move. It was a terrible dream. . . . But I was always afraid then, and I am now, that you do not know me, and when you do, you will hate me. . .

Kathleen's protestation of love was an implicit demand for the reciprocation of love, an attempt to create affection by the very strength of her own feelings. Yet she was so haunted by the fear of rejection (symbolised by a 'terrible dream' of Sylvia walking away from her outstretched arms) that she dreaded the 'hate' her cousin might feel if she were to know her truly.

Freedom from this anxiety could be found in the imagined, happy relationship of a mother and her sick child. A scrap of poetry scribbled in her journal shows Kathleen having recourse to her familiar fantasies:

O mother mine – O mother mine
Snuggle me close and hold me fast
When will the weather again be fine
Shall I really get well at last?

In real life Kathleen could not return to childhood and the security of her mother's arms. But for one brief period she was able to realise another of her recurring fantasies: that of union with a beautiful, tender woman. About a friend older than herself called Edie or 'E.K.B.', Kathleen confided in her journal, 'Caesar [Arnold Trowell] is losing hold of me. Edie is waiting for me. I shall slip into her arms. They are safest. Do you love me?' When some five months later she at last found fulfilment in Edie's arms, Kathleen could write truthfully that 'anticipation [had] become realization'. Just how emotionally climactic the encounter was for the girl who had experienced 'so much Love in imagination; in reality 18 barren years', her journal entry indicates:

> I cannot sleep, because the end has come with such suddenness that even I who have anticipated it so long and so thoroughly am shocked and overwhelmed. . . . Last night I spent in her arms – and to-night I hate her – which, being interpreted, means that I adore her: that I cannot lie in my bed and not feel the magic of her body: which means that sex seems as nothing to me. I feel more powerfully all those so-termed sexual impulses with her than I have with any man. She enthrals, enslaves me – and her personal self – her body absolute – is my worship. I feel that to lie with my head on her breast is to feel what life can hold. . . . In my life – so much Love in imagination; in reality 18 barren years – never pure spontaneous affectionate impulse. Adonis [Arnold Trowell] was – dare I seek into the heart of me – nothing but a pose. And now she comes – and pillowed against her, clinging to her hands, her face against mine, I am a child, a woman, and more than half man.

A separate unpublished entry continues:

> Somehow silently she woke, and came over to me – took me again into the shelter of her arms. We lay down together, still

> silently, she every now and then pressing me to her, kissing me, my head on her breasts, her hands round my body, stroking me, lovingly – warming me . . . to give me more life again . . . . I drew close to her warm sweet body, happier than I had ever been, than I could ever have imagined being – the past once more buried, clinging to her, and wishing that this darkness might last for ever.

But, though the yearning expressed in the fantasy stories for union with a loving female figure had finally materialised, Kathleen's own words contain an implicit recognition that this experience, like those in fantasy, was somehow unreal and incapable of being sustained in the harsh light of day. Daytime in her writing had come to signify reality and the demands of the outer, public world; night-time, or darkness, tended to symbolise the inner realm of fantasy where alone her wishes might be fulfilled. So, in describing her happiness with Edie and wishing that 'this darkness might last forever', Kathleen was unconsciously giving expression to her more profound and hopeless knowledge that it would not.

In fact, Kathleen Beauchamp was, as she recognised in 'Juliet', too much her parents' daughter, too torn between the conventional and unconventional, to be able to escape for long the pangs of conscience. Although she hoped to 'go away again' with Edie, she knew that such love was forbidden, 'poisonous'. Already guilt was manifesting itself when she described in her journal how, while Edie slept, her

> horror of everything seemed to increase. In the yard the very fence became terrible. As I stared at the posts, they became hideous forms of Chinamen – most vivid and terrible. They leant idly against nothing, their legs crossed, their heads twitching. . . . I leaned further out and watched one figure. He bent and mimicked and wriggled – then his head rolled off under the house. . . . I looked at the figure again – it was crucified, hung lifeless before me, yet sneering. Silence profound. This was too awful.

In seeing 'hideous forms of Chinamen . . . sneering', Kathleen's imagination was projecting onto the outer world, and giving vivid shape to, the threatening forces of her own conscience or superego. In a similar way, the child Kezia of Katherine Mansfield's later stories was terrified by the concrete images of her guilt. What suggests that the sneering, 'crucified' figure represented Kathleen's ambivalent feelings about the experience with Edie is her talk of crucifixion in an unpublished section of the same entry:

> Once again I must bear this changing of the tide – my life is a Rosary of Fierce combats for Two – each bound together with the powerful magnetic chain of sex – and at the end – does the emblem of the crucified hang – surely.

To speak of crucifixion was to give utterance to a sense of transgression – and of atonement which must be sought. Psychological restitution had already begun with Kathleen's protest: 'this is really my last experience of the kind, my last'; but the battle within caused her to conclude, 'I ponder my death, my resignation and my passivity.'

Kathleen Beauchamp had good reason to feel depressed. A physically alive young woman who craved affection, she was caught in an intolerable 'double bind'. Perhaps because of her fear of rejection and her linking of sexuality with physical pain and childbearing, normal relationships with young men were unfulfilling; yet compensating relationships with women were fraught with the even worse mental suffering inflicted by shame and guilt. In this situation she attempted to deny her instinctual impulses and resurrect the image of the absent Arnold Trowell: 'I hate everybody, loathe myself, loathe my life, and love Caesar' she wrote in her journal. Just how hollow was the declaration that Arnold Trowell 'must always be everything to me – the one man whom I can call Master and Lover too', her round of frivolous flirtations with other young men in her circle indicates. 'I have been engaged to a young Englishman for three weeks because his figure was so beautiful. I have been tediously foolish many times; but that is past', the journal records.

For some time the pendulum of Kathleen's emotional life continued to swing. Even as she privately admitted her sexual ambivalence, however, Kathleen was repudiating her association with E.K.B.

> But this afternoon has been horrible. E.K.B. bored me, I bored her. I felt unhappy, and I think so did she. But she now

> never took the initiative. And E.K.B. is a thing of the past – absolutely, irrevocably – thank Heaven! It was, I consider retrospectively, a frantically maudlin relationship and one better ended – also she will not achieve greatness. She has not the necessary impetus of character.

But in imagination, at least, there was a gap to be filled; and Kathleen called to mind in the same (unpublished) journal entry, another figure from the past: Maata. Ruth Mantz writes that Kathleen had 'felt ardent toward Maata – she felt she adored her – she worshipped her'. In London there had been a reunion between the two girls which was 'rapturous and romantic'. Now Kathleen wondered,

> Do other people of my age feel as I do . . . so absolutely powerfully licentious, so almost physically ill. . . . I want Maata – I want her – and I have had her – terribly. This is unclean I know but true. What an extraordinary thing – I feel savagely crude – and almost powerfully enamoured of the child. I had thought that a thing of the past – Heigh Ho!!!!!! My mind is like a Russian novel.[1]

The reference to Maata at this time, shortly after her experience with E.K.B., confirms that in real life as well as in fantasy Kathleen was deeply attracted physically to her own sex. A fictional fragment written a year earlier in 1906 shows, moreover, that she had reached the stage of expressing this attraction against a background of realism rather than fantasy. In 'Summer Idylle'[2] the relationship of 'Hinemoa' and 'Marina', two friends resembling Kathleen and Maata, is idyllic precisely because it is rooted in reality. Significantly, the author chose for herself the name of Hinemoa, the Maori girl who, according to legend, swam six miles to join the lover she was forbidden to marry. Depicted as living with Marina by the sea, Hinemoa is shown waking in the early morning and exhibiting a frank sensuality as she watches her sleeping companion:

> Hinemoa bent over her with a curious feeling of pleasure, intermingled with a sensation which she did not analyse. It came upon her if she had used too much perfume, if she had drunk wine that was too heavy and sweet. . . . Marina was wrapped in the darkness of her hair. Hinemoa took it up in her

hands and drew it away from her brow and face and shoulders.

This passage was written about a year before Kathleen's ecstatic physical encounter with Edie. In real life, the attractions of Maata had given way to those of Edie. Arnold Trowell, however, retained his place in Kathleen's imaginative life. When she reacted violently away from women as objects of affection, the thought of Arnold helped Kathleen to deny her lesbianism through a strenuous reassertion of her love for a man. Thus in August 1907, after she had dismissed Edie, Kathleen exaggerated her heterosexual feelings in an unposted letter to Arnold. 'Beloved,' she insisted, 'though I do not see you, know that I am yours – every thought, every feeling in me belongs to you. . . . To me you are man, lover, artist, husband, friend – giving me all – and I surrendering you all – everything.' What is significant about this youthful demonstration of her ability to alternate between a man and a woman – to indulge imaginatively, if not actually, in what she had called 'the whole octave of the sex' – is that such swings were a continuing characteristic of Katherine Mansfield's adult life. Her later, merciless playing off of Ida Baker against Murry was surely an aspect of her deep-rooted propensity to bisexuality.

5 The Consolation of Art

The actual solution Kathleen found for her almost insupportable emotional impasse was the one that she had hit on in 'Misunderstood'. There the child's sickness was forgotten in the shared artistic self-absorption of both the heroine and her creator. Arnold Trowell's artistic success seems from the beginning to have captured Kathleen's imagination. To one who felt undervalued, the rewards of musical accomplishment – attention, admiration, and study in Europe – were alluring. An entry in Kathleen's journal for August 1907 reveals her wanting to share these glories and exploring the idea of marriage to the successful musician as a way of doing so: 'If I marry Caesar,' she told herself, 'I think I could prove a great many things. Mr Trowell said: "She must share his glories and always keep him in the heights." ' But Kathleen had been separated from Arnold for years; almost certainly he was for her by now less a real person than another figure of fantasy, a necessary supporting actor in the continuing drama of her imaginative life. Accordingly, she was by no means broken-hearted when a letter from London finally squashed her dream of marriage to him: 'I felt first so sorrowful, so hurt, so pained, that I contemplated the most outrageous things; but now only *old*, and angry and lonely. . . .'

Openly now, Kathleen determined to become an artist herself. If there was no glory to be had through association with the object of her admiration, she would obtain it anyway – in competition with him. Arnold's first step had been to leave New Zealand. Kathleen resolved to do likewise. 'They have all left N. Z., all of them – my people', she declared. 'I shall somehow or other go, too. You just see.' As if to further deny her dependence on others, she turned for support to her 'other self', to the mirror image and companion with whom she had long conversed. 'Oh, Kathleen, I pity you, but I see that it has to come – this great wrench. . . . Prove yourself strong. Dearest, I hold your two hands, and my eyes look full into yours, trustingly, firmly, resolutely, full of supreme calm, hope and illimitable belief. You must be a woman now and bear the agony of creating.'

The artistic vocation was particularly appealing to the girl for whom role-playing had become a defensive strategy and who, besides, wished to 'try all sorts of lives'. Torn between conventional and unconventional modes of behaviour, between the masculine and feminine sides of her own nature, Kathleen Beauchamp could find no fulfilment in any one prescribed social or sexual role. But as an artist she could be both man and woman: woman in that she would 'bear the agony of creating', man in that she would fight with courage and determination to fulfil her ambitions.

More than anything at this time, Kathleen wanted fame. Fame would be a triumphant vindication of the girl who felt an outsider in her own family; and partially, at least, it would satisfy her craving for love and admiration, free her from the torments of emotional dependence. 'We talked of fame,' Kathleen wrote of two young women in a vignette, 'how we both longed for it, how hard the struggle was, what we both meant to do. I found a piece of paper, and together we wrote a declaration vowing that in the space of one year we should both have become famous.'[1] In real life she dismissed with a certain contempt those who like E.K.B. would not achieve fame. 'I am longing to consort with my superiors', she confided in her journal.

Kathleen had already copied into her journal, together with the maxims of other favourite writers, the exclamation of Marie Bashkirtseff, a young Franco-Russian émigrée artist: 'Me marier et avoir des enfants! Mais quelle blanchisseuse – je veux la gloire.' Part of Marie's attraction for Kathleen was undoubtedly that, through her posthumously published journal,[2] she had achieved a measure of the fame she desired. Moreover, there were certain similarities in temperament. Unashamedly narcissistic and deeply introspective, Marie had decided at the age of twelve that she would record for posterity the unique progress of her own inner life. This meant that for her, as for Kathleen Beauchamp, her life was to be like a continuing novel in which she herself acted the role of heroine. 'It's silly perhaps to praise myself so much', Marie announced at one point in her journal; 'but authors always describe their heroine, and I am my own heroine.' Like Kathleen, she was a decidedly romantic heroine, who, indulging freely in the pleasure of unhappiness, titillated herself with the idea of early death. 'I like to cry, I like to be in despair, I like to be sad and miserable', she admitted. When, by some tragic irony, she indeed lay dying of tuberculosis at the age of twenty-four, Marie justified in the preface to her journal her urge to 'tell everything':

> It is this which has always terrified me. To live, to have so much ambition, to suffer, weep, struggle – and then oblivion! . . . as if I had never been. Should I not live long enough to become famous, this Journal will be of interest to naturalists; for the life of a woman must always be of interest, told thus day by day, without any attempt at posing; as if no one in the world would ever read it, yet written with the intention of being read. . . . And I tell all, yes, all. . . . Else what were the use of it?

Increasingly Kathleen appears to have turned for support of her own attitudes to those writers in whose temperaments she found reflections of herself. The example of Marie Bashkirtseff, with her cultivation of tragic poses and painful emotions, seems to have encouraged Kathleen's habit of exaggerating her personal experiences to the point of artificiality. In the writing of the Decadents, however, especially in that of Oscar Wilde, she found not only confirmation of her own psychological predicaments but also ideas about how to express them. Written about 1907, a fragment called 'The Man, the Monkey and the Mask'[3] reveals the way in which, assimilating the influence of Wilde, Kathleen was grafting features of his work onto the emotional patterns which had taken shape in her adolescent fantasy stories. Obviously derived from *The Picture of Dorian Gray*, 'The Man, the Monkey and the Mask' represents the young author's attempt to give concrete expression to her inner states. Reminiscent of the protagonist in 'Die Einsame', who dwelt 'all alone with her soul', is 'the Man' who has lived for 'a very long time – ten years – twenty years – even more' alone in a fourth-floor room. Although the solitary protagonist's room is conspicuously bare (as if demonstrating his lack of contact with the world outside), 'directly opposite the piano a little black velvet curtain hid the Mask'. The man leads a phantasmagoric existence (like the lady in 'Die Einsame'). Daytime has little meaning for him; only towards evening does he show an interest in the world. 'Late in the afternoon,' the fragment runs, 'the Man crept out of bed and over to the window. . . . Some dark ghost seemed to be confronting his inner self, shrieking why, why and wherefore? Then the night came. . . . Lights woke in the houses opposite. He felt curiously remote from it all – the sole spectator at some colossal stupendous drama.' The man gazes at a young girl meeting and embracing a man in the street below; then,

> the watcher left the window. He staggered across the room, wrenched the black velvet curtain from the mask – 'damn you damn you damn you' [he] screamed, and struck her on her smiling mouth. . . . But the mask crashed down upon the floor in a thousand pieces, and the man fell too, silently. He looked like a bundle of worn out rags.

Because it reflects so closely the psychological condition of the author, the narrative is trancelike and hardly coherent in terms of surface meaning. Yet the emotional logic of the piece is surprisingly lucid. The lonely figure in his fourth-floor room suggests the artist, self-condemned to experience life only as an onlooker. This remoteness is linked to the disturbance of personality which causes 'some dark ghost' to confront his 'inner self' and shriek 'why, why and wherefore?' The ghost, it would appear, is another aspect of the velvet-covered mask – sinister because faceless; and both seem to represent the man's alter ego or double. In this continuing sense of his own duality lies the protagonist's conflict; for the 'colossal stupendous drama' of which he is the 'sole spectator' is really that being acted out within his own psyche. Represented as female, the mask apparently symbolises the feminine aspect of his nature. And it is this with which he is at war. As if reminded by the embrace of the man and woman of his own comfortless, bisexual limbo, he strikes out at the mask. But as the narrative indicates, such an attempt to extirpate the offending aspect of the personality is doomed to failure.

Some of Kathleen's early writing suggests that at times her sense of self-worth sank so low that only suicidal fantasies offered relief from feelings of helplessness. Nevertheless, the very fact that she felt herself to be different from ordinary people appears to have bolstered the conviction, so evident in 'Misunderstood', of her own unique importance. Instinctively, she was transforming the isolation endured by the lonely figures of her fantasy stories into the unconventional stance of the artist. If she felt little in common with the people she met in daily life, she could identify with artists, and especially with 'modern' turn-of-the-century writers who deliberately set themselves apart from conventional society. 'Through the autumn afternoon I sat before the fire in the library, and read, almost a little wildly', she wrote in a poem extolling the companionship to be found in literature.[4]

Having chosen her vocation and determined her goal, Kathleen began systematically preparing herself. At Queen's College she had discovered the writers of the 1890s; at home in New Zealand she continued her search for kindred literary spirits, making notes on the authors and ideas which gripped her imagination. The important revelation of these reading notes[5] is that she was quarrying other writers, not for material, but for ways of expressing emotional states similar to he own. As her adolescent stories indicate, what Kathleen most wanted (or needed) to write about was the hidden, inner life of the mind, especially the conflicts festering within the mind. Her artistic difficulty was to impart form to this raw material, to transmute emotions into literature. A remark on Hawthorne shows that in choosing to tackle this problem she was psychologically self-aware and to this extent in tune with her time. Hawthorne, she noted, is 'with Tolstoi the only novelist of the soul – he is concerned with what is abnormal'. Her cryptic afterthought, 'written with his nerves', recalls Arthur Symons' poem. 'The Modern Malady of Love is Nerves': 'nerves' was the term often used in the 1890s to refer to 'neurosis'.

Kathleen's notes on Walter Pater reveal a fascination with the relationship between art and personality. Of Pater's teaching she observed, 'The Renaissance cultivated personality as we cultivate orchids – striving after a heightening of natural beauty which is [*sic*] but not nature – a perversity which may be poisonous.' Zola, she noted, 'defines Art as nature seen through a temperament'. But it was for an insight into their literary methods that Kathleen seems principally to have been groping as she studied various writers. Her remark that De Quincey made 'a tangled attempt to communicate the incommunicable, his narrative turning back upon itself as it moves', actually foreshadows her own flashback technique in works such as 'Je Ne

Parle Pas Français' and 'A Married Man's Story'. And just as prophetic of her own future artistic development, in which memory came to play such a prominent part, is a comment upon the intensity of Mérimée: 'The Artist becomes an artist by the intensification of memory.'

Kathleen Beauchamp was not only reading during this period, which must be seen as a watershed in her artistic life; she was also writing 'sketches' in which she tried out her literary notions. Fame, or, if not fame, recognition of some kind, was still in the forefront of her mind: 'Now it would be colossally interesting if I could only write a really good work', she told herself; 'Something unusual that would really catch on – a trifle outré in the main – something that would make me really famous.'[6] Perhaps because of her anxiety to 'catch on', she modelled her style on that of such writers as Arthur Symons, whose title 'Silhouettes' she gave to one of her own mood paintings. Quite capable of penning derivative sentences such as 'I want the night to come and kiss me with her hot mouth, lead me through an amethyst twilight to the place of the white gardenia', she nevertheless assured an Australian editor who published some of her sketches: 'they feel very much my own – this style of work absorbs me at present but – well – it cannot be said that anything of mine is cribbed'.[7]

In a sense she was telling the truth; for the moods and feelings conveyed in the sketches are logical extensions of her schoolgirl writing. 'Silhouettes'[8] and a series of three 'Vignettes', for example, focus on a lonely narrator who, from the isolation of her room, looks down at the life in the street below. Such an alienated character was central to Kathleen's fantasy stories, to 'The Man, the Monkey and the Mask', and to the poems 'So I am standing the Test' and 'This is my world, this room of mine'. There is in fact a close similarity between the room described in the latter poem and that in the third 'Vignette'. Drawing the curtain to shut out the outside world, the narrator of the 'Vignette' contemplates her room:

> Strange as I sit here, quiet, alone, how each possession of mine . . . seems to stir into life. The Velasquez Venus moves on her couch ever so slightly; across the face of Manon a strange smile flickers for an instant and is gone, my rocking chair is full of patient resignation, my 'cello case is wrapped in profound thought.

This portrayal of the room and its objects is noteworthy because it shows the young writer in the actual process of discovering the descriptive method which was to become central to her later, mature technique. Inanimate objects in the 'Vignette', as in the later stories, are made to assume human characteristics. They become, in effect, projections of the observer herself as they reflect and heighten her own attitudes. Thus the cello case, the paintings and the rocking chair are given a feminine personality which is friendly and reassuring; they might almost have taken over the role of the mirror face as companion and alter ego. In such accomplished stories as 'The Voyage' and 'Her First Ball', inanimate objects respond to the mood of the young heroines in a similarly friendly manner.

The grotesque and menacing nature of things that seem to come alive is even more striking in Katherine Mansfield's fiction. This depiction of inanimate objects as hostile is similarly foreshadowed in her adolescent writing. In the journal entry describing her night with E.K.B., Kathleen's own feelings of guilt and shame took human form as she looked with horror at the posts of the yard fence coming alive, like 'hideous forms of Chinamen'. And in the 1907 piece 'Silhouettes' the narrator says, 'the bed frightens me – it is so long and white. . . . And the tassel of the window blind moves languidly to and fro. I cannot believe that it is not some living thing.' A corollary of this kind of fantasising, which sees inanimate objects as alive, is the mental distortion which depersonalises human beings. In several of her mature stories, Katherine Mansfield used the technique of turning people into things – and things into sentient beings – to convey her perception of a certain horror underlying the deceptively normal surface of life. The effect is grotesquely funny in 'Bliss', psychologically macabre in 'A Married Man's Story', and emotionally devastating in 'The Man Without a Temperament'. But, as early as the 1907 sketch 'In the Botanical Gardens',[9] Kathleen Beauchamp had experimented with the method. The narrator in this early sketch describes the men, women and children she sees in the gardens as 'meaningless, as lacking in individuality, as the little figures in an impressionist landscape'. The flowers in the gardens, by contrast, are invested with human characteristics.

Another of these sketches written in 1907 confirms the hint given in 'My Potplants', where the lady of the woods and a lily are closely identified, that Kathleen had from a very early period displaced onto plants and objects from the natural world her own stormy sexual feelings. The significant development in 'Leves Amores', however, is that the personification of non-human objects is not spelled out, but only implied. The result is very nearly symbolism. Most suggestive of the technique of symbolist writers is the fact that the force of the story derives from the changed appearance of the wallpaper in a seedy hotel room. Hanging in tattered strips with 'a pattern of roses – buds and flowers – and a frieze [with] a conventional design of birds', the wallpaper underlines the narrator's certainty that 'nothing beautiful could ever happen in that room'. Later in the evening, as the narrator and the woman occupant of the room embrace, the development in their relationship is echoed or symbolised by the change in the wallpaper:

> Lo, every bird upon the bulging frieze broke into song. Lo, every rose upon the tattered paper budded and formed into blossom. Yes, even the green vine upon the bed curtains . . . twined around us in a leafy embrace, held us with a thousand clinging tendrils.

This description may well be the genesis of the scene in 'Prelude' where Katherine Mansfield used a pattern of budding flowers on the wallpaper, in association with bird images, to symbolise Linda Burnell's fear of sexual intercourse and childbirth.

6 Emotion versus Will

A turning-point was reached in Kathleen's life with the publication of the sketches she wrote in 1907. Her father was persuaded to let his self-willed daughter return to England and an artistic career. In coming to his decision, Harold Beauchamp was influenced by the opinion of the journalist Tom Mills. Mills was convinced that he had discovered a genius; but he was uneasy about the sexual overtones of the stories which he categorised as belonging to the 'sex problem type'. Years later he recalled his unsuccessful attempts to deflect the young writer from her exploration of this then tabooed area of human relations:

> I confirmed her own judgement that she could *write*. I went even further and said she was a genius. I had her own word for it, given with all the Beauchamp emphasis, that that was all that was expected from me. . . . One of the few occasions that I raised the question of her literary hopes, aims and aspirations I asked: 'Does this psychoanalysis aspect towards life really and seriously appeal to you? Do you want to put human kind under your mental microscope?' 'Certainly I do!' she replied, with emphasis – and that girl was emphatic in all her expressions. Continuing the discussion she said to me: 'I want to find out actually for myself the reactions of men and women.' 'You mean sexual reactions?' 'Yes, even those!' 'Can't you take those out of books and through your imagination – for those sort of experiments are dangerous for young girls.' She smiled as she retorted: 'There speaks the old man!' Several sequels failed to swerve her from plot, plan or purpose.[1]

Kathleen Beauchamp's parents were even less happy than Tom Mills about the subjects which preoccupied their daughter. Relations became so stormy early in 1908 that the permission to return to England was revoked. Profoundly depressed, Kathleen wrote in her journal, 'I shall end – of course – by killing myself'; and later, 'I purchase my brilliance with my life – It were better that I were dead – really.' But as in previous emotional crises, the need for affirmative, practical action steadied her. 'O, Kathleen,' she exhorted herself,

> do not weave any more of these fearful meshes – for you have been so loathsomely unwise. . . . Be good . . . and brave, and do tell the truth more, and live a better life – I am tired of all this deceit. . . . Don't stay here – accept work – fight against people. . . . PULL UP NOW YOURSELF.

Kathleen was in effect admitting, when she censured herself for untruthfulness and deceit, that avoidance of reality was only frustrating her ambitions. And so was her emotional dependence. 'It is the hopelessly insipid doctrine that love is the only thing in the world, taught, hammered into women, from generation to generation, which hampers us so cruelly', she decided. 'We must get rid of that bogey – and then, then comes the opportunity of happiness and freedom.' That the will must assume dominance over the feelings, that the emotions must be disciplined in the interests of artistic development, she was learning from other writers. 'Independence, resolve, firm purpose, and the gift of discrimination, *mental clearness* – here are the inevitables,' she wrote in her journal. 'Again, Will – the realisation that Art is absolutely self-development'.

About the time of her final departure from New Zealand in July 1908, Kathleen Beauchamp wrote one more story in a manner reminiscent of 'Juliet'; and here she put to the test her new convictions, even as she used the medium of fiction to rearrange yet again the threads of her former relationship with Arnold Trowell. But, whereas Kathleen had been so emotionally involved in the material of 'Juliet' that her writing eddied around the regressive fantasy of death as the solution to personal conflicts, 'The Education of Audrey'[2] exhibits much greater artistic control. Abandoning the device of the first-person narrator, she portrays with near-ironic objectivity the strengths and weaknesses of the heroine whose predicament unmistakably resembles her own. Audrey, seen first through her own eyes, appears a successful and emotionally independent concert singer; but her encounter with Max, a former lover, makes only too plain the difference between her confident self-perception and her very real dependence. If in a sense Kathleen was imagining yet again her own hoped-for reunion with Arnold Trowell, the similarity of Max's advice to Audrey and the author's self-exhortation in her journal suggests that the transformation of this former idol into writer's copy was now almost complete. For Max is less a character in his own right than a representation of one aspect of his creator's psyche: unconsciously, perhaps, Kathleen was personifying in the characters of Audrey and Max the struggle in her own mind between emotion and 'the Will'.

Kathleen Beauchamp's ability thus to divide and personify aspects of her own psyche would appear to be a natural outcome of her habit of conversing with the 'mirror face', of seeing herself, in effect, as two separate people. Audrey is similarly a divided personality. Having received an invitation to visit Max after a separation of four years, she 'walked over to the dressing table, leaned her elbows on the table, her chin in her hand and nodded to the mirror face: "We'll go my dear, and enjoy ourselves, and wear our best clothes".' Buoyed up when she meets Max by 'that wonderful sense of power, of complete confidence in herself, that happiness which always followed her successful concerts', Audrey attempts an objective analysis of the course of their relationship:

> And after the absolute sense of my nearness had worn off, it was easy to put the whole episode away. You realised and how wisely, that you must not be distracted. You thought of me in weak moments as 'poor little girl' or when your pictures failed you, as 'dear little girl'. . . . You see, Max, for a little while I did worship you, lived in a strange and passionate dream of you and of me, believed that love between man and woman was the only thing in the world, instead of a lion in the path I've conquered and walked over. . . . Love is a means to an end. You must have been tossed upon the mighty sea of passion and if you can escape free in body and soul, there lies before you such a wide wind-swept waste of freedom, such promise of happiness in this freedom, that you run forward, your arms outstretched to take the whole world into your embrace.

Audrey, like her creator, has apparently substituted artistic achievement for love as a source of self-esteem. If Max can cast her aside as a distraction from his art, Audrey implies, she can do likewise. If she cannot have him in person, she can possess him through an act of identification – through becoming an artist like him; perhaps, it is hinted, an even more successful artist. And for the love of one man she can substitute the embrace of the whole world. When the focus shifts to Max, however, it becomes clear that Audrey has convinced neither herself nor her former lover. Max, now the more commanding figure, proceeds to instruct Audrey on 'the secret' of becoming an artist:

> Art demands of her disciples absolute slavish obedience, complete surrender of everything in the years of their apprenticeship. But when those years have passed we know that the time has come to realize one's nature perfectly – then to create. . . . You see, my dear girl . . . your experience of life is based upon – forgive me – a little literature and a good deal of morbid imagination.

Thus with clarity Kathleen Beauchamp expressed her perception of the self-discipline demanded by artistic endeavour; with equal objectivity she portrayed the temperamental weakness which stood in the way of achievement. For, childlike in her insecurity, 'Audrey felt intensely angry, also, that her splendid happiness was slipping from her.' Max's thought, 'Could anything be more fascinating than to teach this beautiful child that she might so live her life that each song she sang would be the crystallisation of a wonderful experience', brings the story to its ironic climax. For, under the guidance of the man to whose rejection she owes 'almost everything', the heroine's real education is about to begin. This involves a painful process of self-recognition, as the conclusion of the narrative indicates. 'Why are you crying?' Max asks.

> 'Do you know how I feel? she said painfully – 'as though my philosophy was a thing for sunshine and daylight – and, it is raining now. . . . Yet, I have been happy.'
>
> 'Yes, as a child is happy. Ah! there are heights and depths in Art and Life that you have never dreamed of Audrey. . . .

> One day, sooner or later, if you want to fulfill your destiny, someone will take you by the hand and lead you there, and you will learn.' . . .
>
> She suddenly turned towards him and stretched out her hands – 'Teach me, Max', said Audrey.

In thus reversing the central character's pattern of expectations, Kathleen was using for ironic effect the method of ending her stories which had begun to emerge in her adolescent fantasies. In the fantasy stories, the final reversal is almost an afterthought, a moment of fear or conflict experienced in the face of impending death, or a sudden jerking back to reality of the protagonist who has until then dwelt in a world of fantasy. In the most sophisticated of her 1907 sketches, 'Leves Amores', however, Kathleen seems quite deliberately to have employed the narrator's change in mood – and expectations – to bring the piece to its conclusion. 'The Education of Audrey' confirms the impression that this kind of dénouement was a natural outcome of the division which Kathleen characterised so often as the 'mirror face'. The 'mirror face' was literally a reflection of the separation of personality into two distinct selves; into the ego and the alter-ego; into the self who wilfully engaged in daydreaming, and the self who stood aloof, observing and criticising.

The reversal with which 'The Education of Audrey' closes involves a movement from an unreal to a real perception of the self, when the formerly confident heroine admits that she has been living like a child in a make-believe world. This conclusion is striking; it reveals the author looking at a situation closely modelled on her own from two contrasting angles. Read literally, the ending is ironic, yet somehow convincing: Audrey appears to have been transformed from a young woman, who has discovered her artistic destiny in the act of transcending an emotional crisis, to a child who can only fulfil that destiny through the guiding hand of the man who has rejected her. In thus portraying Audrey, Kathleen seems to have been illustrating with devastating honesty the weaker side of her own dual nature. Counteracting this is her presentation of Max. Outwardly yet another version of Arnold Trowell, he represents, as he speaks, the side of the author's personality which was governed by her determined will. If we see that what appears on the surface to be a reunion between two former lovers is on a deeper level a symbolic confrontation between the ego and the alter-ego, the emotions and the will, the private logic directing the story becomes explicable. Eliot's Prufrock made a similar journey in the attempt to reconcile his two separate selves; for Audrey, as for him, the outcome is only further continued ambiguity.

PART II

1908–1915

7 London and a Dual Existence

In August 1908, Katherine Mansfield, as she now called herself, arrived in England. Soon she had outlined in her journal a story in which she would trace the course of her life. It was to be about

> a girl in Wellington; the singular charm and barrenness of that place. . . . And then to leave the place and go to Europe. To live there a dual existence – to go back and be utterly disillusioned, to find out the truth of all – to return to London – to live there an existence so full and strange that life itself seemed to greet her – and ill to the point of death return to W. and die there. A story – no, it would be a sketch, hardly that, more a psychological study – of the most erudite character. . . .

That particular story was never written; but the remarkable thing about this romantic and sad little outline is that, except for the eventual return to Wellington, what the author imagined for herself did come true. Indeed, a startling aspect of the youthful writing, in which Katherine Mansfield is her own barely disguised heroine, is the frequency with which events she created in fiction took place (if in slightly altered form) in real life. In 1906 she had written to Sylvia Payne of sharing a wish to create her own fate, to 'have power over circumstances'. Katherine may conceivably have been gifted with prevision; but it is more likely that, unconsciously, she tried to seize control over fate by imagining certain events in fictional terms, then enacting them in reality.

Only too often, the outcome of this attempt to translate the omnipotence of fantasy into a genuine power over circumstances was unhappy. For this reason, the single most important aspect of Katherine Mansfield's development, in both the personal and artistic sense, is her steady movement away from immersion in fantasy to a position from which she could record the disastrous effects of dream-living on the lives of her fictional characters. What fantasy had been for Kathleen Beauchamp, art was gradually to become for Katherine Mansfield. Already in 'The Education of Audrey' there had been evidence of a new objectivity. There, as if in anticipation of her new life, the young author had analysed the distance which separated her dream of success from its reality. If her 'songs' were to be 'the crystallisation of a wonderful experience', she acknowledged that there must first be experience; and if her talent was to develop there must be self-development, discipline – and someone to show her the way.

Less explicit, because less affirmative, was the recognition which so dominated 'Juliet': that the aspiring artist needed not only a teacher but also emotional support. This yearning for support was Katherine Mansfield's Achilles' heel: she had an insatiable need for the sustenance of love. An early unpublished notebook fragment graphically illustrates this: 'She faced Max and lifting her arms she stammered, "I must you know I must have love because I cannot live without love you know." ' In the face of such dependence, the isolated stance of the artist was little more than a romantic dream.

The finding of someone who could be, as she had long wished Arnold Trowell to be, lover and companion, intellectual and artistic mentor, was clearly vital to Katherine's emotional stability. Immensely complicating her chance of finding this ideal partner, however, was her sexual ambivalence. Emotionally, if not physically, she kept being drawn into intense relationships with others of her own sex. Before her return to England, Katherine had imagined several alternative modes of life. In 'Juliet' she had depicted herself living in a marriage-like relationship with Pearl, only to succumb to seduction by Rudolf and to die as the result of an illegitimate pregnancy. An unpublished fragment of 1907 shows her deciding to enter a loveless marriage as a means of forgetting 'David' and obtaining security; and 'The Education of Audrey' portrays her as a successful concert singer who must nevertheless seek out her former lover. The close interweaving of Katherine Mansfield's fantasies and her life can be gauged from the fact that in some form all of these possibilities came to pass.

When she first arrived in London, Katherine lived not with 'Pearl' but in a hostel for women. Two unpublished flower poems written while she was there suggest that one very real aspect of her 'dual existence' was a strong attraction towards other women. Flowers she had long associated with the physical beauty of women; and the flower poems, in their expressions of desire and longing, echo the mood of some of her early fantasy stories. Reminiscent of the ending of 'His Ideal', in which consummation is achieved through death by drowning, are the concluding lines of the brief 'Song of the Camellia Blossom': 'I could drown myself in you / Link myself in your embrace.' More physically urgent is the tone of 'Scarlet Tulips':

> Strange flower, half opened, scarlet,
> So soft to feel and press
> My lips upon your petals
> A hated restlessness
> A fever and a longing
> Desire that moves in me
> A violent scarlet passion
> Stirs me so savagely

To some extent, Katherine's need was filled by her former school-friend, Ida Baker. From the time of Katherine Mansfield's return to England in 1908 until her death in 1923, Ida loved her unquestioningly, tolerating her moods and her egotism, encouraging her ambitions. Although Katherine was loath to acknowledge the fact, it was Ida more than anyone else who discharged the functions of the much-needed supporting figure, struggling when called upon to play the part of wife and mother, prepared to remove herself when she was unwanted.

In her determination to lead a dual emotional existence, Katherine (acting like her heroine, Audrey) sought out the family of Arnold Trowell. She might almost have been playing out another fantasy, that in 'Juliet', when, rejected once more by Arnold, she fell in love with his brother instead – and became pregnant. What followed is well-known. Garnett, a young, impecunious musician, was unwilling to marry Katherine. Her response was to worsen the situation by giving life to another fantasy – that in which the jilted heroine agrees to marry a man she doesn't love in the hope of winning back her reluctant lover. It was precisely this that she did with the hapless singing-teacher several years her senior, George Bowden.

When the news reached Katherine's mother that her daughter had precipitously married – and even more precipitously left her husband – she promptly sailed for England. Unable to persuade Katherine to return to George Bowden, Mrs Beauchamp took steps to separate her daughter and Ida Baker: Ida went to the Canary Islands for a holiday, and Katherine to Bavaria. One can only guess at the exact nature of the relationship between the two young women. Recalling the episode, Ida says in her memoirs[1] that Mrs Beauchamp 'felt our relationship was "unwise".' Of Katherine's brief return to her husband some months later, Ida writes: 'I did not know then that George Bowden thought I was Katherine Mansfield's lesbian friend, and the cause of her leaving him in the first place. Indeed, I did not know then what a "lesbian friend" meant.' Mrs Beauchamp apparently did know. When she returned to New Zealand she immediately cut Katherine out of her will.

Katherine Mansfield's response to the pregnancy (about which her mother was probably ignorant) and to the chaos in her emotional and personal life, is hinted at in some brief notebook jottings. As if she had learned her own lessons about the necessity for the will to triumph over the emotions, it was the artist that, even in this very real crisis, remained uppermost. Never one to waste an experience, she almost immediately began dramatising her misfortune. Like 'Kathie', the heroine of an earlier story who burned her hand, Katherine seemed determined to make the most of, even to enjoy, her suffering. 'Sick at heart, till I am physically sick. . . .' she wrote in her journal. 'But *attendez*: you must *not* eat, and you had better not sleep! No good *looking* "fit" and *feeling* dead.' As she struggled to reconstruct her feelings in their most dramatic context, the self which looked on and sought words remained apart from the self which actually experienced unhappiness. Thus, on the evening of Good Friday 1909, she likened herself to Jesus: 'I always, always feel the nail prints in my hands, the sickening thirst in my throat, the agony of Jesus. . . . Only lend me your aid. I *thirst* too – and I hang upon the Cross.'

By her own admission, Katherine deliberately neglected her health on the journey to Bavaria. In view of the negative attitude to motherhood which emerges in her early writing, it seems entirely possible that she acted irresponsibly in the German village where she had to wait out the birth of her child. What is known is that she became ill, and subsequently suffered a miscarriage. John Middleton Murry, amongst others, has asserted that she passionately desired a child. This may have been so towards the end of her life, when childbearing was no longer possible; but Katherine Mansfield's own writing conveys a different impression of her youthful attitude.

A fragmentary story[2] about Elena, a concert singer, and her little son, Peter, is set in Wörishofen where Katherine suffered her miscarriage. Even though it has been dated 1914, it still casts considerable light on Katherine's ambivalent feelings about motherhood. Indeed, the portrayal of Elena reveals that Katherine may have felt some responsibility and lingering guilt over the loss of her child.

Elena, looking out of the window of her German pension one evening, is consumed by a longing to sing. Her child is ill and his eyes implore her not to sing: 'But the knowledge did not take away her longing. . . . I must sing Peter. The longing is much stronger than I – and when she had asserted the fact to herself it became so. It leapt up, cruel and eager.' While his mother sings, the child feels snow 'creeping up to his throat . . . but not to my mouth Mother. Mother, not over my eyes.' Then a doctor comes to her room: ' "I am afraid I am interrupting" he said, and from his voice she thought he was accusing her.' Since the child is found to be dead, there is no doubt about the nature of his accusation.

With more than a little insight into her own nature, Katherine seems to have been depicting in veiled terms the conflict between the vocations of mother and artist. But the conflict is more apparent than real. For the mother's longing to sing is 'far stronger than [her]', thus ensuring that her 'cruel' creative drive will prevail over the welfare of her child.

In a separate section of the disconnected story fragment, Katherine explored the relationship between an artist–mother and her child from a comparatively positive angle. Yet her frank portrayal of the narcissism which causes the heroine to value her son not for himself but for his usefulness in providing an audience is possibly more shocking than the scene describing his death. Elena, as much actress as singer, reflects that 'there is always something wonderfully touching in the sight of a young mother with a delicate child'. Travelling by train with Peter, Elena pretends to be exhausted (as did Katherine Mansfield on her journey to Bavaria) so that she can better enjoy the attention which the child attracts to her:

> She was not really exhausted but her perfect sense of the dramatic fitness of things prompted the action. She could not bear that even so small an audience . . . should go away indifferent or unsatisfied. She felt bound to play exquisitely for them. Why she even took the trouble to play exquisitely for Peter when he and she were alone together. Sometimes in front of her mirror she played most exquisitely of all.

Peter's function is unequivocal: it is to attract an audience for his mother, and when no one else is present to serve, like a mirror, as a passive substitute. Even so, the mother prefers her own mirror face to her son. It is hardly surprising, then, that, as the train journey nears its end and Elena thinks how much she loves travel, Peter is termed 'the unfamiliar burden'.

8 The *German Pension* Stories

Katherine Mansfield's journey to Bavaria in 1909 was the first of many attempts to escape personal unhappiness through changing her environment. No matter where she lived, it seems, some other place was always preferable. After coming home to New Zealand from school, she could only think of England; within a year of having her wish to return to London fulfilled, she was crying out, 'To escape England – it is my great desire. I loathe England.' The fragmentary story about Elena and Peter, so frank in other ways, suggests that for Katherine travel was a kind of drug, providing an escape from reality not dissimilar to that afforded by fantasy. Elena, as her journey by train comes to an end, thinks about

> these strange pangs of excitement that set upon her at the end of a journey. Any journey – it was always the same. . . . The unknown place to which she travelled had in her head a fanciful image. . . . And although these things never came to pass it did not matter. Faced with reality she did not even regret them. They faded out of her mind until they were forgotten, then on the torn web of the old dream the new dream began silently to spin. . . . Yes, yes, I am coming.

Here, the relationship between travel and fantasy (or the imagination) is admitted openly. In real life there appears to have been a close association between Katherine Mansfield's bursts of creative activity and her journeys of escape. Indeed, from the time of this first removal from England to Bavaria a pattern for writing was established: first there would be an emotional crisis; then the search for release, for a new life as it were, through the change to a more desirable location. Once in that location, the mind of the author would begin reworking with a new objectivity the details of the situation from which she had broken away. But Katherine Mansfield's act in putting her personal unhappiness to artistic use was not merely one of transcendence; it was one of defiant self-affirmation. Whatever else went wrong in her life, she could assert herself as a writer, even as she controlled and refashioned the troubling events in a more satisfactory manner. Although her stories far surpass mere autobiography, at their best they always have their origins in, and in some way reflect, the particular emotional crisis she was endeavouring to overcome.

Katherine's experiences in Bavaria provided her with the material for her first collection of short stories, *In A German Pension*. Published in December 1911, the book made an immediate impact, and it gave its author a firm foothold in the London literary scene. Curiously, in later years she repudiated this first work as a 'succès scandale'. Critical commentators followed her lead. The *German Pension* stories, they said, were uncharacteristic of Katherine Mansfield's writing, not only in their technical awkwardness and strident tone, but also in their thematic concern with sexual relationships and childbearing. The early appeal of the collection, most said, was to the anti-German sentiments felt by Britons in the years preceding the First World War.

Towards the end of her life, Katherine Mansfield had private reasons for not wanting the book republished. Yet, from the time of its first reissue in 1920, *In a German Pension* has remained continuously in print. The failure of some commentators and anthologists to see this work as an integral part of the Mansfield corpus would appear unrealistic, then. In fact, neglect of these stories has distorted the picture of Katherine Mansfield's artistic development. In spite of their ostensible focus on the manners and attitudes of German men and women, the stories reiterate in their themes Katherine's youthful uneasiness about relationships between the sexes; and they are clear forerunners of some of the great stories in which sexual ambivalence remains thematically central. But the enduring interest of the collection lies in the intuitive grasp of female psychology which informs the stories.

Into her caustic portraits of German people, whether at work or at play, Katherine Mansfield poured her own emotional reactions to the sad affair with Garnett Trowell, to her hasty marriage, and to the trauma of pregnancy and miscarriage. Her response to pregnancy was primarily physical. 'My *body* is so self-conscious', she commented in her journal before leaving London. 'Je pense of all the frightful things possible – "all this filthiness".' In Bavaria she described 'a terrible confusion in your body which affects you mentally, suddenly pictures for you detestable incidents, revolting personalities'. A preoccupation with the physical aspects of the relations between men and women is to the fore in the *German Pension* stories. Especially striking is the way in which a portrayal of the Germans' gross eating habits barely disguises a persistent correlation between the devouring of food and the sexual devouring, as it were, of a woman's body. In such stories as 'Germans at Meat', 'Frau Brechenmacher Attends a Wedding', 'At Lehmann's' and 'Bains Turcs', Katherine Mansfield reveals an overwhelming fear of physically dominant men and of male sexual appetite, often through the symbolism of food.

Some commentators, seeking to dismiss as an aberration what they considered the 'distasteful' aspects of the *German Pension* stories, have argued that Katherine Mansfield was writing under the alien influence of Beatrice Hastings, the ardent woman's liberationist from the *New Age*. But the appearance of closely related themes in both her mature works and her youthful writing suggests otherwise. Anxieties about physical relations – anxieties which she came increasingly to express in terms of eating – are evident in the juvenilia. Even as a girl there seems to have been a link in her mind between food and physical dominance. Resenting her father's dominating presence in 1906 and precociously aware of his sexual appetite, she had written disgustedly of his behaviour at meal times: 'A physically revolted feeling seizes me. . . . He watches the dishes go round, anxious to see that he shall have a good share.'

In the *German Pension* stories, Katherine Mansfield made little attempt to disguise her private obsessions. 'Germans at Meat' focuses upon the links between sexuality and eating. The narrative, a rather contrived conversation around a pension dinner-table between the German guests and the prim young English narrator, has the ostensible purpose of exposing the gustatory greediness of the Germans. It is not the satirical asides of the narrator, however, which give the piece its interest: it is the tension which develops between her and the physically dominant 'Herr Rat' as the two engage in ambiguous small talk. Herr Rat, anxious like Harold Beauchamp to 'have a good share' of the food, is unpleasantly aggressive as he boasts: 'As for me, I have had all I wanted from women without marriage.' What he wanted from women is never spelled out, but he relentlessly details the quantities of food needed to satisfy his appetite. The narrator's revulsion against Herr Rat and his physical appetites is conveyed indirectly as a German widow elicits from her the information that she is a slight eater and a vegetarian. 'Who ever heard of having children upon vegetables?' exclaims the widow. The correlation between food and sexuality becomes explicit when the widow says that while she herself has had nine children, her own achievement cannot be compared with the feat of a friend who 'had four at the same time. Her husband was so pleased he gave a supper-party and had them placed on the table.'

'Frau Brechenmacher Attends a Wedding' is an undisguised attack upon the sexually dominant male. In portraying the indignities and the suffering heaped upon women in marriage, Katherine Mansfield might almost be dramatising her own expressed belief that 'it is the hopelessly insipid doctrine that love is the only thing in the world, taught, hammered into women, from generation to generation, which hampers us so cruelly'. If the polemic which informs the work is sometimes too direct for comfort, the very sharpness of the narration makes this an unforgettable story. The author illustrates her theme in terms of two women, one who has endured marriage for years and one who is about to be married. In the opening section of the story, Frau Brechenmacher is shown rushing to and fro at the command of her bullying husband. Her husband's name suggestive of one who 'breaks', Frau Brechenmacher must attend the wedding to witness the ritual preparation for the breaking of yet another women's spirit.

It is through the symbolism of food that Katherine Mansfield again drives home her meaning. The bride, who has been deserted by the father of her illegitimate child and who is now being forced into an arranged marriage, has 'the appearance of an iced cake all ready to be cut and served in neat little pieces to the bridegroom beside her'. She might almost be the victim of some primitive sacrifice, such is the effect of the explicit linking of male sexuality and cannibalism. When Herr Brechenmacher presents the newly-weds with a silver coffee pot containing 'a baby's bottle and two little cradles holding china dolls', the latent cruelty of the wedding-feast reaches a climax. Lifting the lid, the bride seems to understand the meaning of the gift; she 'shut it down with a little scream and sat biting her lips'.

Frau Brechenmacher, instinctively empathising with the girl in her humiliation, imagines that 'all these people were laughing at her . . . all laughing at her because they were so much stronger than she was'. The operative word is 'stronger', and the story ends with the focus on the older woman and her fear of physical abuse. Her husband, eating greedily on their return home, reminds his wife of the trouble she gave him on their wedding-night: 'You were an innocent one, you were. . . . But I soon taught you.' Just what the woman, now mother of five children, has been taught is conveyed by the closing sentence: 'She lay down on the bed and put her arm across her face like a child who expected to be hurt as Herr Brechenmacher lurched in.'

Frau Brechenmacher's fear of her physically dominant husband (and her refusal to eat with him) shows in primitive form attitudes which Linda Burnell displays towards her husband in the later story 'Prelude'.

Another *German Pension* story, 'At Lehmann's', shows Katherine Mansfield exploring with a similar unsubtle emphasis on physicality the theme of initiation (a theme which in altered form is central to such later stories as 'The Little Governess', 'Her First Ball' and 'The Garden Party'). Sabina, the servant girl at Lehmann's café, is innocent about the facts of life: 'She knew practically nothing except that the Frau had a baby inside her, which had to come out – very painful indeed. One could not have one without a husband – that she also realised. But what had the man got to do with it?' The climax of the story is of course Sabina's sudden understanding of what the man *had* got to do with it, and the shattering of her childish naïveté and illusion. There is a degree of dramatic irony in the girl's failure to see any link at first between her excitement at the attentions of a visiting young man, whose 'restless gaze wandering over her face and figure gave her a curious thrill deep in her body, half pleasure, half pain', and Frau Lehmann's ugly body in the final stage of pregnancy. But making quite sure that she – and the reader – make the connection is Katherine Mansfield's juxtaposition of the girl's first kiss with the 'frightful, tearing shriek' that heralds the birth of the baby. Shrieking too, Sabina pulls away from her would-be lover and rushes out of the room.

Again and again in the *German Pension* stories Katherine Mansfield underlines her sense that sexual love for women is fraught with physical danger. Victims of the stronger sex, women face the ultimate exploitation: the burden of constant childbearing. Her attempts to find a solution to the problem in fictional terms are various. In 'The Child-Who-Was-Tired', the servant girl (who performs the duties of mother) finally smothers the baby which will not stop crying. But the answer which appears most frequently in these stories is an avoidance of normal heterosexual relations. Widows are singularly blessed. In 'Frau Fischer' the character of that name is a widow, and the 'fortunate possessor of a candle factory'; equally fortunate is Frau Hartmann, the owner of a pension. 'We are such a happy family since my dear man died', she tells her guests. Pretending to be married – to a sea captain who is conveniently away on long voyages – the English narrator of the story announces that, for her part, she considers 'child-bearing the most ignominious of all professions'.

Women's revenge on men, in one form or another, is a thematic element in many of the *German Pension* stories. And lesbianism, or something very close to it, is the alternative to domination by men which Katherine Mansfield explores in 'The Modern Soul' and 'Bains Turcs'.

In dealing with bisexuality, Katherine Mansfield was entering difficult territory. She was not only exposing in fiction the motivations of women whose psychology resembled her own; she was writing about a subject which in the aftermath of the Wilde trial was considered morally wrong, if not 'forbidden'. As a result, there is no urgent presentation of a message in 'The Modern Soul' and 'Bains Turcs'. Rather the author is concerned so to disguise and encode her theme that the stories can be read on two levels: at a superficial level which appears to present satiric caricatures of German men and women, and at a deeper level where psychological dramas of some complexity can be seen unfolding. There is an ambiguity, then, in the texture of these two stories which reveals itself in devious plot structures, confusing shifts of point of view, innuendo and a heavy reliance upon symbols – especially symbols connected with eating.

'The Modern Soul' is about the ambivalent relationship of a narcissistic young actress, Fräulein Sonia Godowska, with her mother on the one hand and with a conceited middle-aged professor on the other. Observing and commenting on the behaviour of this group is the English narrator. As the story opens, the focus is on 'Herr Professor'. Exhausted from trombone-playing in the woods, he is depicted greedily devouring a bag of cherries. From the outset his conversation is spiced with innuendo that leaves us in little doubt about the correlation between his prowess as an eater of fruit (so obviously symbolic of a woman's body) and his sexual prowess. 'There is nothing like cherries for producing free saliva after trombone playing, especially after Grieg's *Ich Liebe Dich*', he announces happily. At a concert that evening it becomes clear that the Professor (who has bragged about the quantity and variety of fruit he has eaten in the present location) intends Fräulein Godowska as his next conquest. 'To-night you shall be the soul of my trombone', he tells her. His reappearance with the trombone symbolically underlines his desires: he 'blew into it, held it up to one eye . . . and wallowed in the soul of Sonia Godowska'.

Amusing though the ridiculous portrayal of this character is, the impact of the story hinges on the reader's perception of the trap which is prepared for him. After the concert it is not the Professor but the narrator whom Fräulein Sonia singles out for a walk in the woods. To her the actress confides that she is 'furiously sapphic.' The focus now shifts from the Professor's expectations to the confused psychology of the woman whose sexual inversion is bound to thwart him. 'Not only am I sapphic,' she continues, 'I find in all the works of all the greatest writers . . . some sign of myself – some resemblence.' If a combination of sapphism and narcissism nourishes her creative 'genius', so, apparently, do Sonia's intensely ambivalent feelings for her mother. Terming Frau Godowska her 'tragedy', the daughter insists, 'I love my mother as I love nobody else in the world – nobody and nothing! Do you think it is impossible to love one's tragedy? "Out of my great sorrows I make my little songs", that is Heine or myself.'

The ending of this story whose secret subject is the frustration of a conceited man's sexual desires is fittingly ironic. Sonia reveals that the attachment to her mother precludes any normal relationship with a man; besides, 'genius cannot hope to mate'. What she would like is to marry 'a simple, peaceful man . . . who would be for me a pillow'. By casting the unwitting Professor in this role, Sonia effectively turns the tables on him. The exploiter is about to become the exploited.

Out of her own inner knowledge, Katherine Mansfield portrays in 'The Modern Soul' not only the battle of the sexes. She probes, in her characterisation of Fräulein Sonia, the longings of an immature woman who, like a little girl, wishes to marry her father and retain sole possesion of her mother. And whether she knew it or not, she illustrates the link between a neurotic fixation on childhood, bisexuality and creative endeavour.

'Bains Turcs', although published some time after the *German Pension* collection, belongs with the group of stories that Katherine Mansfield wrote out of her experiences in Bavaria. Like the earlier works, it has a German cast of characters seen through the eyes of a self-conscious English narrator; and it conveys a disparaging attitude towards men. More directly than in 'The Modern Soul', Katherine Mansfield contemplates in 'Bains Turcs' the alternative to marriage offered by lesbian relationships. But here too the author approaches her dangerous theme with some evasion, relying heavily on the concealing devices of word associations and picture-language, or symbols. The overall effect of the story is dreamlike, so that it is difficult to determine the deliberateness with which we are being allowed a glimpse into the characters' unconscious minds. What we do gain from a close reading of 'Bains Turcs' is a strong sense of Katherine Mansfield's ability to tap, for the purposes of fiction, the workings of the unconscious mind.

Reminiscent of Cerberus, the many-headed dog guarding the entrance to Hades, the cashier at the entrance to the Turkish baths gives an immediate impression of dominance with her 'masses of gleaming orange hair – like an over-ripe fungus bursting from a thick, black stem'. Such luxuriant fecundity suggests that this is a place ruled by women; and indeed, the only man in the establishment, an elevator attendant, is likened to a 'dead bird'. In contrast to the cashier, by whom he is scolded, the man seems impotent. A 'tiny figure disguised in a peaked cap and dirty white cotton gloves', he is referred to derisively by the narrator as 'the figure', 'the midget' and 'the creature'.

The train of thought which depersonalises the man before reducing him to the level of an animal takes another direction when the narrator, who has come to enjoy the baths, settles into the comfort of the 'Warm Room'. 'Yes, it might have been very fascinating to have married an explorer', she thinks, 'and lived in a jungle, as long as he didn't shoot anything or take anything captive. I detest performing beasts.' The implication is that, while man in the shape of a sexless elevator attendant can be an object of mockery, man in the shape of a sexually virile predator (who might take the narrator captive) is a definite threat. Mentally attempting to render this imaginary male impotent too, the narrator reduces him to the level of a 'peforming beast'.

Having thus dismissed the opposite sex, the narrator turns her attention to two women in the baths whose looks and behaviour suggest an attractive substitute for marriage. With their 'gay, bold faces, and quantities of exquisite whipped fair hair', they seem to exist in an exclusively happy world of their own. Their shared act of handling and eating mandarins, as they scrutinise and discuss laughingly the bodies of the other bathers, accentuates their apparent intimacy. The other women in the room, as if signalling a veiled recognition of the lesbianism implicit in this scene, vented 'the only little energy they had . . . in shocked prudery at the behaviour of the two blondes'.

But, as if the theme were coming too close for comfort, the focus shifts from the perceiving mind of the narrator to a new character, 'a short stout little woman with flat, white feet, and a black mackintosh cap over her hair'. Mackintosh Cap demonstrates an obsessive concern with the two blondes: 'They're not respectable women – you can tell at a glance. At least I can, any married woman can.' Then she launches into an account of her own marriage and the five children who have been born to her in six years. Yet her championing of the married state is belied by a physical interest in her own sex she is unable to suppress. 'Are you going to take your chemise off in the vapour room?' she asks the narrator. ' "Don't mind me, you know. Woman is woman, and besides, if you'd rather, I won't look at you. . . . I wouldn't mind betting", she went on savagely, "those filthy women had a good look at each other." ' The narrator's comment, 'I could not get out of my mind the ugly, wretched figure of the little German with a good husband and four children, railing against the two fresh beauties who had never peeled potatoes nor chosen the right meat', conveys her recognition of the jealousy which underlies the discrepancy between the woman's words and the feelings she exposes. It is the narrator, too, who at the end of the story suggests the psychological interpretation of what we have observed through her eyes: 'And as the two [blondes] walked out of the ante-room, Mackintosh Cap stared after them, her sallow face all mouth and eyes, like the face of a hungry child before a forbidden table.'

Katherine Mansfield has been illustrating in this second section of the story the process whereby a wish that has been repressed by the conscious mind can make its way back to consciousness – in the form of a denial of that wish. Overtly denying her own deepest feelings as she rails at the two lesbians, Mackintosh Cap's longing for a similar intimacy is revealed through the very intensity of her fixation. In the striking final sentence, Katherine Mansfield rounds off the exposure of the woman's character. Appearing momentarily to have regressed to the condition of a baby whose sole interest is in possession of its mother's breast, Mackintosh Cap exhibits the despair of a rejected female child; a despair which can survive in adult life as the repressed longing for a physical relationship with another woman.

The understanding of female psychology which emerges in 'Bains Turcs' is remarkable. But, because the author is herself ambiguously involved in the mental processes of her characters, the story is aesthetically unsatisfying. There is no manifestly logical connection between the narrator's thoughts in the opening scene, her observation of the two blonde women, and the conclusion to the story. Only an interpretation of the symbolism and word pictures can make it clear that all the female characters who appear in the narrative are logically linked by their rejection of men and their accompanying attraction to their own sex.

9 Loneliness and its Dangers

The themes of the stories Katherine Mansfield wrote in Bavaria reflect her sense of being at the mercy of a hostile world in which men force upon their women the endless burden of pregnancy. Only relationships between women appear to offer freedom, security, and a defence against the male threat. Nevertheless, Katherine was desperately in need of a temporary harbour on her return to England in January 1910; and, like the actress in 'The Modern Soul', she turned to a man who seemed safe: George Bowden. Her stay with him was brief. The influential weekly the *New Age* published four of her German stories, providing a measure of the recognition she sought; then, after an operation for peritonitis, Katherine left her husband for good. It was with Ida Baker that she now chose to live.

Her journal reveals that once again she was consumed by a need to write:

> This almost mad longing to work is gnawing at me. . . . A frightful intolerable agony overcomes me – I feel that I must be alone now, that a book has *got* to be written – but the difficulty is that I am not yet free enough to give myself uninterrupted hours. Oh how damnable it is.

One of the damnable aspects of Katherine Mansfield's life was the ill health which was already plaguing her; another was the familiar need for a close, sustaining relationship. Ida, apparently, could not stave off the loneliness which Katherine described in a poem published in May 1910:

> Now it is Loneliness who comes at night
> Instead of sleep, to sit beside my bed.
> Like a tired child, I lie and wait her tread. . . .

From her circle of friends Katherine chose the young writer William Orton to fill the gap in her life. Orton was hopelessly in love with another woman, Lais, and therefore unobtainable in any ultimate sense, but he and Katherine shared an intense mental relationship. Both of them, he explains in his autobiography,[1] lived in two separate worlds: the real world and the world of fantasy. Sharing an imaginative delight in letting 'things speak for themselves' and a preference for literature 'overloaded with associations, significances, inner meanings, symbolisms', they were, says Orton, 'happy together in this artist's world'. But in their private worlds they were separately 'leading lives of passionate intensity'. While he remained in love with Lais, Katherine, still in search of 'experience', continued to explore other physical relationships.

Ida Baker's observation that 'in moments of most intense living there was always a part of herself which stood aside, looking on, noting all', is vividly borne out in Katherine's dramatic record of one sexual encounter about this time. 'When the bells were striking five,' she wrote,

> the Man came to see me. He gathered me up in his arms and carried me to the Black Bed. Very brown and strong was he. . . . It grew dark. I crouched against him like a wild cat. Quite impersonally I admired my silver stockings bound beneath the knee with spiked ribbons, my yellow suede shoes fringed with white fur. How vicious I looked! We made love to each other like two wild beasts.

The contrast between the calculated account of this meeting of bodies and Katherine's description of Orton's mistress, Lais, is revealing. 'Lais has just been', Katherine wrote in another part of her friend's journal. 'She is so beautiful that I see no other beauty, and content myself with the sweet Lais. Her slim body in the grey frock – her hands cradling her vivid hair – she lay on the yellow pillows. . . . We are the three eternities – Michael and Lais and I'.

But none of the 'three eternities' really was happy. 'Sometimes I think hopelessly that we will never be together', Katherine eventually wrote. 'I want to begin another life; this one is worn to tearing point.' And so the strange love triangle came to its inevitable end.

During the period between her break with Orton and her meeting with John Middleton Murry, Katherine is thought to have experienced another pregnancy – and an abortion. The poems that she wrote at this time show that she was emotionally adrift, 'like a lost child'. In this crisis, as in later, more desperate ones, her thoughts turned back to childhood and the time when there had been a strong man to call upon for help. Poignantly, the poem 'To God the Father' expresses the speaker's capitulation to an authority-figure who, though ostensibly God, is remarkably like a father. Calling arrogantly at first on 'the little pitiful God' to 'Come down from your place, Grey Beard / We have had enough of your play-acting', she finally requests his love and protection. 'It is centuries since I believed in you', she admits:

But today my need of you has come back.
I want no rose-coloured future,
No books of learning, no protestations and denials –
I am sick of this ugly scramble,
I am tired of being pulled about –
O God, I want to sit on your knees
On the all-too-big throne of Heaven,
And fall asleep with my hands tangled in your grey beard.

The poem moves from an attitude of adult rejection and even scorn to childlike contrition, and finally dependence. Essentially the same feelings are expressed in 'The Storm'. Here the 'ugly scramble' becomes Katherine's sense of being mercilessly buffeted by the elements, and a tree takes the place of the father-figure:

I ran to the forest for shelter,
Breathless, half sobbing;
I put my arms round a tree,
Pillowed my head against the rough bark.
'Protect me', I said. 'I am a lost child.'

During this period of emotional limbo, Katherine Mansfield wrote one notable story, 'The Woman at the Store'. The story's toughness recalls the other, determined side of the 'lost child'.

While critics have noted the work's harsh, naturalistic elements, they have generally passed over its larger significance in the pattern of Katherine Mansfield's artistic development. 'The Woman at the Store' is a milestone because here, for the first time in a major story, she consciously turned back to New Zealand for the subject-matter and setting of her narrative.

'An artist becomes an artist through the intensification of memory', she had written before leaving her own country. Lonely and homesick in 1911, Katherine was once again seeking escape from the dissatisfactions of reality. This time it was not fantasy which came to her aid as an artist, but memory. Her memories were not nostalgic recollections dredged up as fiction, however. So vivid and immediate do the contours of the New Zealand landscape, the colour of the sky, the heat of the relentless summer sun appear in 'The Woman at the Store' that she might almost be reliving her own experiences. And to an extent she was. Not long before her departure from New Zealand in 1908, Katherine joined a camping party which ventured into the sparsely settled back-country of the Ureweras, and in a journal[2] she recorded impressions of the places and people she had seen. It was these precisely remembered details of her own country that she used to shape the external world of her narrative. In her later New Zealand stories she was to do the same.

The internal world of 'The Woman at the Store', however, is very much her own. Manifestly linking this story to those which arose out of the Bavarian episode is the same outrage at the biological helplessness of women which characterises 'Frau Brechenmacher'. The grim lot of the New Zealand woman who keeps an isolated store is presented with far greater objectivity than in the earlier work; but it is still a sympathetic female narrator who observes and comments obliquely upon the circumstances of the central character. Through the narrator's eyes we are made aware of the concupiscence of one of her male travelling companions, Jo. In a state of mounting excitement, he rides towards the store where there is reputedly a woman 'who'll promise you something else before she shakes hands with you'. Undeterred by the ugly physical appearance of the woman – 'you felt there was nothing but sticks and wires under that pinafore' – Jo schemes to win her sexual favours that evening. 'Dang it!' he argues bluntly, 'she'll look better by night light – at any rate, my buck, she's female flesh!' As it turns out, it was as female flesh, too, that the woman's absent husband had abused her. Once 'as pretty as a wax doll' the wife who has been married six years and had four miscarriages rails against the man who took what he wanted, then left her on her own: 'Over and over I tells 'im – you've broken my spirit and spoiled by looks, and wot for – that's wot I'm driving at.'

The source of the emotional tension in the story is not the dramatic unfolding of the woman's unhappiness, however: it is the powerful double irony which gradually becomes evident. The woman, who in her loneliness makes elaborate preparations to sleep with Jo, does not realise that he is as much a sexual exploiter as her husband. But, if she is deceived by the visitor, whom she terms 'a gent', an even greater surprise may await him. While Jo shares the woman's bed, the narrator, her other companion, and the woman's half-crazy child doss down for the night in the store. There the child draws for the visitors a picture her mother has forbidden her to draw: one of 'the woman shooting at a man with a rook rifle and then digging a hole to bury him in'. The narrator's resulting unease conveys her realisation that this woman (who first greeted the travellers with a gun in her hand) harbours an hostility towards men which might cause her to strike again.

'Millie', which was written over a year later in 1913, is a companion piece to 'The Woman at the Store'. This story, too, is set in New Zealand and focuses on the confused emotions of an uneducated married woman. Murder is crucial to the plot structure of both narratives, not for itself but because it enables Katherine Mansfield to explore the complex nature of a woman's vindictiveness towards men. An important difference between the two works, however, is the extent to which the readers' sympathies are manipulated and directed. While we are not asked to condone the woman at the store's murder of her husband, our pity is aroused by Jo's cynical exploitation of her, the woman's bitter story about her married life, and the narrator's own sympathy. By contrast, in the more psychologically complex portrayal of Millie, the reader remains at a greater distance from the central character and at the end it is the woman, rather than the men in the story, who is implicitly judged.

Katherine Mansfield builds up her portrait of Millie with considerable subtlety: only gradually does it become clear that the key to Millie's character is her barely conscious resentment at being a woman. Alone in her house when the story opens, she thinks idly about a murder that has just been committed locally, then about her own childlessness. 'Well, *I've* never missed them', she concludes. Barred from motherhood, Millie demonstrates a certain toughness and familiarity with the world of men when she is startled by a noise from the wood-pile. A gun in her hand, she rushes outside shouting, 'I seen yer. . . . I'll teach you to play tricks with a woman.' Anger and a latent hostility towards the opposite sex are present in her threatening manner. But an unexpected reversal takes place. Millie perceives that the intruder is only a wounded boy with eyes full of pain and terror, and, even as she realises that he is Harrison, the hunted murderer, she decides to hide him. 'Nothing but a kid. An' all them fellows after 'im. 'E don't stand any more of a chance than a kid would. . . . They won't ketch him. Not if I can 'elp it. Men is all beasts.'

The woman's repetition of the word 'kid' would imply that an unsuspected motherliness has motivated her decision; it is her statement 'Men is all beasts' which suggests a more psychologically profound explanation. Inwardly bitter against the sex before whom she feels helpless, Millie has a sense of kinship with the boy who is at the mercy of the same force. The horror of the story lies in her paradoxical change of mood later that night. While the unsuccessful lynch party are asleep in the house, she lies awake hoping for the boy's escape. But a dog's barking rouses the men and they call on the woman to bring a lantern.

> And at the sight of Harrison in the distance, and the three men hot after, a strange mad joy smothered everything else. She rushed into the road – she laughed and shrieked and danced in the dust, jigging the lantern. 'A-ah! Arter 'im, Sid! A-a-a-h! Ketch him, Willie. Go it! Go it! A-ah, Sid! Shoot 'im down. Shoot 'im!'

This is one of the most shocking and startlingly effective endings Katherine Mansfield ever wrote. What she has described is the process by which a woman's emotional identification with the victim has changed to one of identification with the aggressor. In the excitement of the chase, Harrison no longer seems to Millie a helpless being like herself but a representative of his sex, almost literally a 'beast' in whose hunting down she exults. With almost mindless unleashing of her hatred the story comes full circle. For it was Millie who in the beginning had first threatened the man with a gun.

10 Middleton Murry and the Theme of Childhood

Katherine Mansfield's meeting with John Middleton Murry marked a major turning-point in her life and writing. In 'The Education of Audrey' she had imagined the already accomplished man who would instruct her in the secrets of becoming an artist. Murry, an Oxford undergraduate who was attempting to launch an avant-garde literary magazine, must have appeared the personification of her fantasy: as an intellectual he had an educational background which might supplement her own, and as an editor he was in a position to further her literary ambitions.

Perhaps more important, he and Katherine seemed emotionally matched. She dreaded male dominance; and, as Murry himself later admitted in his autobiography, 'there was little of the conquering male about me'. Recognising that she was the stronger, Katherine assumed the dominant role in their alliance. It was she who invited the young man to become a lodger in her flat, and she who eventually suggested that they become lovers. Many years later, Katherine was to assert bitterly in her journal that she had been the man and he had been the woman in their relationship. 'When we first met,' she said, 'it was I who kept him, and afterwards we'd always acted (more or less) like men-friends.'

This was the kind of relationship she herself seems to have wanted, however. A youthful autobiographical fragment called 'Three Twentieth Century Girls' hints that Katherine even as a girl had cultivated a masculine pose. Described as having 'developed a tendency to appear masculine, to the great amusement of the rest of the family', the young heroine of the piece is found crying over a novel; embarrassed she 'stoutly denied such "feminine weakness" and turned the conversation into a different channel'. George Bowden, Katherine's first husband, commented on this masculine streak.[1] 'She had an extreme and almost masculine sense of independence', he said, and before their marriage 'enjoyed being a bachelor along with us'. This was part of her attraction for him. 'Katherine', he wrote, 'found in me not only sympathy but an inclination to anticipate her own broad outlook that the marriage tie should further her emancipation rather than in any way cripple it.' Murry had his own emotional reasons for welcoming a companionship rather than a fervent love-relationship with Katherine Mansfield. 'It is true that I did not want to be Katherine's lover', he explained in *Between Two Worlds*. 'The truth is', he continued, 'that I was now afraid of sex, simply because I had been badly hurt by it. I had suffered mentally and physically, and wanted to forget. . . . It was marvellous to me to have Katherine as my companion.'

From the outset, Katherine and Murry were united by a sense that as children they had been unjustly treated. As if to make up for this, they pretended that they were really children still and able to compensate to each other for what they had suffered in the past. Murry published his own self-pitying story, 'The Little Boy', in the August 1912 issue of *Rhythm*; Katherine's complementary story, 'The Little Girl', was published in the October 1912 issue. In 1912, too, 'New Dresses' was published, although this, together with two slighter childhood pieces, 'Mary'[2] and 'How Pearl Button Was Kidnapped', had been written in 1910. Perhaps it was inevitable that in 1912 Katherine should attempt to analyse with some seriousness her ambivalent feelings about childhood. In mid-1911 her parents, two sisters and brother arrived in England for an extended visit; and their presence probably resurrected memories of the bitterness she had borne them. It was less than four years since she had gained release from the restrictions of family life. Neither time nor events had intervened sufficiently to blot out the jealousies and misunderstandings which had accompanied her departure.

All Katherine Mansfield's early stories about childhood reveal that she carried a heavy burden of resentment. She resented her more attractive and lovable sisters, her brother for being born a boy, her mother for not seeming to love her, her father for meting out too much punishment and too few favours. The importance of 'Mary', 'How Pearl Button Was Kidnapped', 'New Dresses' and 'The Little Girl' is that they are precursors of Katherine Mansfield's most famous stories, 'Prelude' and 'At the Bay'. Appearing undisguised in the early works are the psychological tensions which, in softened form, give the mature portrayals of childhood their remarkable power. As if recognising the revelatory nature of these stories, however, Katherine Mansfield chose not to republish them in her lifetime.

Rivalry between sisters is the dominant theme of the frankly autobiographical piece 'Mary'. Using her own childish nickname, 'Kass', for this first-person account of the relationship between herself and her sister 'Mary', the author looks with more pity than objectivity at her youthful self. Kass had certain natural advantages over her sister. She was 'a strong, fat little child who burst [her] buttons and shot out of [her] skirts to grandmother's entire satisfaction'. And she was clever at schoolwork, especially at poetry. Mary, on the other hand, was a 'weed'. Her continuous cough meant constant doses of medicine (and attention from mother), and she was hopeless at school. But in spite of her handicaps Mary was the more fortunate sister. She loved everybody and was loved in her turn, 'the centre of admiring popularity' at school and of affection, if not favouritism, at home. The story centres on Kass's unhappy attempt to win an extra share of love for herself. One day she heroically decides to transfer her own poetry prize to the unsuspecting Mary; but, because the sacrifice must be kept a secret, it backfires. She is mocked at school while her sister gains additional popularity; and at home Kass's doleful looks are interpreted as jealousy. In bed that night she wept: 'Nobody loved me. Nobody understood me, and they loved Mary without the [prize] and now that she had it I decided they loved me less.'

Written in the same year as 'Mary', the fable-like 'How Pearl Button Was Kidnapped' reads like an attempted answer to the problem posed in the other story. Little Pearl Button allows herself to be stolen from her conventional middle-class home by some fat, affectionate Maori women. With these new 'parents', the little girl enjoys not only the attention lavished on her but also the pleasure of warm, physical contact: 'She nestled closer in the big lap. The woman was warm as a cat. . . . Pearl had never been happy like this before.' The fantasy behind the story is that of the unloved child who dreams of running away and finding a more satisfactory family. But, as in the fantasy stories of the adolescent Katherine Mansfield, reality intrudes on the dream so that it ends in reversal and disappointment. In Pearl Button's case, 'a crowd of little blue men [come] to carry her back to the House of Boxes'.

'New Dresses' is a far longer story which compares a child's bad, real parents with her good, substitute parents. Thinly disguising Annie and Harold Beauchamp as Anne and Henry Carsfield, Katherine Mansfield portrays both parents unfavourably. The mother, making expensive new dresses for her daughters Rose and Helen when the story opens, favours the older girl, and shows almost positive dislike of Helen. Helen is not to have lace on her cuffs because she is careless with her clothes; the girl's stuttering irritates her mother, who terms it merely an affectation; moreover, Helen must be kept away from her baby brother because she frightens him. Capping the mother's antagonistic feelings towards her daughter is the sight of a book left outside in the damp night air: she determines to complain about the girl to her husband.

The father in his turn is portrayed as boastfully self-centred, ungenerous and obsessed with his baby son to the exclusion of Helen. Finding his wife making expensive dresses for the girls, he angrily questions her about their cost and justifies his displeasure with reference to their son: 'How do you think I can buy Boy a chair or anything else – if you chuck away my earnings like that?' Later, after a family excursion to church, Henry invites Doctor Malcolm home to dinner because he has 'asked after Boy so intelligently'. When the visitor shows an interest in Helen, however, her father admonishes the girl, 'You mustn't be a plague to people who are not members of your own family.'

In contrast, the grandmother and Doctor Malcolm understand and defend the child. The grandmother, who wonders why Anne and Henry 'want to hurt Helen's feelings', insists on putting some lace on her dress too. She reminds her daughter that she herself stuttered as a child, and that Helen is highly strung: 'She wanted to speak her mind to Anne once and for all about the way she and Henry were treating Helen. . . .' For his part, Doctor Malcolm prefers Helen to her favoured sister, Rose. After Helen's new dress has mysteriously disappeared, it is he who acts the role of fairy-godfather and contrives to have a new one made in time to avert the impending punishment.

'New Dresses' is an unsubtle story, too obviously biased against the heartless parents. But Katherine Mansfield's insights into the psychology of the young girl who feels unloved are penetrating. 'The peculiar way she treats Boy, staring at him and frightening him' reflects Helen's jealousy of the envied male child. Her carelessness in tearing the dress which has created such friction between her parents is an almost deliberate act of retaliation against the mother who cares more for her daughter's clothes than she does for her feelings. Besides being a way of revenging herself on her parents, the destruction of the dress is a desperate bid for some of the attention which is lavished on her siblings. For this reason the whipping which her father 'promises' Helen the next day is as much a reward for her naughtiness as a punishment, and affords the child a kind of perverse pleasure. The grandmother intuitively understands this and treats Doctor Malcolm's arrival with an identical new dress less as a reprieve than as a disappointment. ' "How thoughtful of you, Doctor!" said the old woman. "I'll tell Anne I found it under my dolman. . . . But of course Helen would have forgotten the whipping by to-morrow morning, and I'd promised her a new doll. . . ." The old woman spoke regretfully.'

The story ends with the reversal of expectations so typical of Katherine Mansfield's fiction. 'Don't seem to have got any forrader than doing Helen out of a doll' are Doctor Malcolm's final puzzled words. Aesthetically, the ending is weak because attention is deflected from the major characters in the family drama to a supporting character. And yet there is a certain logic to the conclusion. Doctor Malcolm, the observer, is accurately echoing the puzzlement of the reader, who, without the psychological key to the events acted out before him, fails to grasp their connection.

The emotional focus of 'New Dresses' is on the child's relationship with her mother. 'The Little Girl' centres firmly on the child Kezia's feelings about her father. Harold Beauchamp always loomed large in Katherine Mansfield's life. When she was young, he was a figure of authority whose dominance must be resisted, but as she grew older he came increasingly to seem a source of strength as well as restraint, of emotional stability as well as firmness. 'I feel towards my Pa man like a little girl', Katherine wrote to Murry in 1913. 'I want to jump and stamp on his chest and cry "You've *got* to love me." When he says he does, I feel quite confident that God is on my side.'

Written in 1912 either during or shortly after her parents' visit to England, 'The Little Girl' is a hauntingly intense story whose emotional power stems from the author's re-examination of her childhood relationship with her father. From the outset, he is established as an awesome personage. 'To the little girl he was a figure to be feared and avoided', the story opens. Through the child's own eyes we are shown why this should be so. Although father is a domineering man, who, like Herr Brechenmacher, signals his presence in the house through a stream of commands, it is less his verbal than his physical dominance which overwhelms the girl. 'He was so big – his hands and his neck, especially his mouth when he yawned. Thinking about him alone in the nursery was like thinking about a giant.' Try as she might, Kezia cannot avoid father. She receives his 'perfunctory' kiss every morning and is summoned in the evenings to pull off his boots. On Sunday afternoons she is sent to the drawing-room to have a 'nice talk with father and mother'.

The central incident in the story involves father's birthday, for which Kezia is instructed to make a pincushion. Unwittingly, she tears up his 'great speech for the Port Authority' as stuffing for the pincushion. Despite her protestations that she has been making him a present, father furiously sends her to bed to await a whipping. ' "Oh, no, no!" she screamed, cowering down under the bedclothes' as he came towards her with a ruler. For all grandmother's comforting, 'the child never forgot'; and, indeed, there appears to be a link between this punishment and the nightmares which torment Kezia. One night when mother and grandmother are away, 'the same old nightmare came – the butcher with a knife and a rope who grew nearer and nearer, smiling that dreadful smile'. The surprise dénouement occurs when she wakes from the nightmare to find father at her bedside. Uncharacteristically kind, he takes her into his own bed. 'Half asleep still, still with the butcher's smile all about her, it seemed, she crept close to him.' Deciding that father is 'not so big, after all – and with no one to look after him', Kezia sighs and says, 'What a big heart you've got, father dear.'

On the surface, the story seems to be one of childhood misunderstanding happily resolved. The combination of details together with the symbolism indicates, however, that we are being given a far more sophisticated insight into the workings of a child's mind. Kezia's stuttering, which so irritates father, can be seen as an expression not just of fear but also of hostility. The same repressed hostility causes her apparently accidental destruction of his speech. As if recognising this, he will brook no excuses when he punishes her. But hate is interwined with love and the need for love, as the ambivalent picture of the nightmare butcher signifies. Physically threatening her in the dream with a knife and rope, he smiles as if to convey benevolent intentions. Similarly, the father who so terrifies his daughter appears loving when he takes her into his bed.

It is the resemblance of Kezia's closing words – 'What a big heart you've got, father dear' – to those spoken by Little Red Riding Hood to the wolf which suggest the deepest, psychological meaning of the story. Implicit in this unconscious reference to being devoured is the child's inability to separate her need for paternal love from her fear that the price of emotional satisfaction is to be killed and eaten. For her, as for an infant, love and food are emotionally indistinguishable. What seem to confirm this interpretation are the insistent references in the narrative to the mouth. There is father's morning kiss, followed by a sense of relief at his departure; his loud voice (especially in church) and Kezia's own stuttering response. Thinking about father's size, it is his open mouth which seems particularly big. An implicit association emerges, too, between Kezia's likening of him to a giant and the fairy story about the giant who killed and ate children. When the child, however unconsciously, attempts to get even with her father, it is by destroying his 'great speech'.

In the context of the chronic anxiety which unfolds in the story, the concluding reconciliation between father and daughter is more apparent than real. Assuredly, the act of being taken into father's bed gratifies the little girl's secret desire to replace her mother as the object of his love, just as the reality of physical contact with his body allays her frightening fantasies. But what does not change is the ambiguous image of father as a butcher on the one hand, and as a wolf dressed in kindly guise on the other.

11 Reality versus Dream

In the same issue of *Rhythm* as 'New Dresses' and 'The Little Girl', Katherine Mansfield published a satirical piece called 'Sunday Lunch'. Here she unleashed against the London 'arty' set the bitterness which, in more restrained form, echoes through her stories of childhood. The very sharpness of her attack in 'Sunday Lunch' indicates that it was motivated by more than a desire to exhibit her cleverness: behind it one detects the jealousy which is revealed again and again in the stories based on her own childhood. Katherine's problem as a writer was that, although her talents were being noticed, she did not feel at home in London literary circles. These were dominated by the socially exclusive Bloomsbury group; and, although she herself had grown up in a privileged, upper-class family, she was personally unknown in London, and, what was worse, a colonial. For one as ambitious as Katherine and as much in need of acceptance, such exclusion was galling.

Her aggression against the literary world in 'Sunday Lunch' takes the form of a 'biting' sarcasm and an unequivocal use of the metaphor of eating to depict the destructive competitiveness of the arty set. 'Sunday Lunch is the last of the cannibal feasts', the sketch begins. 'It is the wild tremendous orgy of the upper classes, the hunting, killing, eating ground of all the George-the-Fifth-and-Mary artists.' The would-be artists' 'air of immense unconcern' is belied when they begin to eat:

> With kind looks and little laughs and questions the cannibals prick with the knife. . . . With ever greater skill and daring the cannibals draw blood, or the stuff like blood that flows in their veins. But the horrible tragedy of the Sunday lunch is this: however often the society kills and eats itself, it is never brave enough to consider itself well eaten.

Thus Katherine Mansfield ascribed to the artistic world, of whose power she was only too conscious, the same desire to devour and annihilate which had inspired her portraits of German males, and which was implicit in the child's conception of her father. Like the parents who were goaded to punish, society began to fulfil her expectations. A period of comparative stability ended abruptly when the publisher of *Rhythm* vanished, leaving a debt to the printers of £400. As if masochistically anxious to have their conception of themselves as unfairly harassed children confirmed, Murry and Katherine shouldered the debt. Bravery, Katherine Mansfield had declared in 'Sunday Lunch', was to submit to aggression, to allow oneself to be eaten. In paying over to the printers her total allowance she did just that; for it is probable that the privations which ensued lowered her resistance to the consumption that was to kill her.

From all accounts, the life of Katherine and her partner was financially and personally turbulent in 1913. Almost certainly they must have moved to Paris in December 1913 in the hope of escaping their troubles and finding a more satisfying life. But this proved only a dream. Unable to make a living in Paris, Murry returned to England in February 1914 and accepted a position with the *Westminster Gazette*.

Emotionally as well as financially, Katherine Mansfield's life was by now thoroughly intertwined with Murry's. His sense of social inferiority and his self-described terror of life fed her own tendency to stand apart from a world by which she felt rejected. A natural concomitant, then, to Katherine's lashing out against those in a stronger position than herself was a withdrawal with Murry into a world of their own making: a world where they avoided as much as possible 'society', which, with its power of censure or approbation, was an extension of the parents who gave, or more often withheld, love.

Nothing illustrates more clearly the extent to which this private world was based on fantasy than 'Something Childish But Very Natural', the one story Katherine wrote in Paris in 1913. Fantasy plays an important part in Katherine Mansfield's mature fiction; but with the exception of 'The Tiredness of Rosabel', written in 1908, and two uncollected pieces, 'A Fairy Story' (1910) and 'The House' (1912),[1] the stories she wrote during her first few years in London are for the most part unrelievedly realistic. 'Something Childish', however, bears unmistakably marks of Katherine Mansfield's association with Murry. Murry seems to have deflected her thematic concerns away from the trauma of heterosexual relations towards the earlier traumas of childhood. More important, he gave her a new subject for fiction: their own emotional relationship. 'Something Childish' is the first of a group of fine stories, including 'Je Ne Parle Pas Français', 'The Man Without a Temperament' and 'A Married Man's Story', in which the author examines in fictional guise her attitude to the man she lived with. It is also the first major story in which fantasy is used in conjunction with realism to soften, even to disguise, the pain of reality.

Katherine Mansfield had moved far from the dreamlike stories of her adolescence when she came to write 'Something Childish'. Instead of fantasy controlling the mind of the author, it becomes a theme to be treated with artistic objectivity. Closely interwoven with the theme of fantasy is the ambiguous love relationship of two young people, Edna and Henry. After meeting accidentally, the couple are drawn together by a realisation of their mutual need. Alienated from their families as well as from the world at large, both feel misunderstood and very much alone.

But their ripening friendship is threatened by Edna's shrinking from any physical contact with Henry. 'Every time he . . . even asked for her hand she shrank back and looked at him with pleading frightened eyes as though he wanted to hurt her.' Edna, who before their meeting had 'made up [her] mind that [she] didn't care for – men at all', finally tells Henry, 'It's not that I'm frightened of you . . . it's only a feeling, Henry, that I can't understand myself even. . . . Somehow I feel if once we . . . held each other's hands and kissed it would be all changed. . . . We wouldn't be children any more.' And so Henry is forced to play Edna's game of make-believe, of children pretending to be adults. Life assumes for him a quality of dreamlike, insubstantial happiness in which time stands still and reality is kept at bay. Since to admit of any progression in the relationship is to break the bubble and destroy the dream, Henry must struggle against the reality of his physical longing for the girl he loves.

In this situation, the boundary lines between fantasy and reality, between sleeping and waking, and ultimately between living and not-living become blurred. The narrative itself, as if imitating the mental state of the protagonists, becomes increasingly dreamlike and ambiguous. Caught up in this ambiguity is the character of Henry, to whose thoughts we are given access. While we sympathise with his yearning to break out of the dream which falsifies his life, we remain aware that in the opening scene he adopted as his own the escapist sentiments expressed in a poem, 'Something Childish But Very Natural'. The message of the poem is that, while thoughts or wishes cannot transcend reality, the state of sleep or dream does allow the creation of one's own world.

Henry's crisis occurs one day when he and Edna are walking in the woods. 'Ever since waking he had felt so strangely that he was not really awake at all, but just dreaming.' Although he tries to reinforce their pretence by imagining himself and Edna as 'two very small children', a longing to break through the unreality of the relationship overwhelms him. 'He wanted to kiss Edna . . . and kiss her until he'd no breath left and so stifle the dream.' And so he ignores the warning from his subconscious mind about some other dream in 'a dark place'. Joyfully he accepts at face value Edna's declaration (made in the 'deceptive' evening light) that she loves him and has 'quite got over the feeling'. As a result, they agree to rent a country cottage and live together – as brother and sister.

'Something Childish' concludes with Henry, let down by Edna's failure to arrive, sitting on the doorstep in a state which might be sleep or death. There is an inevitability about this ending in which Henry is returned to the condition of the speaker in the poem. For one thing, Katherine Mansfield has enclosed the story in a framework of fantasy or magic: any concluding reconciliation between the demands of fantasy and those of reality would entail the breaking of the spell, the destruction of the dreamlike mood which is so integral to the narrative. On the thematic level, there is built into the story an almost irreconcilable conflict between Henry's love of dreaming and his real-life needs. He and Edna have come together precisely because they believe themselves to be quite different from ordinary people. Since the make-believe existence they build is based on this premise, any move towards accepting themselves as normal human beings is bound to threaten, if not destroy, their relationship.

The deathlike ending of the story is reminiscent of the endings Katherine Mansfield as a girl contrived for her fantasies.

Whenever she was unable to adjust the needs of fantasy to those of reality, she chose for her character that state in which no adjustment is necessary. In her slight 1912 piece 'The House', Katherine had once again ended a fantasy, this time that of a poor office girl who dreams of a perfect home, husband and child, with the protagonist's sudden death. The significant difference between her attitude to fantasy in the two stories is that in 'The House' she herself weaves a fantasy and concludes it abruptly and unconvincingly; in 'Something Childish' there is evidence of greater objectivity. Artistically in control of her theme, she conveys implicitly her own understanding that fantasy-living, at best, merely postpones the final reckoning.

12 Role-playing

If 'Something Childish' is indicative of Katherine Mansfield's growing awareness that fantasy-living was a kind of living death, the story also conveys the impression of some premonitory insight into the development of her relations with Murry. Indeed, the disillusioned return of the couple from Paris in February 1914 seems to have marked the close of one chapter in the alliance between them. Their relationship was incomplete. And this they could no longer gloss over merely by indulging the insubstantial happiness of existing together in a world of their own making. Murry by his own admission felt inferior to Katherine. Now, after the Paris fiasco, he was desperately anxious to prove his own worth and achieve a measure of independence from her. 'I was, in a sense, rebellious even against the love that bound me to Katherine', he writes in his autobiography; 'even to her, I surrendered unwillingly. I wanted to guard my personality against her. . . . An impulse of resistance and withdrawal had grown up in me. . . .'

Murry had reason to feel inadequate in 1914. The collapse of *Rhythm* and its successor, the *Blue Review*, had left him adrift professionally. Hating the casual journalism by which he was forced to live, he hated even more being chronically short of money. His inability to earn a living diminished him in the eyes of the world; and it made him vulnerable to Katherine's scorn. Katherine, never a true bohemian, and accustomed by her upbringing to the luxuries as well as the necessities of life, was always in want of money. Deliberately, she had rejected masterful men such as her father who might have offered her luxury at the price of freedom. What she wanted was the best of both worlds: a sufficiently submissive partner, yet one who, while devoted to herself, could sustain her materially and further her ambitions. Murry was now failing on all counts. Using her allowance, they drifted from one dismal abode to another; then, after moving to a cottage in Buckinghamshire near their new friends, the Lawrences, the situation deteriorated still further. Not only did the contrast between the more fortunate position of the Lawrences (who were enjoying the fruits of literary success) and their own poverty exacerbate Katherine's discontent: Lawrence's attempt to draw Murry from her sphere of influence into his own deepened her resentment.

As he explains it in *Between Two Worlds*, Murry was reacting away from Katherine and searching for some sense of identity among men. Shunning other people, he indulged in bouts of intensive self-probing with Lawrence and Gordon Campbell. Lawrence, who criticised Murry (among other things) for 'not taking *Sex* seriously', appears only to have worsened his feelings of inferiority. 'It was Campbell whom I set on a pinnacle,' he admits, 'that he might haul me out of my own sense of nothingness. . . . I desperately wanted him to "believe in me". . . . Ultimately it did not matter to me whether Lawrence "believed in me". . . . And, alas, ultimately it did not matter to me if Katherine believed in me.'

Katherine's own ambiguous involvement with Ida Baker made it difficult for her to counter this new development. When all was well in her relationship with Murry, Ida was pushed to the background; but whenever Katherine's fears of abandonment were reactivated, as happened in 1914, Ida again became important in Katherine's emotional life. Guilt and a kind of remorse echo through a journal entry dated March 1914, shortly before Ida left England for an extended visit to Rhodesia. 'Have I ruined her happy life? Am I to blame?' Katherine asked herself.

> She gave me the gift of herself. 'Take me, Katie. I am yours. . . .' Yes, I am altogether to blame. . . .
>
> To-night I saw her all drawn up with pain. . . . So I helped her to bed. . . . And as I tucked her up, she was so touching . . . that it was easy to stoop and kiss her. . . . 'Oh!' she sighed, 'I have dreamed of this.' (All the while I was faintly revolted.) . . . 'This is Paradise, beloved!' Good God! I must be at ordinary times a callous brute. It is the first time in all these years that I have leaned to her and kissed her like that. . . .
>
> Ah, how I long to talk about it, sometimes – not for a

> moment, but until I am tired out and have got rid of the burden of memory.

Implicit in the entry is a comparison between Ida's unquestioning love and Murry's lack of understanding – and perhaps his lack of physical desire. On an emotional level, Ida clearly offered some kind of continuing alternative to Murry. But, because Katherine's attraction to her own sex was dangerous, it had to be quickly denied. Just as she had once repudiated E.K.B. after recording a physical encounter, so she now turned against L.M. and privately blamed her for the unhappiness she felt:

> When I get by myself, I am always more or less actively miserable. Nobody knows, or could, what a weight L.M. is upon me. She simply drags me down and then sits on me, calm and huge. The strongest reason for my happiness in Paris was that I was safe from her.

Yet in spite of this assertion Katherine could record quite happily, only two days later, an excursion around London with Ida. The next day she noted, '[Ida] left at about 9 p.m. having dressed me. When I leave her hands I feel hung with wreaths.'

Such was Katherine's fickleness, however, that only a week after Ida had left England she was telling herself, 'My letter to L.M. was a great effort. She seemed somehow "out of the running". . . . I wish I lived on a barge, with Jack for a husband and a little boy for a son.' A few days later, happy for the moment in her relationship with Murry, she added ambiguously, 'L.M. seems to be simply fading away. I can barely remember her objectively: subjectively she is just the same.' Perhaps the most vivid description of Katherine Mansfield's confused mental state in 1914 is to be found in Murry's account in his autobiography of an intense discussion between them towards the end of that year. After a session with Campbell, Murry felt that he was suffering from a dislocation of the personality. Katherine said she shared his feeling:

> I have always been attempting to be myself since I was a child. I always wanted to 'get down to myself' when I was seventeen. From twenty to twenty-four, certain moments of music, a tree waving outside, seemed to take me to myself. I

> realised by their contrast with me at other moments that there was a self to get to.

Her difficulty in integrating and communicating with this divided personality Katherine expressed metaphorically. 'I see it like a misty river flowing out of the beyond', she told Murry, 'and I am like a little figure running in the mist on the bank, knowing that there is a bridge to be found, but not knowing for the mist whether to go right or left.'

Whether the role-playing in which she habitually indulged was a result of this chronic indecision about her personality, or whether the sense of being self-divided was a natural concomitant of role-playing, is debatable. What seems certain is that from an early age Katherine cultivated the outward manifestations of a dual personality. While one side of the self withdrew from the outside world, the other would participate on its own terms, acting a part with the conscious intention of deceiving. To Sylvia Payne she had confided that impersonation was almost a necessary condition for writing. Others observed Katherine's indulgence in play-acting. One school-friend remembered her as a strange girl with 'a knack for withdrawing into herself completely from those around her . . . mimicry was her strong suit and her sense of drama was faultless – she could think herself into any part'.[1] George Bowden vividly recalled Katherine Mansfield's startling changes in personality. At one evening gathering, he reminisced, she appeared

> dressed in more or less Maori fashion. . . . There was something almost eerie about it, as though of a psychic transformation rather than a mere impersonation. At such times her facial lineaments might seem altered, and in trying to understand her complex personality this is a factor to be reckoned with.[2]

A story fragment written in 1915 and called 'Dark Hollow'[3] suggests that psychic transformations of the kind Bowden describes occurred when Katherine was feeling particularly insecure. Faced with situations of stress, she would be seized with the desire to escape momentarily from her own circumstances by acting out some part she had imagined. It is exactly this that Nina, the heroine of 'Dark Hollow', does. Telling the male companion she has been living with, 'Money won't fall through the ceiling onto the quilt, you know. . . . And you bloody well won't milk me any longer . . . I've done with you', she pretends to leave him. Once away, Nina admits to herself the part she is playing: 'This has happened to you before and will happen again and again – and again.' After she meets Louise, a former friend, Nina begins acting in earnest. Inventing a hard-luck story of illness, a broken marriage and a stillborn child, she gains the other girl's sympathy. Then, secure in the comfort of Louise's home,

> a mysterious sense of well-being filled her. It did not matter how long this lasted. At any rate for the time she had dropped out of her own world and all its beastliness, and that was enough. . . . The funny thing was that Louise believed her story – had taken it all so simply and naturally that Nina began to have a faint feeling that it was true. . . . How I sobbed, she thought admiringly.

In all probability, the mood of the piece reflects Katherine's actual relations with Murry during the closing months of 1914 and the early part of 1915. Providing little in the way of emotional support, Murry's contribution to their finances was so meagre that in January 1915 Katherine wrote in her journal:

> For this year I have two wishes: to write, to make money. Consider. With money we could go away as we liked . . . be as free as we liked, and be independent and proud with nobodies. It is only poverty that holds us so tightly. Well, J. doesn't want money and won't earn money. I must.

Depressed, and left emotionally isolated by Murry's involvement with Gordon Campbell and his seeming indifference to her needs, Katherine began casting around for alternative sources of love. There was L.M.: 'The ghost of L.M. ran through my heart, her hair flying, very pale, with dark startled eyes'; but there was also Francis Carco, Murry's Parisian friend, with whom a correspondence had begun. With his 'warm sensational life', Carco seemed to offer the best chance of happiness. Impassioned letters were exchanged, and mentally Katherine prepared to leave Murry. 'For him I am hardly anything except a gratification and a comfort', she wrote in her journal. 'He doesn't know me himself – or want to. . . . Jack, Jack, we are not going to stay together. I know that as well as you do. . . . What we have got each to kill – is my *you* and your *me*. That's all.'

In the pages of her journal, Katherine tried to convince herself that it was the romantic Frenchman whom she really loved: 'Yes, love like this is a malady, a fever, a storm', she declared. By February 1915 she had determined to go to Carco in France. Her decision was essentially an unreal one, an attempt (like Nina's) to escape unhappiness by trying out another life. Murry, 'curiously certain that she was deceiving herself', made no attempt to prevent her flight. Indeed at a Christmas party in 1914 he himself wrote a scenario of their separation and joined Katherine in performing it.

In January 1915, before her departure, Katherine Mansfield produced her own scenario of the affair she was contemplating. A long rambling story, 'Brave Love', is akin to 'Dark Hollow' in its portrayal of the narcissistic role-playing of the female protagonist. Valerie Brandon's own thoughts reveal her as a thoroughly unpleasant character, a pretender who toys unscrupulously, even sadistically, with men vulnerable to her charms. Mitka, a shy young Russian sailor, is her latest victim, and she extracts from him the fervent declaration, 'I would do anything in my power to help you.' Not seeing the signs of insincerity in her face, 'the strange mingling of relief and scorn and amusement', he joyfully accepts her offer of a 'secret friendship'. 'Ah God, what bliss this is', he thinks. 'I who have never had a friend, who have never had anyone to wholly love.' The pathetic irony of the situation is painfully evident as further disclosures reveal the extent of Valerie's egotism. Bored and dissatisfied with her steady companion, Evershed, but unwilling to give him up because he offers a certain security and besides, is 'worth any amount of money', she is seeking merely the diversion of a romantic passion. In the cause of this passion Mitka (whom as part of the game she has agreed to marry) is 'to be sacrificed'. To a friend, Mildred, she admits frankly, 'If once I've touched a thing I can't let it go until I've tried to break it or to see if it can break me.'

The closing scenes of the drama Valerie has initiated take place in Marseilles, where Mitka lies ill. Thinking, 'He'd be an awfully charming lover – after my commercial bulldog', she goes to his lodging. If the sordidness of his tenement house dispels her romantic expectations, the affair nevertheless works out to her advantage. For Valerie has brought the unknowing Evershed with her to Marseilles, and when she returns to their hotel he is distraught. 'I never thought a man could be such a fool over a woman', he blurts out. 'Why, I thought you'd done it on purpose. Brought me here and then skeedaddled.' Not displeased with this reaction, she replies smoothly, 'on the contrary. . . . I believe I'm really falling in love with you.'

For all its insight into the motivation of a particular type of heartless young woman, 'Brave Love' is an aesthetically weak story. Besides the element of melodrama, the working out of the plot shows such an absence of intellectual control that it might almost be the enactment of a wish-fulfilling fantasy. To be sure, Valerie Brandon is shown up for what she is, but, as the ending indicates, the author is quite unprepared to pass judgement on her heroine; indeed, she appears to be in league with her.

Katherine Mansfield never lost her interest in the thought processes of women who were deliberate pretenders. Written at the height of her career in 1920, the sophisticated 'Poison' is thematically a direct descendant of 'Brave Love'; there are elements, too, of Valerie's play-acting in Beryl in 'Prelude' and 'At the Bay', in Miss Brill, in the female characters from 'Psychology', 'Bliss' and 'Marriage à la Mode' and even in the effeminate Mr Reginald Peacock and Raoul Duquette. Never again, however, did Katherine Mansfield portray so nakedly the cruel deception of others, nor did she so self-indulgently suspend moral judgement.

It is significant that neither Katherine nor Murry (who printed nearly everything else) ever saw fit to publish 'Brave Love'. The story was far too damning, reflecting as it did the author's relations with actual people. Mitka, the shy, affectionate Russian, appears to be modelled upon Koteliansky, with whom Katherine conducted a flirtation between 1914 and 1916. Thanking him for the present of a dress in February 1915, she wrote, 'It makes me feel that wonderful adventures might happen if only one is dressed and ready.' Wondering what she can give him in return, she closes the letter with 'one thing if you want it is yours to keep . . . your loving friend'.[4]

If Katherine's inspiration for the guileless Mitka was Koteliansky, who genuinely loved her, the episode in which the heroine goes to France to test out her potentially 'charming lover' was surely based upon the rendezvous she was planning with Francis Carco. Although the ending of 'Brave Love' suggests that in her heart of hearts she anticipated no lasting relationship with Carco, there is a hint of the other ways in which he might serve her purposes. As an 'awfully charming lover' he might relieve her boredom with Murry as a lover; better still, he might arouse Murry's jealousy and rekindle his need of Katherine. For, although Evershed in the story has plenty of money, he quite clearly is cast in the mould of Murry. In fiction as well as in real life, Katherine was playing off one person against another, attempting to harness the jealousy she was so prone to herself.

'Cynical, but wonderfully brave, ready to risk anything for the sake of an experience', was how Murry in *Between Two Worlds* described the woman who left him in February 1915 in pursuit of her new romance. Katherine's stay with Carco lasted a bare ten days, and experience was her only gain. The actual love affair appears to have been no more fulfilling than any other, nor was there the compensation of making Murry jealous. Only Katherine's return to her steady, if inadequate, companion resembles the dream she had woven around her romantic adventure. Emotionally Murry retained the upper hand, for, as he himself writes,

> the truth [was] that I did not need Katherine in the way she then believed she required to be needed. . . . I was self-sufficient in some odd and partial fashion. . . . The feeling she awakened and kept alive in me was more important to me even than herself.

Out of her short-lived but happy sojourn with Murry in Paris in 1913, Katherine Mansfield had written 'Something Childish But Very Natural', a work tinged with sadness as it describes the first encounter of youthful dream with adult reality. Her return visit to France with another lover, Carco, was a very different emotional experience. In its aftermath Katherine struggled to come to grips with her feelings in a new story. It is significant that in 'The Little Governess' she deals much more harshly with the heroine who cannot distinguish between truth and wish-fulfilment. Almost certainly, the darkening atmosphere of this story reflects the author's bitter mood of humiliation and self-condemnation.

On her way to a post in Germany, the little governess is portrayed from the outset as another immature character. Apprehensive about travelling abroad for the first time, she is warned by the woman in the Governess Bureau: 'it's better to mistrust people at first rather than trust them, and it's safer to suspect people of evil intentions rather than good ones.' When a porter with an 'insolent voice' grabs her bag and ushers her onto the train to Munich, she takes the advice literally. 'Sure he was a robber', she resolutely refuses payment. In contrast to her hostile attitude towards the porter is her friendliness to an elderly man who enters the carriage. Because he appears old, well-dressed and extremely courteous, her vigilance is relaxed. Wanting a protector, she allows herself to believe that he is one as he offers her magazines, deplores the conduct of the youths next door, and buys her strawberries when the train stops: 'it was while she munched the berries that she first thought of the old man as a grandfather. What a perfect grandfather he would make! Just like one out of a book. . . . When she had eaten them she felt she had known him for years.' Deluding herself thus that her wishes are fact, she tells him everything about herself and her appointment in Munich. Only for a moment after she has accepted his invitation to go sightseeing does she feel, then quickly dismiss, some misgiving: 'After all, she really did not know him. But he was so old and he had been so very kind – not to mention the strawberries.'

It is not the old man, therefore, but the waiter at her hotel in Munich who bears the brunt of her mistrust: she dismisses him curtly without the expected tip. In sharp contrast to her treatment of menials who expect gratuities for their service is her happy response to the generosity of the old man, now mentally become 'her grandfather who had asked her to spend the day'. Like a real grandfather with a child, he indulges the little governess with morning tea, lunch and ice-cream. She responds, as he lavishes ever more food upon her, by lapsing into such a state of childishness that 'her grateful baby heart glowed with love for the fairy grandfather'. And 'fairy' in the sense of 'unreal' grandfather he indeed proves to be. Enticing her home with the promise of yet another gift, he finally asks:

> 'And are you going to give me one little kiss before you go?' . . . She sprang up, but he was too quick and he held her against the wall, pressed against her his hard old body and his twitching knee and, though she shook her head from side to side, distracted, kissed her on the mouth.

Rushing tearfully back to the hotel, the little governess finds herself stranded.

The irony which overlays the story is obvious. One with so much to learn as the little governess has no business to be starting out as a teacher. But the real theme of the work is childhood: not chronological childhood, but the unnatural prolongation of emotional childhood in an adult woman. If there is a horrifying depravity about the aging roué who deceives his victim so elaborately, the little governess is in her own way equally perverse. There is an infantilism about the pleasure with which she responds to the care of the motherly stewardess and the 'warm rocking' motion of the Channel boat. Acting like a spoilt child in her refusal to pay the porter and the waiter, she regresses ever further into greedy dependency as the fantasied 'grandfather' plies her with food. This mental perpetuation of the condition of childhood is on one level an attempt to evade responsibility; but the young woman's self-deception about her companion is also a defence against another childish fantasy: that of becoming the object of a father-figure's love. For, while the attentions of the old man have resembled those of a man courting, the coquetry of the little governess suggests that she has been instinctively aware of this. First she 'peeped at him through her long lashes' and decided that 'he was really nice to look at'. Blushing 'a deep pink colour that spread slowly over her cheeks' when he initiated conversation, she is shown smiling prettily, and dimpling at him. Later she allows her hand to lose itself 'in the big brown suède ones'. As if she were indeed a young woman in love, she finally tells him, 'this has been the happiest day of my life. I've never even imagined such a day.'

As long as the little governess's repressed wishes are kept within the realm of 'fairy' or 'storybook', her enjoyment with the old man is unlimited. When he attempts to make love to her, however, and fantasy threatens to become reality, she reacts with horror and outrage. Such is the inner truth of the story that its effect is unpleasant. For as she wrote it, Katherine Mansfield appeared to spare no one: neither her protagonist, nor herself, nor her readers. Indeed, in this punishment of the little governess one is tempted to see the author's vicarious self-castigation for her own folly in misconstruing the honeyed words of Carco. He had been no more the 'fairy' grandfather, come to relieve her suffering with Murry, than the old man in the story. Content to explore the condition of fantasy-living in 'Something Childish', she unmistakably condemns it here.

Katherine's visit to Carco, and two other trips to Paris – not for the purposes of romance but for writing – brought to an end what she called her 'three years' idyll' with Murry. Her letters to Murry from Paris reveal the beginning of a psychological pattern that was to become even more familiar as time passed: an assertion of her emotional dependence on him which alternated with a disillusioned striving to overcome that dependence. As if to force him to reciprocate her love, she filled letter after letter in March 1915 with declarations of her own deep feelings. When he did not reply in kind, Katherine's demand for love became more urgent. 'Oh, Jack, write often. I am *lost*, *lost* without letters from you.' A few days later she put her case more clearly: 'Here's a confession. I cannot write if all is not well with us – not a line. I do write in my own way through you.'

The letters Katherine wrote to Murry during their next period of separation still protest her love; but they reflect a deepening disillusionment. 'You and I still love each other, but you haven't the need of me you had then, and somehow I do always have to be "needed" to be happy.' As invariably happened when Murry failed to live up to her expectations, Katherine began casting around for other sources of consolation, other people to fill the gap in her life – and to taunt him with. During her first visit alone to Paris she wrote to him about calling on Beatrice Hastings: 'there arrived "du monde", including a very lovely young woman, married and *curious* – blonde – passionate. We danced together.' But Ida Baker's devotion provided the most telling contrast to Murry's lack of warmth. 'You sent me a letter from Lesley [Ida] which was simply marvellous', Katherine wrote to him insinuatingly. 'There is something quite absolute in Lesley. . . . She's about the nearest thing to "eternal" that I could ever imagine. I wish she were not so far away.'

L.M. was still in Rhodesia; but Katherine's brother, Leslie, was now in England training as an army officer. His visits to her later that year assuaged her sense of isolation. Eagerly, after so many months of dissatisfaction, Katherine welcomed someone from her own background. In the company of her brother, she could turn back the clock and recreate in memory the time when (for all her rebelliousness) she had known the security of a family and a comfortable home. Memory, idealised, was like fantasy: a source of consolation and a means of escaping the present. It was also a means of self-discovery. Her brother's companionship during those brief months in the latter half of 1915 set in motion the process of Katherine Mansfield's reconciliation with the family and the country she had so bitterly rejected.

PART III

1915–1918

13 Death of Little Brother

Katherine's newfound happiness with her brother proved just as insubstantial as the happiness experienced by the heroines of her early fantasy stories.

In October 1915 Leslie was killed, and the shock was so traumatic that it constituted a turning-point in her life, 'a complete upheaval' as Murry stated. From at least the age of fourteen she had reacted to personal unhappiness with fantasies of her own death; and now, with so little hesitation that it seemed she had been merely waiting for the cue, there came the declaration that she too must die: 'Awake, awake! my little boy', Katherine wrote in her journal.

> I want to write down the fact that not only am I not afraid of death – I welcome the idea of death. I believe in immortality because he is not here, and I long to join him. First, my darling, I've got things to do for both of us, and then I will come as quickly as I can. . . . To you only do I belong, just as *you* belong to me. . . . I give Jack my 'surplus' love, but to you I hold and to you I give my deepest love. Jack is no more than . . . anybody might be.

Unable to live any longer in the house where Leslie had spent his last leave, Katherine, accompanied by Murry, went off to the south of France to nurse her grief. There, in effect, she contemplated suicide:

> I think I have known for a long time that life was over for me, but I never realised it or acknowledged it until my brother died. Yes . . . I am just as much dead as he is. The present and the future mean nothing to me. . . . Why don't I commit sui-

cide? Because I feel I have a duty to perform to the lovely time when we were both alive. I want to write about it, and he wanted me to.

This was an extreme reaction, one which (in the opinion of friends) was hardly justified by the actual relationship between Katherine and her brother. She was six years older than Leslie and had – until 1915 – seen little of him after her departure for school in England. Margaret Woodhouse, to whom Katherine had talked often of her family during her early London days, commented that 'the little brother was too young then to interest her much except as a charming child'.[1] An old family servant, Rose Ridler, when interviewed in Wellington, said that as children Leslie and Katherine were not attached; and this opinion was corroborated by Katherine's friend E.K.B. Leslie was the boon companion of Chaddie, not Katherine, she remembered. Both Murry and Frieda Lawrence thought that her brother was for Katherine mainly a symbol. 'Her brother was not so supremely important to Katherine Mansfield. He was a symbol and a part of that world of Innocence and Truth and Beauty which only love could comprehend', Murry wrote in *Between Two Worlds*. Less vaguely, Frieda observed: 'This brother, I believe, became a symbol to her of all her unfulfilled affection. She made something of him, I think, that he never was.'[2]

It is Katherine's writing which provides a clue to the profound psychological significance of the disaster. Except in two slight pieces, 'The Wind Blows' and 'The Apple Tree',[3] which she wrote shortly before Leslie's death, he had hardly figured at all. Three notable exceptions are 'A Fairy Story', 'New Dresses' and the poem 'The Grandmother'. In the poem the speaker longs to be in grandmother's arms in the place of little brother. Leslie was a rival, then, for the affections of the beloved grandmother; and it is as a rival that he also appears in 'New Dresses'.

'A Fairy Story', published in *Open Window* in December 1910, provides a commentary on the significance of Leslie's death which is all the more remarkable for its prefiguring of what actually came to pass. 'It was the old story of the woodcutter's daughter, but he was by no means a prince', opens the piece, which reads like a sophisticated version of one of Katherine's adolescent fantasies. Transforming her parents into the harmless 'woodcutter' and 'woodcutter's wife', Katherine depicts herself as their only child. When the kindly woodcutter finds a baby boy lying in the meadow, he brings him home to his wife to be 'a playmate for my baby daughter'. Displeased with her husband's gift, the wife burns his dinner – but consents to rear the infant. Apparently the same age, the boy and girl grow up as twins. But, while the boy becomes a romantic dreamer like his father, the girl models herself upon the 'exceptional' mother, who is also an intellectual. While the boy indulges in childish fantasies, she learns 'words of three syllables'; and latter, while he reads 'What the Moon Saw', the girl reads Shakespeare and Milton, Dickens and Tennyson. The girl's education is completed when 'the Wanderer' comes to stay. He teaches her about Omar Khàyyàm, Arthur Symons and the maxims of Wilde. Then a 'new life began for the girl'. One night, she and the boy discuss their future. 'I am going to find myself', the girl declares. In contrast, the boy wants to

> find the world . . . the people, the great battles, the streets, the dragons and hidden places. All are to belong to me. I am going to be so famous that when I ride past on my white horse, the people will point at me crying, 'See, there he goes, the boy who has found the world; the boy who has conquered the world.' And I shall sit in a bower made out of my laurel wreaths, and you shall be the queen and hold my hand.

Two years later, after their parents have died, the boy announces that he 'must begin to learn to find the world. I must read all the great books that have been written. . . . And you shall mend my clothes, Girl, and cook my little meals.' The girl rejects this virtual offer of a marriage which entails subordination. Instead she runs all the way to London and to the Wanderer who helps her to become a great actress. All the people point at *her* and cry, 'See, there she goes – the Girl who has found herself, the Girl who has conquered the world.' In bed at night, however, she cries for 'the Boy in the little hut on the hill'; and he spends all his days and half his nights reading in the effort to catch up with her. 'One night, as he sat by the fireplace a great mountain of books, from the mantlepiece above, fell on him and killed him.' In the midst of her triumphs, the girl refuses the Wanderer's offer of marriage and rushes back to the hut. ' "Oh, I have been a fool", cried the Girl, "I do not want myself and I do not want the world, but just the Boy, the Boy." ' Then she finds the boy, laid by an 'old ghost' upon her own bed: '"Oh, my dear", said the Girl, kissing him on the mouth – and her heart broke.' Together, the boy and girl are buried in a great meadow.

'A Fairy Story' is another version of the childish 'family romance' in which the pattern of family relationships is re-arranged in a manner satisfactory to the dreamer. In accordance with her deepest wishes, Katherine has relegated her father to the background and eliminated from the story the sisters who in real life were rivals for the parents' affection. Placing herself in the foreground of the narrative, she ensures from the first her advantage over the boy. For she is the legitimate child, he a foundling. As the children grow up, the girl retains her superiority. She resembles the remarkable mother who is 'very "up" in everything'; but the boy becomes an impractical dreamer – like the father. The girl's affinity with the mother, who encourages her daughter's precociousness (she 'never allowed her to touch the housekeeping or dishes – "You must be very advanced", she always said') gives her a virtual monopoly of this parent's attention. Moreover, the boy as a baby was accepted but not welcomed by his foster-mother; and the wife, who died 'cutting the leaves of "A Wife Without a Smile" ' seems to have little in common with her husband: 'Why she had married the woodcutter was always a little vague.' As the children grow up, then, there is no rivalry between the boy and the girl. Only when the two young people are left to plan their own lives does the boy begin to assert himself. Wishing to 'find the world', he assigns the girl a traditional, wifely position. But she, who has been taught by her mother to reject that role, usurps the brother's ambitions; and in what amounts to a reversal of sexual identities accomplishes both her goal and his.

The relationship of brother and sister is at once central to the story and extremely ambiguous. Because the two children are not related by blood, the boy is able to think of the girl as his 'queen' and future wife. The girl appears to reciprocate her brother's feelings when she refuses the Wanderer's offer of marriage and decides that she only wants 'The Boy'. There is a certain retributive logic in the girl (whose rejection of femininity has indirectly caused the boy's death) herself dying of a broken heart. But her death is not just a punishment for symbolically castrating her brother by taking over his masculine role: it is also the inevitable ending of a story of implicitly incestuous love.

In 'A Birthday', another story written in 1910, Katherine Mansfield achieved an even more drastic reversal of sexual identities. Although the narrative is ostensibly about a German husband's self-concern during the birth of his son, other evidence suggests that the author was reconstructing here her own birth – as a boy. Changing Annie Beauchamp's name to 'Anna Binzer', and including a grandmother in the household, Katherine accurately reconstructs the physical setting of the Wellington house in which she was born. Built on the edge of a gully, the Beauchamp house looked over a breakwater on one side. The only way to the city was over a suspension bridge spanning the gully; and at the end of the street there was a public house. In the story Andreas Binzer looks out of his window over a gully; later, as he goes to call the doctor, he crosses a suspension bridge and passes a public house on the corner. As he waits for the child's birth, he views from his dining-room 'the breakwater of the harbour'. It is Sunday; and Andreas reflects that Anna is giving birth to her third baby in four years. Outside the wind rises and the doctor observes, 'A great pity – this storm. You know climate has an immense effect upon birth. . . . Good weather is as necessary to a confinement as it is to a washing day.' These details are significant. Katherine Mansfield was born on a Sunday, the third child in four years; and all her life she believed (incorrectly) that she had been brought into the world during a storm. If Doctor Erb's remarks about the influence of climate upon a woman in labour reveal an attempt to rationalise her mother's rejection, Andreas Binzer's joy at the prospect of gaining a son shows only too clearly why Katherine coveted identification as a male: ' "A boy?" ' Binzer thinks, ' "Yes, it was bound to be a boy this time. . . ." Of course he was the last man to have a favourite child, but a man needed a son. "I'm working up the business for my son! Binzer & Son!" ' When he hears that the third child is indeed a son, 'A glow spread all over Andreas. He was exultant.'

In their different ways, both 'A Fairy Story' and 'A Birthday' demonstrate Katherine's envy of the only male child in her family and her wish that she, rather than Leslie, had been born a boy. Wanting to take her brother's place, she probably fantasised his elimination, just as she had fantasised the elimination of her father. Possibly in her unconscious mind the images of her father and brother, the two males in the family who were also competitors for the love of mother and grandmother, were hardly separable. Although Katherine fictionalised the death of Leslie only in 'A Fairy Story', she wrote more than once of her father's death. It is his elimination which in 'My Potplants' clears the way for the writer's idyllic love-relationship with the lady of the woods; the fragmentary piece about Juliet Delacours depicts the child witnessing her father's death; and a later *Scrapbook* piece called 'Kezia and Tui', describes the adolescent Kezia quarrelling with her father and openly wishing for his death.

In 'Kezia and Tui' the intensity of Kezia's hatred of her father is paralleled only by the intensity of her love for the grandmother. ' "I wish that he was dead – Oh, what Heaven that would be for us!" ' Kezia thinks. 'But she could not imagine that sort of person dying. . . . No, that sort of person seemed too real to die. She worried the thought of him until she was furious with rage. "How I detest him – detest him!" ' What the girl wants is her grandmother: 'She saw herself sitting on the Grandmother's lap and leaning against the Grandmother's bodice.' After school Kezia seeks her out: ' "Sweetheart, listen", she said. "It's no good saying I'm sorry because I'm not. . . . I hate that man and I won't pretend. But because you're more –" she hesitated, groping for a word, "more *valuable* than he is, I won't behave like that again." ' The word 'sweetheart' is highly suggestive. The adolescent girl speaks as if she were the grandmother's lover, and as such is entitled both to monopolise her attention and to assume the role of a man. Later Kezia rejects her friend Tui's suggestion that they go to Sydney together with the reply, 'No, Grannie and I are going to live by ourselves when I grow up, and I'm going to make money out of flowers and vegetables and bees.' There seems to be an association, then, between the death of the hated father and Kezia's sole possession of the much needed mother-substitute; moreover, this necessitates the girl's assumption of the male role as provider.

Guilt for her hostile feelings towards the men in her family probably heightened enormously the natural grief Katherine Mansfield felt over the death of her brother. Occuring after months of unhappiness with Murry, his death must have seemed in some odd way the logical outcome of her years of battling with male adversaries. Barely repressed wishes for their destruction had informed the emotional content of several short stories; suddenly, it was as if these wishes had been realised. Katherine had been preoccupied since childhood with fantasies of her own death; now, as though the primitive law of talion was demanding punishment in kind for her 'crime' against another's life, she passed sentence upon herself. Perhaps because Leslie's death merely confirmed her belief in the inevitability of such a punishment, she could declare quite honestly, 'I think I have known for a long time that life was over for me. . . .' To determine to follow her brother in death (as the girl had followed the boy in 'A Fairy Story') was to make reparation for her transgression.

From a psychological point of view, it is hardly surprising that in the months following this personal tragedy Katherine Mansfield experienced one of the happiest periods of her adult life. Even as she called herself 'just as much dead as [Leslie]' she probably experienced a remission of guilt, her determination to die being received unconsciously as if it were an act. There was even a sense in which she could benefit from what had happened. For the rival *had* been removed, her father's male line extinguished; and the daughter who had already begun to 'conquer the world' had less need of self-pity now that she was in a position to replace the son in her parents' eyes. It was after her brother's death, therefore, that she wrote her first really affectionate letter to her father since she had left New Zealand:

> Our dear one, when he was here, seemed to bring me so near to you. And talking of you with him I realised afresh each time how much I love and admire you, and how very much you mean to me. Forgive my childish faults, my generous darling Daddy, and keep me in your heart. . . . I am happier. Not that the loss of our darling one is any less real to me. It never can be, and I feel that it has changed the course of my life *for ever*, but I do feel very strongly that I fail in my duty to his memory if I do not bear his loss bravely, and I could not bear to fail him.[4]

If the tragedy enabled Katherine to effect some kind of inner reconciliation with her father, there was a sense, too, in which the over-evaluation of her dead brother could be used as a weapon against Murry for his seeming lack of love. When he had been preoccupied with his relationship with Gordon Campbell and D.H. Lawrence, Katherine had tried to retaliate by leaving him for Francis Carco. But in a humiliating fashion the ploy had rebounded against her. Now she bestowed on her brother a love which excluded Murry: 'You know I can never be Jack's lover again. You have me. You're in my flesh as well as in my soul', she wrote that October. Four months later a sense of almost physical communion with Leslie was still strong: 'The night before, when I lay in bed, I felt suddenly passionate. I wanted J. to embrace me. But as I turned to speak to him or to kiss him I saw my brother lying fast asleep, and I got cold. That happens nearly always.'[5]

Leslie, dead, became a kind of imaginary companion and lover whom Katherine bound to her, and used against Murry, as she could use no man in real life. By displacing what she mainly valued from being loved onto loving, she temporarily acquired a degree of emotional independence from her partner. And this acted as a subtle punishment of him. Murry's own words show just how effective it was. For, after three weeks of being shut out of Katherine's emotional life, 'outcast and disconsolate' he returned to England:

> He, [Leslie] though dead, was far more real and near to her than I was now; and that was anguish to me. . . . I could not confess how unbearably it hurt me to have my place taken by another – even though he was dead, and her brother, it made no difference at all; except that I felt I must not make it a grievance against her. . . . Now, indeed, I knew what jealousy was.

Murry's jealousy was not unfounded. Katherine had toyed with the idea of a marriage-like relationship between brother and sister in 'A Fairy Story'. Now she directed towards Leslie a flood of longing which, as the language of her journal reveals, contained incestuous overtones. In 'A Fairy Story' these overtones had been kept at bay by the absence of blood ties between brother and sister. Only in death were they united. In real life, Katherine fantasised a similar unification with her dead brother at the same time as she transformed him mentally into her idealised lover. The last lines of the poem 'To L.H.B.' show her in the act of spiritualising their relationship, of counteracting incest-related anxieties by raising Leslie to the level of a figure of worship, a kind of Christ:

> By the remembered stream my brother stands
> Waiting for me with berries in his hand . . .
> 'These are my body. Sister, take and eat.'

Central to the poem is the image of poisonous berries which the brother tempts his sister to eat. This is significant because eating, in Katherine Mansfield's writing, is a persistent metaphor for sexuality in its most destructive aspect. Here, the danger associated with eating the 'poisonous' berries, called 'Dead Man's Bread', is quite explicit; yet the poem ends with the brother's Christlike injunction to 'take and eat'. The invitation is to share his death and also, the symbolism implies, to enter into an act of physical communion.

The cloak of mysticism allowed Katherine to disguise the real nature of her feelings for Leslie by turning him into an object of worship. Art now became a religion in whose practice she felt herself a kind of high priestess; through art she would immortalise her brother, if not bring him back to life. 'Grace' or salvation could only be attained to the extent that she had earned it through the atonement of work. 'When I am not writing I feel my brother calling me, and he is not happy', Katherine wrote in her journal. 'Last night I dreamed of him and Father Zossima. Father Zossima said: "Do not let the new man die." My brother was certainly there. . . . I knelt down by the bed. But I could not pray. I had done no work. I was not in an active state of grace.'

All through Katherine Mansfield's life, devastating personal crises were followed by a burst of creative activity. Now, in Bandol with Murry (whose jealousy and fear of losing Katherine had caused him to rejoin her), writing became a cathartic experience and a means of self-discovery. It was also Katherine's way of achieving a sense of communion with Leslie. 'The thought of you *spiritually* is not enough to-night. I want you by me. I must get deep down into my book, for then I shall be happy. Lose myself, lose myself to find you, dearest.' To find Leslie was to find an identity they had shared, as New Zealanders: 'I want to write about my own country till I simply exhaust my store', she wrote in her journal.

> Not only because it is a 'sacred debt' that I pay to my country because my brother and I were born there, but also because in my thoughts I range with him over all the remembered places. I am never far away from them. I long to renew them in writing.
>
> Ah, the people – the people we loved there – of them, too, I want to write. . . . But especially I want to write a kind of long elegy to you.

Leslie, spiritualised, was not only the inspiration of Katherine's writing; he was now the unseen auditor, the imaginary companion whom she had so often conjured up:

> Dear brother, as I jot these notes, I am speaking to you. To whom did I always write when I kept those huge complaining diaries? Was it to myself? But now as I write these words and talk of getting down to the New Zealand atmosphere, I see you opposite to me. . . . Yes, it is to you. . . . Each time I take up my pen *you* are with me. You are mine. . . . you believe in me, you know I am here. Oh, Chummie! put your arms round me. . . . You know how unhappy I have been lately. I almost felt: Perhaps 'the new man' will not live. Perhaps I am not yet risen. . . . But now I do not doubt.

When she brought together the ideas of Leslie resurrected and herself as 'risen', reborn a 'new man', Katherine was reasserting her identification with her brother. The figure of the shadowy 'other self' or double who had appeared in 'Die Einsame' as the 'lady all alone with her soul', and in 'Juliet' and 'The Education of Audrey' as the heroine's 'dream face' or 'mirror face', she now personified as Leslie.

Just such an unconscious personification had probably caused Katherine to depict him as a virtual twin in 'A Fairy Story'. Writing in her journal in 1915 she mused, 'We were almost like one child. I see us walking about together, looking at things together with the same eyes. . . .' Inasmuch as the boy and girl in 'A Fairy Story' represented the opposing sides of Katherine Mansfield's personality, they *were* one child. They are also true fictional doubles. The most revealing aspect of Katherine Mansfield's creation of these doubles, from the biographical point of view, is her allocation of personality traits. In defiant reversal of sexual identities, she assigned to the brother in the story the very attributes she most criticised in herself. He, instead of she, is rejected by the mother at birth; he indulges in fantasies and dreams as she had done in childhood; but, most damning of all, he is a passive character, feminine in his emotional dependence. The ending of 'A Fairy Story' is inexorable, then. The girl must join her brother in death because she cannot escape sharing the fate of one who is, in effect, the other side of herself.

14 'Prelude'

The months which followed Leslie's death were, in Murry's words, 'the happiest time of our life together – one to which we looked back, with love and a certain incredulity, in after years'. It was during this period, at Bandol in the South of France, that Katherine Mansfield wrote the first draft of her longest and most considerable story, 'Prelude'. The immediate inspiration of 'Prelude' was Katherine's desire to 'renew' in her writing the country and the people she and her brother had shared. Yet there is also a sense, too, in which the work represents her attempt to reconstruct in fiction the permanence and security of the home she had repudiated and in real life could not replace. More importantly, the story is an act of extended self-analysis; an attempt to explore in greater depth than ever before (or again) her feelings about life within that home as it had conditioned and shaped her own personality.

Depicting three days in the life of the Burnell family as they move from one house and settle into another on the outskirts of rural Wellington, 'Prelude' is a story whose apparently simple surface is constantly belied by an underlying psychological complexity. Themes that Katherine Mansfield had dealt with separately in her earlier writing are brought together here in a sustained form; and they are centred unequivocally on the interrelationships of the family. What a comparison of 'Prelude' with the much longer first draft (printed separately by Murry as 'The Aloe') reveals is how potentially explosive are the emotional conflicts which run through the work. So intricate is the patterning of 'Prelude' that the obsessive nature of these conflicts is masked and controlled. Almost certainly, it was to achieve patterning and control that Katherine Mansfield eliminated, in her final version, passages which too openly laid bare conflicts that she preferred to convey less directly, through the nuance of association and symbol.

The ordering of 'Prelude' is most obvious in its structural division into twelve episodes during the course of which certain thematic ideas are introduced, brought to a climax, and either resolved or allowed to subside. Unifying these episodes, and providing a natural transition between them, is the repeated appearance of objects or activities which have symbolic meaning. Birds of various kinds are the most pervasive symbols in the story; but almost as important are the plants, trees and flowers of the natural world. As in Katherine Mansfield's previous stories, food and eating carry emotional overtones. Fantasising, moreover, is the single most significant activity indulged in by virtually all the characters: fantasy is at once the medium through which the author explores the minds of her fictional people, and a linking device which helps integrate the various threads of the story.

On the surface, 'Prelude' is a story about life as it occurs in the most unified and secure of circumstances – within the supportive structure of the family. There is the house where each member has his place, the motherly grandmother who sees to the family's domestic needs, and the father who provides for their material welfare. Belying the apparent security of this external framework, indeed demonstrating its fragility, is a disturbing pattern of contraries. Juxtaposed to the orderly existence within the house is the disorder Kezia encounters outside in the natural world; in contrast to the safely humdrum outer lives of the characters are their disturbingly conflict-ridden inner lives; and, as if echoing this division, the world which appears safe and familiar by day assumes hidden, fearful characteristics at night. Even in daytime, there is a strange tendency for things to appear the reverse of what they really are; inanimate objects and plants take on human attributes, while people are seen or treated as if they are mere objects.

Such a reversal of perceptions accords with the duality of feeling and the ambivalence experienced by some of the characters. The ambivalence of Linda Burnell, who loves her husband by day but hates him at night, is shown most explicitly; Beryl Fairfield's ambivalence towards her sister and brother-in-law and towards her friend, Nan Pym, is also conveyed. Indeed, it is through the character of Beryl that Katherine Mansfield chooses to portray the duality of character – the division between the 'true self' and the 'false self' – which serves to emphasise all the other dualisms of the story.

If there is a constant impression of flux in 'Prelude', it is because the narrative moves from the public life of the characters to their private fantasies just as inevitably as the day blends into night. In the fantasies of Linda Burnell, Beryl and Kezia, relationships with the opposite sex are more or less explicit. Central to the public life of the story, and influencing the interrelationships of the entire family, however, are the bonds between mother and daughter. These are complex, for they involve the relationship of Linda and her unmarried sister to their mother, Mrs Fairfield, and that of the three Burnell children to Linda herself as well as to their grandmother.

In the first three episodes, attention is focused upon the subtle interaction of Linda, the young mother, and her daughter, Kezia. Dominating the relationship between these two principal characters (and affecting the emotional movement of the entire story) is Linda's abdication of the role of mother. Almost casually, in the opening paragraph, Katherine Mansfield establishes the abnormality of Linda's feelings as she distinguishes between the 'hold-alls, bags and boxes' which are 'absolute necessities', not to be let out of her sight for one instant, and the two younger children, for whom there is no place in the buggy. ' "We shall simply have to leave them. That is all. We shall simply have to cast them off", said Linda Burnell.' Mentally devaluing her children, Linda interchanges in imagination the 'tables and chairs standing on their heads on the front lawn' with Lottie and Kezia, to whom she longed to say, 'Stand on your heads, children, and wait for the storeman.'

Kezia's anxiety at separation from the mother and grandmother who drive off with the favoured older sister, but without her and Lottie, is expressed in her cry, 'I want to kiss my granma good-bye again.' In 'The Aloe' grandmother comforts her with 'It's all right, my darling. Be good.' But in 'Prelude' Katherine Mansfield underlines the child's sense of abandonment by portraying the grandmother as being too absorbed in Linda's needs to reply. Unobtrusively, the working out of psychological cause and effect is conveyed through the succession of events and through the reiteration of certain motifs in different contexts.

Thus there is an implicit comparison between the motherliness of Mrs Samuel Josephs, in whose care Kezia and Lottie are left, and Linda's lack of concern for her children. And the rivalry among the many Samuel Josephs children acts as a reminder that, in the Burnell family (as in the Beauchamp family), there are grounds for competition. Only lightly, in 'Prelude', is the existence of discord among the Samuel Josephs children sketched in; in the earlier version, 'The Aloe', there is a more detailed reference to the 'pitched battle' which 'every single one of them started . . . as soon as possible after birth with every single other'.

'Prelude' depicts a tearful Kezia caught up in the other children's aggressiveness during tea, and we learn that 'she did hate boys'. The lengthier description of her stay with the Samuel Josephs family in 'The Aloe' explicitly links her distress at being separated from mother and grandmother with her fear of being left helpless and exposed to physical attack. A comparison of the two versions shows that Katherine Mansfield took pains in 'Prelude' to cover the psychological tracks of her characters. For example, she eliminated from 'Prelude' a description of the Samuel Josephs children as 'jump[ing] out at you from under the tables, through the stair rails, behind the doors, behind the coats in the passage'. In very similar words, however, she describes Kezia's subsequent fearful encounter with 'IT'. Exploring the empty Burnell house after tea, the child imagines in her parents' darkening bedroom that 'IT was just behind her, waiting at the door, at the head of the stairs, at the bottom of the stairs, hiding in the passage, ready to dart out at the back door.'

In 'The Aloe', a sharply drawn scene indicates a relationship between Kezia's haunting fantasy and her fear of physical aggression. After tea, she takes revenge upon her tormentors. Cunningly she devises a 'new game' in which the other children must compete to see who can chew up first the stamen of an arum lily. 'The Samuel Josephs suspected nothing. . . . Savagely they broke off the big white blooms. . . . She flung up her hands with joy as the Samuel Josephs bit, chewed, made dreadful faces, spat, screamed, and rushed to Burnells' garden tap.' Symbolically, the destruction of the 'big white blooms' parallels the little girl's barely conscious fear of being assaulted. By tricking her enemies into devouring the burning, phallic stamens she has turned the tables and successfully warded off attack.

The motif of rushing things is picked up again in the third section of 'Prelude' when Kezia talks to the storeman during the drive home. Here, as he explains the difference between a sheep and a ram, the overtones become more obviously sexual. 'A ram has horns and runs for you', he tells the child. And she answers, 'I hate rushing animals like dogs and parrots. I often dream that animals rush at me – even camels – and while they are rushing, their heads swell e-enormous.'

In 'The Aloe', Linda seems intuitively aware of these secret terrors. She greets the children's belated arrival at the new house with 'Are those the children? . . . Have either of them been maimed for life?' In 'Prelude' the apparently illogical question is omitted. Instead the mother's lack of interest – which also has power to maim – is emphasised. ' "Are those the children?" But Linda did not really care; she did not even open her eyes to see.' As she tends the sleepy children, it becomes clear that the grandmother has taken over Linda's maternal responsibilities. Kezia's special relation to her grandmother, whose bed she shares, is suggested but not dwelt upon in 'Prelude'. We are merely told that, when the old woman lay down beside her, 'Kezia thrust her head under the grandmother's arm and gave a little squeak.' The bedtime scene continues in 'The Aloe', however, with Kezia whispering, ' "Who am I?" . . . This was an old established ritual to be gone through between them. 'You are my little brown bird", said the Grandmother. Kezia gave a guilty chuckle.' In effect, Kezia's question is an attempt to compensate for her abandonment earlier in the day by asking 'Who am I to you?' The reassurance that she is indeed her grandmother's favoured child is what produces (in view of the sibling rivalry) her guilty chuckle.

Inexorably, the movement of 'Prelude' is towards a series of revelatory scenes in which repression is lifted, and Kezia, Linda and Beryl are brought face to face with their hidden anxieties. There is an inevitability and aesthetic 'rightness' about each revelation; yet so subtle is Katherine Mansfield's introduction and reiteration of key remarks, actions and symbols that tension mounts almost unnoticeably. The details of day-to-day living impart a deceptively matter-of-fact appearance to the surface texture of the narrative, and hardly more obtrusive is the infiltration of objects from the natural world into the characters' dream life. Thus, on the second day of the story, Linda Burnell awakens to the sound of birds whose calls have become part of her dream. The dream unravels and she becomes aware of Stanley dressing; but the bird image merges into her waking thoughts and releases a succession of involuntary disclosures. In the dream, Linda had been walking with her father when he showed her a tiny bird in the grass. Picking it up, she stroked its head. 'But a funny thing happened. As she stroked it began to swell . . . it grew bigger and bigger. . . . It had become a baby with a big naked head and a gaping bird-mouth, opening and shutting.'

The image of the bird which when stroked becomes a baby is one of intercourse and pregnancy. But although Linda's wish, as she looks round her bedroom, that 'she was going away from this house, too . . . driving away from them all in a little buggy', recalls her desertion of the children the previous day, it is not at this stage explicitly related to her dream. Nor is her perception of Stanley as 'a big fat turkey'. From this point on, however, the idea of pregnancy and its ramifications is one which recurs with mounting intensity – even as the bird image acquires symbolic significance for the other characters, too.

Just as the parrots on the wallpaper had seemed alive to Kezia the previous night, so does the poppy on the wallpaper which Linda, still lying in bed in the morning, traces with her finger. Repeating the stroking gesture of her dream, 'she could feel the sticky, silky petals, the stem, hairy like a gooseberry skin, the rough leaf and the tight glazed bud. Things had a habit of coming alive like that.' Then the sight of the washstand jug that 'had a way of sitting in the basin like a fat bird in a round nest' reminds her of the bird dream. Consciously, now, the phallic imagery of the swelling bird and the sticky poppy is elaborated in a menacing sexual fantasy which reads as a more elaborate version of Kezia's 'IT'.

> . . . the strangest part of this coming alive of things was what they did. They listened, they seemed to swell out with some mysterious important content, and when they were full she felt that they smiled. . . . Sometimes . . . she woke and could not lift a finger . . . [because] THEY knew how frightened she was. . . . What Linda always felt was that THEY wanted some-

> thing of her, and she knew that if she gave herself up and was quiet . . . something would really happen. . . . She seemed to be listening with her wide open watchful eyes, waiting for someone to come who just did not come, watching for something to happen that just did not happen.

The meaning of Linda's dream and of her fantasy is left as oblique for us in 'Prelude' as it is for her. Katherine Mansfield omitted a long passage from 'The Aloe' where a glimpse of Linda's present relationship with her mother, and her past relationship with her father, helps explain her feelings. After Stanley has left for work, the young wife is depicted in 'The Aloe' as regressing to a state of childlike dependency. '. . . playing with her breakfast', Linda refuses even to look at the kitchen and pantries of the new house: 'I don't want to. I don't care', she tells her mother. Needing to remain a child herself, Linda's rejection of the role of mother is underlined in her refusal to take any part in the feeding of her family.

This portrayal in 'The Aloe' of Linda's immaturity is sharpened by a flashback which projects her retreat from marriage (signified by a constant losing of her wedding ring) against the background of her ideal, non-sexual relationship with her father. As a child, she had been 'his darling, his pet, his playfellow. . . . He understood her so beautifully and gave her so much love for love that he became a kind of daily miracle to her, and all her faith centred in him.' Sitting on his knee, she used to plan: 'When I am grown up we shall travel everywhere – we shall see the whole world – won't we, Papa? . . . And we shan't go as father and daughter. . . . We'll just go as a couple of boys together – Papa.' Reality destroyed this dream of being both the central figure in her father's life, and a boy, when Stanley Burnell came courting. The year her father died, Linda married.

In such passages Katherine Mansfield analysed fairly explicitly in 'The Aloe' the workings of her characters' minds, spelling out the connections between their past experiences and their present thoughts and actions. When she revised the story as 'Prelude', the explanatory sections were largely eliminated and symbols were left to carry the weight of psychological meaning.

The new house, around which the action of the story takes place and in terms of which the characters are shown defining themselves, is itself a kind of symbol which imposes unity on those who live under its sheltering roof. Sharing the symbolic attributes of the house is Mrs Fairfield, the real mother of the story and the pivotal figure upon whom all the others depend. There is something archetypal about her, as she creates security, order and pattern both in the dwelling and in the emotional lives of its inhabitants. Significantly, she, whose maternal presence must counteract the private anxieties of those in her care, wears at her throat the emblem of 'a silver crescent moon with five little owls seated on it'. Since Linda has refused the responsibilities of motherhood, Mrs Fairfield has, in effect, five daughters: Linda, Beryl and the three little Burnell girls.

Emphasising the implied contrast between the two mothers is Linda's appearance in the kitchen on the first morning at the new house. Of Mrs Fairfield, 'It was hard to believe that she had not been in that kitchen for years; she was so much part of it. She put the crocks away with a sure, precise touch. . . . When she had finished, everything in the kitchen had become part of a series of patterns.' While the older woman is invariably concerned with the preparation and serving of food, Linda shows hardly more interest in eating than she does in satisfying the needs of others. On the first night in the new house, the young wife sits apart and refuses the meaty chops which Stanley and Beryl devour with gusto. In 'Prelude' (as in 'The Aloe') she merely picks at the breakfast her mother prepares, asking childishly, 'Beryl, do you want half my gingerbread?'

While Linda, in the orderly kitchen reflects that 'There was something comforting in the sight of her [mother] that . . . she could never do without', and refuses to 'go into the garden and give an eye to [her] children', Kezia, outside in the garden, is exploring the disorder of the natural world beyond the house. Kezia's sensibility is linked with that of her mother by the pattern of symbolism. Her secret terror, 'IT', is paralleled by Linda's fantasised 'THEY'; the rushing animals and parrots she so dislikes because 'their heads swell e-enormous' become in her mother's dream life the swelling bird, the poppy with the 'fat bursting bud' and the 'things' which 'swell out with some mysterious important content'. Sharing an emotional dependence on

Mrs Fairfield – sharing, in effect, the same mother – both Linda and Kezia want freedom their first morning at the new house. Earlier, Linda had wished to escape from the bonds of family life; now Kezia escapes her bossy older sister and wanders off alone into the 'spread tangled garden' where 'she did not believe that she would ever not get lost'.

The inherent duality of the story is evident in the symbolism of the garden. Divided by the drive leading up to the house, the garden has two sides with many little paths on either side. 'On one side they all led into a tangle of tall dark trees and strange bushes . . . that buzzed with flies . . . this was the frightening side, and no garden at all.' In contrast, on the other side 'there was a high box border and the paths had box edges and all of them led into a deeper and deeper tangle of flowers.' With its tangle of tall, masculine trees, the frightening side of the garden suggests the uncontrolled fantasy worlds of Kezia and her mother; the other side, with its ordered box borders and profusion of sweet smelling flowers, corresponds to the security and reassurance that Mrs Fairfield provides.

With their connotations of order and disorder, the opposing sides of the garden suggest the divided human psyche, alternately overwhelmed by private fantasy but also participating in the public life of the family; seeking independence and separateness on the one hand yet dependent upon a nurturing maternal presence on the other. The island 'that lay in the middle of the drive, dividing the drive into two arms that met in front of the house' is like a bridge between the two sides.

Significantly, the mother and child, who are at once separate and the same, experience their only moment of direct communication as they stand in front of the island, gazing at the aloe tree which is the central symbol of the story. Asked 'Mother, what is it?', Linda 'looked up at the fat swelling plant with its cruel leaves and fleshy stem'. The mother, with a smile and half-shut eyes, tells her daughter that the plant is an aloe, which flowers only once every hundred years. Linda's smile suggests a secret empathy with the aloe. By an act of displacement, Kezia's 'Mother, what is it?' registers in her mind as 'Mother, what are you?' Partly answering the question is the description of the aloe. Linda's obsession with pregnancy is reflected in the 'fat swelling' of the plant. Its leaves are 'split and broken . . . cruel'. Similarly Linda herself is broken, apathetic and uninterested in life around her, cruel in her rejection of the children. As the plant clings with 'claws' to the earth it grew from, so she clings selfishly to her mother; and, like the aloe with its 'blind' stem and leaves which seem to be 'hiding something', Linda half-shuts her eyes. She too is hiding something.

There is a suggestion, in this depiction of Linda's first encounter with the aloe tree, that while looking at it she has experienced a degree of self-understanding. With dramatic inevitability 'Prelude' progresses towards an exposure of what is psychologically hidden, towards the crystallisation, by means of a catalytic symbol, of the characters' only partly understood anxieties. On the third and final day of the story, Kezia, Linda and Beryl, in a moment of revelation, confront their innermost selves. Kezia's secret fears are the first to come to a head. Her dislike of the teasing Samuel Josephs boys, and the similarity of her fantasies to those of Linda's, indicate that her anxieties (perhaps transmitted from her mother) are based upon a fear of sexual attack. And, indeed, the game which the three little girls play with their boy cousins Pip and Rags Trout is a childish imitation of adult sexuality. 'Mrs Smith' tells 'Mrs Jones' about the new baby which 'came so suddenly that I haven't had time to make her any clothes, yet. So I left her. . . .' Lottie, significantly, doesn't want to play 'hospitals' with the boys 'because last time Pip had squeezed something down her throat and it hurt awfully'.

The climax occurs for Kezia when Pat, the handyman, offers to show the children 'how the kings of Ireland chop the head off a duck'. As the headless duck begins to waddle 'Kezia suddenly rushed at Pat and flung her arms round his legs. . . . "Put head back! Put head back!" she screamed.' If the child's reaction is overcharged, it is because she (like the female characters of Katherine Mansfield's earlier stories who unconsciously empathised with the suffering of another) has put herself in the place of the headless duck.[1] Her distress at being 'abandoned' by her mother, at being teased by the Samuel Josephs boys, at encountering the fearful, imaginary 'IT', has merged, together with her unpleasant thoughts of rushing animals with swelling heads, into the one overwhelming horror of the decapitation. Yet the shock is purgative. Now that the vaguely dreaded physical attack has been vicariously experienced, her anxiety diminishes.

Light relief from this tense scene comes when the focus shifts to Alice, the servant girl. The element of fantasy, which is so prominent in the working out of the story's psychological themes, recurs in the portrayal of Alice. For her, however, fantasy is a source not of terror but of comforting mastery. In 'Prelude' the episode where Alice peruses her dream book in the kitchen and then composes a series of imaginary conversations in which she mentally gets even with the haughty Beryl is followed directly by a depiction of the whole family eating the duck at dinner. But in 'The Aloe' there is an intervening scene in which Mrs Fairfield and her daughters – the married Doady Trout, Linda and Beryl – are depicted sewing together. Here Katherine Mansfield probes at greater length the phenomenon of fantasy-living. Like other long excisions from 'Prelude', this passage is important for the light it throws on the author's original conception of her characters' psychology, as well as on the aspects of family life which preoccupied her.

Fantasising or day-dreaming is common to Kezia, Linda, Beryl and Doady. All four youthful characters are sharply differentiated; yet their sharing of certain traits suggests that, besides being members of the same family, they may also represent different stages in the emotional development of the author's own troubled personality. For Kezia and Linda, fantasising is an almost involuntary activity, one in which some external object or event causes repressed anxieties to rise to the surface of their minds. But for Beryl and Doady it is a conscious indulgence which allows them to escape from daily routine and gratify, at least in imagination, their unfulfilled wishes. Doady Trout, the bored suburban housewife who lives on the sofa wondering 'why it was that she was so certain that life had something terrible for her . . . until by and by she made up perfect novels with herself for the heroine, all of them ending with some shocking catastrophe', is remarkably similar to the adolescent author of 'Juliet'. Katherine Mansfield might almost be parodying her own early creation when she depicts the Dickensian sentimentality of Doady's imaginings: 'Her child would be born dead, or she saw the nurse going in to Richard, her husband, and saying: "Your child lives *but*" – and here the nurse pointed one finger upwards like the illustration of Agnes in *David Copperfield* – "your wife is no more." '

It is significant that Doady's destructive fantasies are implicitly attributed to envy. More often than not, the imagined tragedy would befall not Doady herself but some member of her family. As if envious of the Burnells, she imagines their new house on fire and her mother appearing for a moment at the window before 'a sickening crash'. While she keeps such day-dreams a 'profound secret', the jealousy that she feels for Linda is less easily concealed. When Linda laughs off her spiteful suggestion that the new house 'will be very damp in the winter', the smouldering rivalry between the three sisters bursts into the open. 'What can you expect from Linda', says Doady bitterly. 'She laughs at everything – everything.' Beryl, who 'felt her anger like a little serpent dart out of her bosom and strike at Linda', joins in the attack:

> 'Why do you always pretend to be so indifferent to everything?' she said. 'You pretend you don't care where you live, or if you see anybody or not, or what happens to the children or even what happens to you. You can't be sincere and yet you keep it up – you've kept it up for years. In fact' – and she gave a little laugh of joy and relief to be so rid of the serpent, she felt positively delighted – 'I can't even remember when it started now'.

Perhaps because they revealed too much, Katherine Mansfield eliminated from 'Prelude' the two 'Aloe' scenes in which she had explicitly depicted sibling rivalry. Yet competition for possession of the mother-figure is clearly a motivating factor in the psychology of her female characters. Beryl and Doady, in 'The Aloe', are shown resenting Linda's retreat from adulthood and her virtual monopoly of their mother. It is Linda herself, however, who in this earlier version of 'Prelude' is made to suggest the relationship between her own behaviour and Kezia's emotional well-being. As if supporting Beryl's accusations, Linda appears to recognise Kezia's separation anxiety, and cruelly reinforce it. 'Your Mother doesn't care, Kezia, whether you ever set eyes on her again. She doesn't care if you starve. You are all going to be sent to the Home for Waifs and Strays to-morrow', she cynically teases.

In 'The Aloe' there is an easing of emotional tension – and a preparation for the next episode – as the sewing scene closes with another reference to birds. To her son's question, 'Mum . . . which would you rather be if you had to – a duck or a fowl?', Doady replies, 'I'd rather be a fowl – much rather.' Katherine Mansfield eliminates from 'Prelude' any such open correlation between a human being and a duck. Such a correlation, however, is psychologically central to the scene at dinner that night when Stanley Burnell carves the duck whose killing has so shocked Kezia. Stanley's enjoyment of the roast duck emphasises his carnal appetite. In contrast to his wife, who is uninterested in eating, Stanley (like the *German Pension* males) is invariably associated with food. Portrayed on the first evening eating a chop and 'picking his strong white teeth', he returns from work on the second day devouring a bag of cherries, 'three or four at a time, chucking the stones over the side of the buggy'. His present to Linda that night is 'a bottle of oysters and a pineapple'. As if there is for him an unconscious association between food and procreation, the sight of his children at supper reminded him of the son he wanted; and he 'tightened his arm round Linda's shoulder'.

As he carves the duck at dinner on the third day, Stanley openly refers to it as a child: 'this must have been one of those birds whose mother played to it in infancy upon the German flute. And the sweet strains of the dulcet instrument acted with such effect upon the infant mind.' Thus by subtle association Kezia's traumatic experience earlier that day is linked with her father's attitude to food – and with Linda's reponse to her husband. For, as if she understands the underlying symbolism of the carving scene, Linda sits apart after the meal. Her mounting emotional tension expresses itself in an unspoken warning to two moths: 'Fly away before it is too late. Fly out again.'

This, then, is the setting for the climactic scene in which Linda, contemplating the aloe tree, admits to consciousness her own deepest feelings. All the imagery of the story – birds, plants, food, swelling head and grotesquely human inanimate objects – has been leading up to this moment. As she gazes up at the aloe in the moonlight, Linda's rejection of the children, her longing for escape, and her clinging to Mrs Fairfield, all coalesce as aspects of her polarised feelings for Stanley. On the previous day, she had envied the impenetrability and maleness of the tree.

Now, when the moon is full and 'the house, the garden, the old woman and Linda' are all 'bathed in dazzling light', mother and daughter seem to be enclosed in a world exclusively their own; and the budding aloe appears as a feminine symbol, a ship.

> 'Do you feel it, too', said Linda, and she spoke to her mother with the special voice that women use at night to each other as though they spoke in their sleep or from some hollow cave – 'Don't you feel that it is coming toward us?' She dreamed that she was caught up out of the cold water into the ship with the lifted oars and budding mast. . . . Ah, she heard herself cry: 'Faster! Faster!' to those who were rowing.

The empathy of mother and daughter contrasts with the emotional gulf between Stanley and Linda. Full moon, house and garden are all feminine symbols; but the aloe-as-ship represents the womb itself. Only there, between mother and unborn child, could there be communication 'at night . . . in their sleep . . . from some hollow cave'. Like the island on which the aloe grows, the earth to which it clings, the ship symbolises the prenatal world which protects and nourishes; and it is to the safety and nothingness of that world that Linda wishes to return. 'Nobody would dare to come near the ship or to follow after', she thinks as she looks at the 'long sharp thorns that edged the aloe leaves. . . . Not even my Newfoundland dog . . . that I'm so fond of in the daytime.'

The dualities which so pervade 'Prelude' are brought sharply into focus as Linda confronts the difference between her day-time and night-time feelings for Stanley:

> He was too strong for her; she had always hated things that rush at her, from a child. There were times when he was frightening – really frightening. When she just had not screamed at the top of her voice: 'You are killing me.' And at those times she had longed to say the most coarse, hateful things . . .
>
> 'You know I'm very delicate. You know as well as I do that my heart is affected, and the doctor has told you I may die any moment. I have had three great lumps of children already . . .'
>
> Yes, yes, it was true. . . . For all her love and respect and admiration she hated him. . . . It had never been so plain to

> her as it was at this moment. There were all her feelings for him, sharp and defined, one as true as the other. And there was this other, this hatred, just as real as the rest.

The scene is central in that, as Linda comes to understand and admit openly the meaning of her fantasies, the separate threads of the story are drawn together. Her secret happiness at casting off the children is symptomatic of a stronger, but hitherto suppressed, desire to be free of the sexual role imposed by marriage to Stanley. Haunted by fears of sexual intercourse and childbearing, and transmitting these to Kezia through her rejection of motherhood, Linda seeks refuge in regression to a state of asexual, childlike dependence upon her mother. But a return to childhood, in the sense that Linda really desires it, is possible only in death; as if recognising this, her attitude is essentially nihilistic: 'And why this mania . . . to keep alive at all? . . . What am I guarding myself for so preciously? I shall go on having children and Stanley will go on making money. . . .' Like the aloe, which earlier seemed 'becalmed in the air', Linda is herself becalmed. Forced to accept a life that leads nowhere, with only fantasies of escape as an outlet, hers is a kind of living death.

Linda's admission of her divided feelings about Stanley throws into relief all the other patterns of opposites in 'Prelude'. Philosophically central to the story is the idea that objects and people can appear in two different and contrasting guises. As opposed to the way things really are, there is the way they seem when viewed through the distorting lens of fantasy. Fantasy, in its ability to transmute reality, is like the coloured-glass window Kezia peeped through at the empty house. First she saw a blue lawn, then a yellow. When a yellow 'Chinese' Lottie came into view, she wondered, 'Was that really Lottie? Kezia was not quite sure until she had looked through the ordinary window.' In the same way, such objects from the natural world as birds form part of the narrative's realistic backdrop when viewed through ordinary glass; when viewed through the coloured glass of fantasy they become children – children waiting to be born, demanding attention, or vulnerable to potentially aggressive males.

Fantasy causes food, too, to take on ambiguous connotations. Greedily devoured by Stanley, it conjures up the threatening sexual love that Linda fears. But, when given by a mother as nourishment to her children, food symbolises love in its life-sustaining capacity. By the same token, however, the deliberate withholding of love (as Linda withholds love from her children) is a symbolic act of murder.

For all the understanding with which Linda Burnell's plight is depicted, the symbolism of 'Prelude' unequivocally damns her for being an unloving mother. The focus shifts, in the final episode, from the close family group of grandmother, parents and child to Linda's unmarried sister, Beryl. Beryl's prominence in the closing section, and her characterisation, have puzzled some critics. Sylvia Berkman believes that Katherine Mansfield 'had some difficulty in presenting a successfully integrated character', and that this trouble arose because she ' "made up" more of Beryl Fairfield than of any other character in the story'.

It is the author's adolescent writing which provides the key to Beryl's characterisation and importance. Both physically and emotionally, there is a remarkable similarity between Beryl and the heroine of 'Juliet'.[2] This suggests that Beryl is, if anything, less 'made up' than any other character in 'Prelude'. Katherine Mansfield, like other writers of her generation, repeatedly cast herself as a central character in her fiction. Her private difficulty in 'Prelude' is that she is at once recreating the tensions she had felt among her own family – and attempting to reconstruct her life within the confines of that family. Because her life had been divided into two distinct phases – her years as a child before she left for school in England, and her later brief residence in New Zealand as a young woman – she needed two separate characters to represent both versions of herself. In Kezia she created an idealised version of herself as a child; onto the figure of the real Aunt Belle who lived in the Beauchamp household she grafted aspects of her own rebellious young womanhood.

Given the psychological coherence of 'Prelude', it is peculiarly fitting that the story which opens with the temporary – but painful – physical desertion of the child by her mother, and which goes on to account for that desertion in terms of Linda's inner conflicts, should be rounded off with a portrayal of the far-reaching effects of emotional insecurity on the adult Kezia-as-Beryl. What is emphasised in this closing episode is Beryl's hopeless inner division.

Beryl, like Linda, fantasises about her own sexuality. Seeing in marriage a solution to her unfulfilled life, she imagines on the first night at the new house that a young man is outside watching her undress. When, in a sexually suggestive gesture, he offers her a bouquet and 'thrust his head among the bright waxy flowers, sly and laughing', she cries, 'No, no', and embarks on a less frightening daydream. Beryl, like Linda, is the victim of sexual ambivalence; and her behaviour is marked by conscious play-acting. Fundamentally narcissistic, she is reminiscent of Juliet (and other early Mansfield heroines) in her substitution of self-adoration for mature love. Thus, on the evening of the second day, she plays the guitar and thinks, 'If I were outside the window and looked in and saw myself I really would be rather struck.' In the absence of an external admirer, she enjoys her own beauty in the mirror. The final scene of 'Prelude' depicts Beryl once more gazing at her reflection. 'Yes, my dear,' she tells the mirror face, 'there is no doubt about it, you really are a lovely little thing.'

There is barely a hint in 'Prelude' that the young woman's self-admiration is a substitute for the adoration of her friend, Nan, to whom she has been writing. Katherine Mansfield excised a passage in 'The Aloe' which conveys fairly explicitly the repressed lesbian relationship between the two. At boarding school, it had been the fashion for the girls to brush Beryl's lovely hair.

> But nobody brushed it as beautifully as Nan Fry. . . . She shook it out, she yielded it up to Nannie's adoring hands. Slowly she brushed, with long, caressing strokes. . . . She would say with a kind of moaning passion . . . 'It's more beautiful than ever, B. It really is lovelier than last time.' . . . She seemed to send herself to sleep with the movement and the gentle sound. . . . But nearly always these brushings came to an unpleasant ending. Nannie did something silly. Quite suddenly she would snatch up Beryl's hair and bury her face in it, and kiss it, or clasp her hands round Beryl's head and press it back against her firm breast, sobbing: 'You are so beautiful!' . . .
>
> And at these moments Beryl had such a feeling of horror, such a violent thrill of physical dislike for Nan Fry. . . . She didn't even try to suppress her contempt and her disgust. . . . Nan Fry seemed to understand this. . . . And the *more* curious

> thing was that Beryl let her brush her hair again, and let this happen again . . . and again there was this silly scene between them . . . never referred to in the day time.

This flashback into Beryl's past throws light on both her narcissism and her role-playing. Secretly she enjoys Nan's caresses; but shame and anxiety about indulging in 'forbidden' behaviour force her to repudiate both Nan and the self which accepts such love. Struggling to deny her lesbian impulses, then, she mentally separates her personality into a day and a night self. The night self she calls her 'false self' and blames for her unhappiness. If there is an uncertainty in Beryl's characterisation, it is because the vital information about her guilty relationship with Nan has been dropped from 'Prelude'. Shown bitterly castigating her falseness, and the self which is 'silly and spiteful and vain', the admission that she shows off to visitors and flirts with Stanley hardly accounts for the intensity of her condemnation.

Not only does 'The Aloe' indicate the real reason for Beryl's self-castigation; it also reveals the importance Katherine Mansfield attached to her character's sense of inner division. The idea of a false or second self is one which recurs in her writing. More openly than in any other story, she analyses in 'The Aloe' the phenomenon of the 'false self' – in terms suggesting Dr Jekyll's possession by Mr Hyde:

> The Beryl who wrote that letter might have been leaning over her shoulder and guiding her hand – so separate was she: and yet in a way, perhaps she was more real than the other, the real Beryl. She had been getting stronger and stronger for a long while.
>
> There had been a time when the real Beryl had just made use of the false one to get her out of awkward positions – to glide her over hateful moments. . . . But that was long ago. The unreal Beryl was greedy and jealous of the real one. Gradually she took more and stayed longer. Gradually she came more quickly, and now the real Beryl was hardly certain sometimes if she were there or not.

A note on the manuscript of 'The Aloe' indicates that Katherine Mansfield had an actual double in mind. 'What is it that I'm getting at?' she asked herself. 'It is really Beryl's *Sosie*.

The fact that for a long time now, she hasn't been even able to control her second self: it's her second self who now controls her.' Beryl's second, or false, self in 'Prelude' is no worse than a naughty child; that described in 'The Aloe' is sinister, because uncontrollable. Through the metaphor of the double, Katherine Mansfield is trying to convey the extent to which Beryl has assumed a defensive mask to hide her guilt and insecurity. The psychological price for this protection is a continuing sense of unreality.

The author's comment on the 'Aloe' manuscript – 'I want to get at all this *through* her. . . . To suddenly merge her into herself' – implies that she wanted Beryl to break through her repression, to confront herself and in a moment of self-revelation to admit the unpleasant truth. In 'Prelude' Beryl is indeed accorded, like Linda, a climactic flash of insight. This occurs when she looks at herself once more in the mirror, not to admire but to ask, 'what had that creature in the glass to do with her?' But with Beryl repression is only partially lifted, the problem of sexual ambivalence only partly faced. As if to underline this, our last glimpse of Beryl is of her asking a series of questions that can only be answered in the negative: 'Shall I ever be that [real] Beryl for ever? Shall I? How can I? And was there ever a time when I did not have a false self?'

Beryl is shown to have no true identity; and in the closing lines of the story her character almost merges with that of Kezia, her younger self. Kezia, remaining in the room after she has called Beryl to lunch, metaphorically enacts the answer to her aunt's anguished questions. As if she were continuing the dialogue between the two selves, she admonishes the calico cat she has placed on the dressing-table with a cream-jar lid over its ear: 'Now look at yourself.' When the cat falls to the floor, with the undamaged lid, the child is overcome with guilt for a crime imagined – not committed. Her tip-toeing from the room, 'far too quickly and airily', is symbolic of the inner confusion which will continue to torture Beryl and which bodes ill for Kezia as well.

At the heart of 'Prelude' is a pessimism about the ability of human beings to control their fate. Although Linda can bring into the open her true feelings about Stanley, she has no power to alter her circumstances. Beryl can neither face up to her self as she really is, nor effect any change in her own personality. If

'Prelude' is one of Katherine Mansfield's greatest stories, it is partly because she creates a group of characters so psychologically believable they might be living people. Delicately investigating the nature of character, she represents the mysterious processes of the inner life to suggest how personality is determined by events far back in childhood. As Katherine Mansfield portrays them, human beings – especially women – are doubly beset: they are at the mercy both of external circumstances and of the internal conflicts that fester beneath their conscious minds. Bringing these to the surface can be a cathartic experience which affords some relief. Yet people have little power to change what they are. And, for the dilemma of the emotionally ambivalent women whose social destiny is marriage, Katherine Mansfield can provide no answer.

15 Garsington as Fiction

After their return from France in 1916 (at the behest of Lawrence), the harmony that had developed between Katherine and Murry since the death of Leslie was shattered. While Murry buried himself in his work at the War Office, Katherine indulged the bohemian side of her nature. Seeking adventure, she entered into new flirtations, attended shady parties, and took strange jobs. At the same time as she was seeing something of Bertrand Russell, she was acting for the movies and, according to Vera Brittain,[1] giving amateur stage peformances at the lesbian club called 'The Cave of Harmony'. By 1917, Katherine was living apart from Murry. L.M. again filled the gap in her friend's life, sleeping in Katherine's studio apartment, and obligingly removing herself when there were visitors.

While L.M. remained for Katherine something of a convenience, the person she could always fall back on when all else failed, Lady Ottoline Morrell was quite a different matter. Letters had been exchanged between the two women since Murry had left the Garsington Christmas party in 1915 to join Katherine grieving in Bandol. From France early in 1916 Katherine had written to Ottoline:[2] 'I have been writing to you ever since the day when Murry came and said "There's a perfectly wonderful woman in England" and told me about you. . . . I long to meet you. Will you write to us again?' Following her unhappy return to Cornwall, Katherine lost no time getting in touch with Ottoline. 'I really long to come. *I do hope that you will like me*', she wrote before her first visit to Garsington.

Katherine was instinctively drawn towards Ottoline; and again and again in 1917 she wrote to her of the love she felt. 'How can I tell you what it is to be with you and to enjoy your presence', she said after one meeting. But commingled with Katherine's expressions of love ('I wish you were here. . . . I would tell you that I loved you and you would believe me') are her fears of losing Ottoline's love. Running through her letters to Ottoline, as through her schoolgirl letters to Sylvia Payne, is a tragic sense of love doomed to disappointment. Indeed, the feeling in one letter written in August 1917 is reminiscent of that expressed towards the beautiful lady in the adolescent fantasy 'My Potplants':

> Quite suddenly, just after you had been so near, so thrilling and so enchanting – for no reason that I can explain away – it was as if the light changed, and you vanished from me. I wandered about in the wood among the wild smelling bushes and sometimes I thought I saw the dark plume of your hat, or your lips or your hand but when I went toward you – you *were* not.

In the same letter, Katherine says that Murry came to see her that evening: 'He showed me a handkerchief you had given him. I took it in my hand and the scent of it shook my heart – yes, just as if I had been a young person profoundly in love with you.'

Independently, during that year of their living apart, Katherine and Murry visited Garsington; and independently they poured out their feelings for Ottoline in letters that were virtually love letters. At the end of 1916, Murry confessed to Ottoline his 'queer suspicion that I must be in love with you'. In a later letter he wrote: 'I won't worry you with another attempt to analyse all the feelings that are stirred up in me the moment that my mind is busy with you. . . . I am only the more sure that I am in love with you.'[3] Sometime in August 1917, Ottoline's memoirs reveal, the bubble burst. Katherine and Murry had made a late summer visit to Garsington, and Katherine suggested that Murry stay on alone for a week's holiday. One evening, Ottoline records, 'Murry asked me if he might "come into my heart" '. Although 'quite unprepared for any emotional intimacy with him', she did call him down, later that evening, to share with her the beauty of the moonlit night. After his return to London, she waited in vain for a letter of thanks. None arrived. When Murry eventually did write, it was to refuse, on behalf of himself and Katherine, Ottoline's offer of a cottage at Garsington. Katherine's letters, too, became 'very cold and indeed quite changed from what they had been'; and Ottoline was deeply wounded. ' "Why did he ask to come into my life", I wrote in my

Journal, "and knock and push against the door as he did and then run away? Now you must leave me alone, Katherine and Murry. I bang the door of my heart in your face." '

It was from Dorothy Brett that Ottoline finally learned that Katherine was bitter and angry. 'At last', Ottoline reports, 'I got her to talk.'

> It appeared that on Murry's return from Garsington he seemed exceedingly distraught, and lay on her sofa groaning and sighing. He said he 'was utterly miserable and that the most dreadful thing has happened'. After much pressing from Katherine he told her that I had 'fallen deeply and passionately in love with him'. When she told me this I really laughed. It was so absurd. But at the time to Katherine it was no laughing matter; for here in her eyes was another treachery. Here was this woman, whom she felt she could love and trust, just as bad and treacherous as everyone else and at the first opportunity tried to steal Murry from her.[4]

After Ottoline had succeeded in reassuring her, Katherine's letters became 'quite like her old ones, affectionate and frank. But Murry became like the ghost of a friend'.

So Katherine won the battle for Ottoline. Although the separation from Murry in 1917 had been initiated by her, she was jealous of his growing intimacy with this mutual friend, just as she had been jealous of Murry's earlier, intense relationships with Gordon Campbell and D. H. Lawrence. For jealousy remained a dominant trait in the personality of this childishly insecure woman. Like Kezia, who in 'The Aloe' demanded grandmother's reassurance that she was the favoured child, Katherine Mansfield as an adult needed overwhelmingly to feel herself in sole possession of the ones she loved. Jealous and angry with Ottoline for apparently usurping Murry's affections, she was equally jealous of Ottoline's friendships with other people.

Ottoline was not unaware of this facet of her friend's character. In her diary she wrote: 'She says she likes me, but I have an odd feeling underneath that her liking is shot with suspicion and envy. . . . Bertie Russell warns me that she is a very jealous woman and would like to poison my mind against other people so as to alienate me from them.'[5] In his own autobiography

Russell says of Katherine, 'When she spoke about people she was envious, dark and full of alarming penetration in discovering what they least wished known and whatever was bad in their characteristics. She hated Ottoline because Murry did not.'[6]

What Bertrand Russell saw as the 'dark' side of Katherine Mansfield's personality, others saw as a mask. In a perceptive comment on her friend's contradictory behaviour, Ottoline Morrell wrote:

> Hidden away behind her mask there was a passionate desire for sympathy, a desire which she would not allow herself to indulge in. If it was offered to her it was as a gift is offered to a lonely child, who couldn't quite believe in it, and would hide it away, to keep it for herself alone, to take out and look at when alone, and perhaps to break it to see if it was real.[7]

Dorothy Brett, admitting that she was herself frightened of the 'Bloomsburies' who frequented Garsington, noticed Katherine's defensiveness on one occasion. She had been singing and playing the guitar when she 'thought she felt an antagonistic criticism and abruptly stopped. Everyone tried to get her to sing again, but nothing would induce her, the guard was up, the face became a mask, the eyes watchful, and a sort of discomfort fell upon us all.'[8] Such behaviour was quite deliberate. Like her own characters, Katherine shielded her sensitive inner self by showing the world a mask, or false self. Again and again she urged Murry, as well, to hide his real feelings. 'It's a terrible thing to be alone', she told him in 1917. 'Yes, it is – it is. But don't lower your mask until you have another mask prepared underneath – as terrible as you like – but a mask.'

Whatever their private disagreements, Katherine and Murry retained a sense of being outsiders in the literary circles of Garsington and Bloomsbury. Mentally, they fortified themselves by withdrawing into their own childlike dream world which was free of the threatening adults known as 'Bloomsburies'. For more than they envied Ottoline, Katherine and Murry envied and distrusted the group surrounding Leonard and Virginia Woolf. In letters to each other, and their friends, they vented their hostility. 'They have hurt me terribly', Murry wrote to Ottoline about her Bloomsbury visitors.

> I will have no more of them. Don't think I am bitter against them. . . . But they are not of my kind. And as soon as I begin to feel passionately about things again, I hate them passionately: Gilbert, Clive, Lytton. You must forgive me, for I know that you like at least one of them. And I do too. But that cannot prevent me from seeing in them at times something horrible. . . . I can hear in imagination one of them reading this letter aloud, and laughing a kind of half-laugh and I could kick him.

After the onset of her illness in 1918, Katherine increasingly echoed these sentiments. Her chief reason for becoming legally married to Murry, she told Ottoline in May 1918, was her 'hatred of the human snigger – and in fact, of human beings, especially of the Bloomsbury element in life'. On an earlier occasion Murry had confided to Ottoline, 'It's awfully childish to dream of revenge . . . but I do continually.' In real life, revenge against the 'arty set', against the 'Bloomsburies' – and even against Ottoline herself – was to be not Murry's, but Katherine's. Like Kezia, who revenged herself upon the Samuel Josephs boys by beating them at their own game, Katherine Mansfield got even with her rivals by turning them into copy.

Ottoline Morrell had few illusions about the use Katherine made of her friends. 'When I look back on the many days I spent with her,' she wrote,

> I cannot remember an hour when she was entirely 'off duty', so to speak, from being a writer. . . . It was easy for her with her acute and precise observation to 'take off' and to act scenes which she had seen and turn them into mockery. No one could so impersonate her victims and catch the mannerisms, the talk and the superficial absurdities in people as she could.[9]

Easily recognisable is the genesis of 'Night-scented Stock', a poem Katherine wrote after one visit at Garsington. One stanza describes the country-house setting:

The big dark house hid secretly
Behind the magnolia and the spreading pear tree,
But there was a sound of music – music rippled and ran
Like a lady laughing behind her fan,
Laughing and mocking and running away . . .
'Come into the garden – it's light as day!'

In Ottoline's own words, 'It was a hot moonlight night when we all went into the garden. . . . Katherine walked up and down under the house where the night-scented stock had opened its pale flower, fanning herself with a little black transparent fan.'[10] Katherine Mansfield's transpositions into fiction of situations involving Garsington, Ottoline and her guests are less immediately recognisable. Yet almost certainly elements of these appear in 'Bliss', 'Marriage à la Mode' and an uncollected sketch, 'In Confidence'. In all three stories, criticism is directed towards a woman based to some extent upon Ottoline, and towards a group of arty guests.

'In Confidence', which appeared in the *New Age* in May 1917, is openly satirical. Marigold, the hostess who is entertaining five young 'literary' gentlemen and a woman, Isobel, suspiciously resembles contemporary descriptions of Garsington's hostess. Ottoline had a sometimes theatrical manner of dressing and a penchant for big hats. Marigold, having invited Isobel to walk with her, first 'powders her face, smears a little rouge on her lips and a little black on each eyelid; puts on a string of big green beads and takes them off again; puts on an immense straw hat that looks to have been pelted with its little bunch of cherries, and ties it under her chin with some wide tulle'. As they walk, Isobel responds to Marigold's overtures with only an enigmatic smile. 'How hard it is to break the ice and melt towards each other as one does so long to melt', Marigold rhapsodises.

> Why are we so shy of each other? Have you any real intimate women friends? . . . Women are such traitors to one another, aren't they? One can feel that one is everything to another woman, her dearest friend – her closest – and the most commonplace little man has only to come along and lift a finger for her to betray you, to let you down! . . . . Women might be so

> wonderful together. I often feel I could appreciate a woman far better than any man could – understand her so exquisitely – sympathise so perfectly.

Typical of the reversals which characterise the endings of Katherine Mansfield's stories is the final, ironic twist of 'In Confidence'. Marigold, who has exposed her feelings to Isobel but received no confidences in return, takes revenge by hypocritically turning against her new protegée. 'No,' she tells the literary gentlemen later, 'I shall not ask Isobel again in the summer.' The sketch is a rather cruel, if lighthearted, caricature of a woman who had showed Katherine much kindness. More significantly, the portrait of Marigold who courts Isobel, as it were, and then betrays her, foreshadows the major but enigmatic story 'Bliss'.

The germ of Katherine's central idea in 'Bliss', as with 'In Confidence', seems to have been her own and Murry's relationship with Ottoline Morrell. For the central theme in 'Bliss' – the betrayal of Bertha by the woman with whom she has fallen in love, and by her own husband – parallels the betrayal Katherine fancied she had suffered at the hands of Ottoline and Murry. Katherine's letters to Murry while she was writing 'Bliss' in February 1918 indicate that Garsington and its hostess were very much on her mind, and that her feelings were not generous. On 7 February she told Murry:

> I must write to H. L. [Ottoline] today or she will take great offence and I don't want to have her my enemy. It's too nauseous. But, to tell the truth, it's very difficult, very, to keep it up: the 'atmosphere' at Garsington (which is now explained . . . one knows where the smell comes from, so to speak; it's her false relation with Philip) does offend me unspeakably. I don't feel I *could* go back there. I am always underneath so acutely uneasy. . . . She *is* bloody interesting – the fact she doesn't know she's poisoned, *par exemple*, but I really have got all I want from her.

A few days later she commented: 'I haven't yet written to H. L. and each day I dislike her a bit more.' In a letter dated 22 February Katherine inquired, 'I wonder if you escaped H. L.? She has become to me now a sort of *witch*. I can't write to her.

When I put my pen on the paper it begins to tremble and make crosses and won't go further.' Four days later she wrote, 'I'll make no END of an effort to finish this story called 'Bliss'. I hope you'll like it.' Suggesting in her next letter that Murry spend a weekend at the Waterlows, Katherine added, 'I don't mention Garsington because it's 2 [*sic*] vile.' The following day came her announcement:

> I've just finished this new story, 'Bliss', and am sending it to you. But though, God! I *have* enjoyed writing it, I am an absolute rag. . . . You will 'recognize' some of the people. *Eddie* of course is a fish out of the Garsington pond (which gives me joy) and Harry is touched with W. L. G[eorge]. Miss Fulton is 'my own invention' – oh, you'll see for yourself.

'Bliss' is one of Katherine Mansfield's most discussed and most controversial stories; and it is also among her most ambiguous. With perhaps more conscious artistry than in any other work, she encoded her meanings, using aspects of the ordinary, external world to suggest emotional attitudes and moods not easily expressible. Her success in masking the psychological meaning of 'Bliss' can be gauged from the fact that, while critics have been unanimous about the effectiveness of her witty caricature of London's pseudo-bohemian 'art set', they have been divided about the story's overall significance.

Middleton Murry himself calls 'Bliss' a 'sophisticated failure', reasoning that 'the discordant combination of caricature with emotional pathos' spoils the story. A major problem facing the critic of 'Bliss', his comment would suggest, is the need to reconcile what on the surface appear to be two incongruous narrative threads: caricature and pathos. In the foreground of the story are the emotional expectations of Bertha Young, who is depicted 'waiting for something . . . divine to happen . . . that she knew must happen'. But why, we wonder, should her eventual tragedy be set against the background of a grotesque caricature of the evening's dinner guests?

Only when we recognise the bitter psychological irony contained in the title word, 'Bliss', do the incongruities and elaborate correspondences fall into place. For the truth that emerges from the story is that Bertha Young, just as surely as the other characters, is caught up in a perverse deviation from the natural and social order that not only denies 'bliss' but also mocks the very possibility of its existence. Through a sophisticated pattern of interlocking symbols and double meanings, Katherine Mansfield builds into the narrative the central idea of emotional aberration, of human beings whose lives are off-course.

The first indication that all is not well with Bertha Young occurs in the opening section of the story when her thought, 'Why be given a body if you have to keep it shut up in a case like a rare, rare fiddle', is immediately countered with the confused denial, 'No, that about the fiddle is not quite what I mean.' From the outset, Bertha's blissful feeling of expectancy as she prepares for her dinner party can be correlated with a sexual tension which is constantly denied and repressed. And, married woman though she is, the comment later that evening by one of the guests – 'Why doth the bridegroom tarry?' – suggests that her dinner party might almost be a wedding-feast.

If Harry Young is the implied bridegroom, Bertha, with her air of emotional expectancy, is surely the bride. Sensuously she arranges a bowl of fruit, admiring the 'two pyramids' she has made of 'these bright round shapes.' Love is central to her consciousness when, after a brief telephone conversation with her husband, his echoed remarks intermingle with thoughts about Pearl Fulton, with whom 'Bertha had fallen in love . . . as she always did fall in love with beautiful women who had something strange about them.' Bertha's physical desire is expressed almost openly as 'she surprised herself by suddenly hugging [a cushion] to her, passionately, passionately'. Spared an examination of her feelings by the immediate contemplation of 'a tall, slender pear tree in fullest, richest bloom', Bertha dresses that evening to resemble the tree: 'A white dress, a string of jade beads, green shoes and stockings. It wasn't intentional.' Perhaps not intentional, either, is the resemblance of the white dress to a wedding dress. Yet for the young woman whose immaturity gives her a virginal quality, whose apparent sexual frigidity has made her relations with Harry that of 'good pals', this night when she comes to desire her husband 'for the first time in her life' might almost be her wedding night.

What complicates, indeed confuses, this relatively straightforward interpretation of the story is the appearance of Pearl Fulton: 'all in silver, with a silver fillet binding her pale blond hair', she too is dressed like a bride. Yet the relationship which appears to develop in the course of the evening is not between either woman and Harry, but between the two women themselves. With Pearl, whose touch 'could fan . . . start blazing . . . the fire of bliss that Bertha did not know what to do with', Bertha experiences a mounting sense of intimacy. While Harry and his modern friends, 'writers and painters and poets or people keen on social questions', typify the artificial 'civilisation' that Bertha twice calls 'idiotic', Pearl appears to understand instinctively the other woman's identification with the beauty of the natural world.

Epitomising this beauty is the 'tall, slender pear tree in fullest richest bloom', the tree which, with its 'wide open blossoms', Bertha now sees as 'a symbol of her own life'. Her bliss becoming a 'brimming cup', Bertha's excitement increases as she thinks of the pear tree which 'would be silver now, in the light of poor dear Eddie's moon, silver as Miss Fulton, who sat there turning a tangerine in her slender fingers that were so pale a light seemed to come from them'. There is a congruence of specifically feminine imagery in the association of the pear tree, the moon, Miss Fulton and the tangerine she so seductively handles. Believing that Pearl shares her mood, and that 'this does happen very, very rarely between women. Never between men', Bertha waits for her friend to 'give a sign'. The moment comes when Miss Fulton asks, 'Have you a garden?'

> And the two women stood side by side looking at the slender, flowering tree. Although it was so still it seemed, like the flame of a candle, to stretch up, to point, to quiver in the bright air, to grow taller and taller as they gazed – almost to touch the rim of the . . . moon.
>
> How long did they stand there? Both, as it were, caught in that circle of unearthly light, understanding each other perfectly, creatures of another world, and wondering what they were to do in this one with all this blissful treasure that burned in their bosoms and dropped, in silver flowers, from their hair and hands?

The psychological significance of the scene derives from the fact that, just as Bertha has been consistently linked with the pear tree, so Pearl, dressed in silver and with her fingers emanating a silver light, has been associated with the moon. In her perception of the tree's insistently phallic appearance as it stretches and seems 'almost to touch the rim of the . . . moon', Bertha-as-tree seems to have fantasised a moment of physical communion with the other woman. This vicarious sexual fulfilment is the climax, then, of the bliss which, fanned by her sensual arrangement of the fruit into two breast-like mounds, her exhilaration at the sight of the pear tree, at the scent of jonquils and the cool touch of Miss Fulton's arm, has been mounting all day; this is the 'something . . . divine . . . that she knew must happen . . . infallibly'. Almost immediately, however, the falling action of the story begins. For Bertha's sense that they are 'creatures of another world' is also a recognition that there is no possibility of a union between two women in this one.

If the lesbianism implicit in the symbolism of this episode is by ordinary standards a deviation from the natural order, and therefore perverse, so is Bertha's suppression of her instinctual feelings as she decides to 'try to tell [Harry] when we are in bed to-night what has been happening. What she and I have shared.' Her attribution of the physical excitement she has experienced to a sexual desire for the husband with whom there is so little emotional rapport is even more perverse. As she imagines bed that evening, Bertha's thoughts indeed resemble those of a bride – virginal and reluctant:

> something strange and almost terrifying darted into Bertha's mind. And this something blind and smiling whispered to her: 'Soon these people will go. The house will be quiet – quiet. The lights will be out. And you and he will be alone together in the dark room – the warm bed. . . .'

In this context, the dinner party *is* like a wedding celebration: Bertha's own bizarre wedding celebration, in which, repressing the welling hatred she feels for Harry, she prepares to consummate with him the physical love she feels, but may not express, for Pearl Fulton.

What the ending of the story makes evident is that a tragic triangular relationship exists between Bertha, Harry and Pearl Fulton; and that in this relationship it is Pearl, not Harry, who is the pivotal figure. Bertha, whose bisexuality is symbolised by her identification with the pear tree in both its feminine and masculine aspects, is betrayed not by her husband only but by the woman who, cold and chaste like the moon, has falsely intimated a reciprocity of mood. Bertha had thought to tell Harry 'what she and I have shared': the cruellest irony of the story is that, although separated emotionally from her husband in almost every way, she and Harry share a love for the same woman.

'Bliss' is a complex work partly because Katherine Mansfield used symbol and ambiguity deliberately to obscure the full sexual significance of her narrative, and partly because the story operates on two emotional levels. In the foreground there is the sympathetic, if ironic, portrayal of Bertha Young which is in itself a study of a repressed and divided personality. Repressing the real nature of her feelings for such beautiful women as Pearl Fulton on the one hand, and for Harry on the other, Bertha indulges in the most blatant self-deception. Part of her defence against facing up to the truth is the role-playing which causes her to cultivate a kind of childish immaturity. This is expressed in her self-conscious desire to 'take dancing steps on and off the pavement, to bowl a hoop'; in the thought, when she visits her child in the nursery, that she is 'like the poor little girl in front of the rich little girl with the doll'; and in her girlish happiness at such superficial pleaures as finding 'a wonderful little dressmaker', and at having a cook who 'made the most superb omelettes'. The same, almost deliberate, naïveté enables her to reject the flashes of insight which occur when she is off guard. For instance, her thought 'Why have a baby if it has to be kept . . . in another woman's arms?' is dismissed as easily as is her suspicion that there is more to Pearl Fulton than meets the eye. Only too readily does Bertha accept at face value Harry's deprecatory remarks about Miss Fulton, even though one such remark before Pearl's arrival is followed by a 'tiny moment, while they waited, laughing and talking, just a trifle too much at their ease, a trifle too unaware'.

Bertha's instinctive, natural self prefers the unspoilt beauty of the garden to the intellectualised falseness of 'civilisation'; yet the immaturity which is responsible for her role-playing causes her to acquiesce in the behaviour of Harry and his guests. Against the almost grotesque background of their appearance and conversation, the emotional abnormality of her feelings for Pearl Fulton is projected; and the contrast reveals that, while Bertha is a pitiful figure, her falseness is of a different order from theirs.

Imagery associated with the world of the garden – trees, flowers, fruit and moonlight – is used to define Bertha; but the conversation of the others is dominated by unpleasantly ambiguous references to food and sexuality. Harry's dismissal of Bertha's ingenuous remarks about Pearl with such replies as ' "liver frozen, my dear girl', or "pure flatulence", or "kidney disease" ', implies both an obsession with the alimentary processes and a diseased personality. Apparently unable to give love in the normal domestic sense ('don't ask me about my baby. I never see her. I shan't feel the slightest interest in her until she has a lover'), the man's gross delight in food points to the strength of his carnal appetite, even as the language used to describe it conveys the impression that for him sexual love and eating are virtually interchangeable.

> It was part of his – well, not his nature, exactly, and certainly not his pose – his – something or other – to talk about food and to glory in his 'shameless passion for the white flesh of the lobster' and 'the green of pistachio ices – green and cold like the eyelids of Egyptian dancers'.

Even more implicitly cannibalistic is the description of Mrs Norman Knight, whose monkey coat 'so upset the train that it rose to a man and simply ate me with its eyes'. The image of human beings as something to be devoured is continued in the Norman Knights' repeated references to the scene in the train as 'creamy', and in Bertha's distorted perception that the wife's dress resembles 'scraped banana skins' and her earrings 'little dangling nuts'. Mrs Norman Knight's own obsession with food is revealed in her desire to use 'a fried-fish scheme' in the decoration of a room, 'with the backs of the chairs shaped like frying-pans and lovely chip potatoes embroidered all over the curtains'. Even the conversation about literature revolves around correspondences with food: romantic writing is associated with seasickness; and the '*incredibly* beautiful' (in Eddie Warren's eyes) first line of 'Bilk's *new* poem called "Table d'Hôte" ' is 'Why Must it Always be Tomato Soup?'

If the pervasiveness of the food imagery suggests that in this perverse milieu people feed on each other as mindlessly as animals do on food (and the idea of animalism is reinforced by references to the grey and black cats, to monkeys, phoenixes and a spider), it is clear, too, that sexual relations are governed by a kind of mindless perversity. Calling each other 'Face' and 'Mug', the Norman Knights appear sexually interchangeable. Eddie Warren, the writer, is an effeminate young man whose story of a '*dreadful* experience with a taxi-man', a '*bizarre* figure with . . . *flattened* head *crouching* over the *lit-tle* wheel' is full of sexual innuendo. Such innuendo, in fact, governs the conversation. Castration and mutilation are implied in the description of 'the weirdest little person' someone met at 'the Alpha show'. 'She'd not only cut off her hair, but she seemed to have taken a dreadfully good snip off her legs and arms and her neck and her poor little nose as well.' Almost as explicit is the idea of rape and castration in the mention of '*A dreadful* poem about a *girl* who was *violated* by a beggar *without* a nose in a lit-tle wood.'

In this context, the depiction of Harry as he embraces Miss Fulton at the end of the evening is grimly ironic. His 'nostrils quivered; his lips curled back in a hideous grin', and he resembles nothing so much as an animal about to pounce and devour its prey. What the symbolism of 'Bliss' makes clear is that this story is neither the 'modish anecdote' nor the 'sophisticated failure' that some critics have suggested. With its nightmarish overtones, the work is one of Katherine Mansfield's most horrifying psychological studies: a near-surrealistic portrait of an immature woman caught up in a web of perversion from which there can be no escape.

Unable to correspond with Ottoline while she was writing 'Bliss', Katherine re-established contact once the story was finished. Obviously suffering from a guilty conscience, she apologised in her own oblique way for the treachery of which only she was aware:

> I have taken this tiny piece of paper in the slender hope that I may still be able to hide behind it and try (ah! try) to explain my inexplicable silence without falling into too dread a panick at sight of your stern looks of anger and dismay.
>
> Would to God I were *not* this fickle, faithless . . . creature.
> But lady! Pity her – Alas – poor soul: Katherine is curst!

All goes well. . . . She makes merry. She hugs the 'black but beautiful' fire with her dearest and is not lost in gossip of those who are not there. And then, quite suddenly . . . she is shut up in her dark house, and the blinds are pulled down. . . .'

The real tragic part of the affair is that what happens to her while she is so wickedly *out* yet dreadfully *in* she cannot tell or explain. . . .

A curse on my pen! . . . Why aren't I as true as steel – firm as rock? I am – I am – but in my way. And yes, I agree, it is no end of a rum way –

The previous month, Katherine had called Ottoline a 'witch'; now that 'Bliss' was completed and her burden of anger and spite relieved, she guiltily imagined that the 'friends' whom she had so distortedly represented saw her in the same light. Quite genuinely, Katherine seemed unable to account rationally even to herself for her change in mood. She could only think that she was under a spell while writing, 'curst'. As if echoing, indeed explaining, the state of mind which created 'Bliss', she told Ottoline that the beauty of spring tired her out 'with the loveliness of the world. . . . Ah, Ottoline, it has made me realise so deeply and finally the *corruption* of the world. I have such a horror of the present day men and women that I mean never to go among them again.' A few months later, Katherine wrote again to Ottoline of feelings remarkably similar to those of Bertha in 'Bliss':

Why are human beings the only ones who do not put forth fresh buds – exquisite flowers and leaves. I cannot bear to go among them. . . . Really, on some of these days one is tired with *bliss*. I long to tell someone – to feel it immediately shared – felt without my asking 'do you feel it?' Do you know what I mean?

Until the end of her life, Katherine Mansfield continued to write affectionately to Ottoline. One late story, 'Marriage à la Mode', bears witness to the truth of her remark, 'I shall always be haunted by the memory of Garsington'. But the story also indicates the mixed feelings with which Katherine still viewed Ottoline and her circle of friends. In its use of a social situation reminiscent of the life at Garsington, its portrayal of one partner in a marriage at the expense of the other, its caricature of a group of 'arty' guests and its grotesquely symbolic references to food, the satirical 'Marriage à la Mode' is a clear descendant of 'Bliss'. It contains none of the psychological ambiguity which has so puzzled critics of the earlier work, partly because the author did not cast herself emotionally as one of the characters. But the story's origin has aroused debate. Commentators have frequently charged Katherine Mansfield with drawing the actual plots as well as the inspiration of her writing from Chekhov; and it is to Chekhov's 'The Grasshopper' that D. W. Kleine attributes the source of 'Marriage à la Mode'.

The work is not an imitation of Chekhov. Here, as in her other writing, Katherine Mansfield drew upon her own experiences. In 'Marriage à la Mode' these experiences were not emotional, as in the stories where she depicted in disguised form her own intimate relationships with her family or with Murry; they were factual experiences. A comparison of certain external details in the story with real-life scenes which Katherine had witnessed shows this. In character the superficial Isabel in 'Marriage à la Mode' bears little resemblance to Ottoline, yet there is a decided similarity between the situation of the fictional Isabel and William, who have moved from London to a larger house in the country, and that of the Morrells. Like Philip Morrell, William must live in London near his work and only commute home at weekends. Robert Gathorne Hardy writes candidly of Philip Morrell's visits home during the years of the First World War,

> Bruised and unhappy, he would come back to Garsington; no notice was taken of him; those he had befriended and aided seemed to show neither gratitude nor sympathy, tributes which would have alleviated his suffering. Even Ottoline, alas, seems to have failed him here. What he found was a cell of gaiety and happy feasts of the intellect. He was dreadfully hurt: 'Nobody', he told me, 'had the slightest idea of what I was going through.'[11]

Nobody, perhaps, except the ever-observant Katherine Mansfield. In 'Marriage à la Mode', William's wife keeps an extravagantly open house for her flock of arty friends. Thrust into the background when he comes home, William is made to feel a stranger, even an intruder, in his own house.

Ottoline Morrell surrounded herself with avant-garde writers and painters, self-important and aware of their cleverness.[12] Isabel's guests are mercilessly satirised for their artistic pretensions. Dennis Green, for example, is a would-be writer and poseur who persists in referring to his companions as if they were models for still-life paintings. Isabel he labels as 'A Lady in Love with a Pineapple', then as 'A Lady reading a Letter'; Moira Morrison he calls 'A Lady with a Box of Sardines'.[13] Reminiscent of Garsington, too, are the entertainments of Isabel's friends. In 'Night-Scented Stock' Katherine had described the swimming which was a feature of Garsington summers. William, in 'Mariage à la Mode', is left alone with the children after his arrival while 'the others went off to bathe'; and the story concludes with Isabel being summoned to join once more the revelry of the swimmers. Ottoline, who loved dancing and records that she had entertained Nijinsky, kept a great store of fancy clothes for use at her parties; on one occasion when Katherine was present they all danced 'a wild lovely ballet on the lawn'. In the story, Bobby Kane after his swim begins to leap and pirouette on the lawn: ' "I say, Isabel," called Bobby, "would you like me to wear my Nijinsky dress to-night?" '

As in 'Bliss', the imagery of food is central to Katherine Mansfield's caricature of the arty set in 'Marriage à la Mode'. To William, who brings a pineapple and a melon for his children, food is a symbol of loving care. Sharply contrasted with him are the predatory, animal-like guests who greedily devour everything in sight. William has a 'horrible vision of one of Isabel's young poets lapping up a slice [of melon] . . . behind the nursery door', and his worst fears are confirmed. The revellers who meet him at the station are preoccupied with food. At their urging Isabel appropriates the fruit. Later, after a swim, they are 'all starving'. As they devour sardines and whisky, 'William [is] forgotten. . . . Bill and Dennis ate enormously. And Isabel filled glasses, and changed plates, and found matches, smiling blissfully.' But, after William's departure on Monday, even she finds the gluttony disconcerting: 'Isabel couldn't help wondering what had happened to the salmon they had for supper last night. She had meant to have fish mayonnaise for lunch and now . . .'

Katherine Mansfield's use of the symbolism of food and the imagery of eating to portray her characters' insensitivity, indeed their grotesqueness, is hardly surprising. Story after story reveals her profound, irrational revulsion against the alimentary processes. But it is significant, when one considers the genesis of 'Marriage à la Mode', that this portrayal of greediness (heightened for the purpose of satire) accords with Ottoline Morrell's own account of an episode witnessed by Katherine at the Garsington Christmas party in 1916. Ottoline writes that

> The guests, although they had doubtless to put up with meagre diets in their own homes, when at Garsington expected to find food very richly and plentifully supplied, and to have plenty of wine and spirits. There was a dreadful scene one morning at breakfast, when Lytton came down very late and I suppose the appetites of the other guests had been healthy, for he did not find all he required. He lost his temper and turned and rated me angrily for not providing him with sufficient breakfast. Murry and Katherine and several others were present, and we looked at each other surprised and aghast, for there really was ample food. I went to the kitchen and fetched him enough for six men. I know that next day and the succeeding days he had breakfast sent up to his room, piled high with six eggs, ham, fish, scones and everything that could be collected together.[14]

Correspondences such as these indicate that Katherine Mansfield drew far more heavily from life than from literature when she wrote her stories. One of the strengths of great writers is that they instinctively portray human characteristics that are universal. Katherine Mansfield is just such a writer. In describing the greedy 'suitors' who took up residence in the house of another man, devoured his sustenance and tried to usurp his position with his wife, she might just as well have been thinking of Homer's *Odyssey* as of Chekhov's 'Grasshopper'. But in all probability she was thinking about Ottoline and Garsington.

16 'Je Ne Parle Pas Français'

Like 'Bliss', 'Je Ne Parle Pas Français' was written at Bandol, France, in the early months of 1918. These stories were Katherine Mansfield's courageous response to the knowledge that she was securely in the grip of a dreaded disease, tuberculosis. Different though they are in almost every other way, homosexuality is central to the themes of each. Throwing light on this preoccupation are Katherine's tormented relations with Murry and Ida Baker.

The previous year, it was she who had rejected domesticity and chosen to live apart from Murry. Now, more than ever before, she needed the support of Murry's love. Pouring out her own love in letters, she attempted to bind him to her. Although physically unable to bear children, she spoke of having a child. And she resurrected the fantasy that they were themselves children, chivvied by a world that took advantage of their innocence. So they must stick together as 'playmates' and 'live on honeydew and milk of Paradise'. The concomitant of Katherine's renewed longing for Murry was a violent repudiation of Ida Baker. While living apart from Murry, she had readmitted Ida into her life and favour. But, as soon as illness reunited them emotionally, Katherine began to treat L. M. as Murry's rival. Cattily, on Christmas Eve 1917, she flattered Murry with a comparison of his gifts and L. M.'s: 'You have simply covered me with presents lately, and I've given you nothing. L. M. gave me a petticoat – rather like raspberries and currants. Very nice. I let her.'

When she was joined by her woman friend rather than by Murry in Bandol, Katherine justified the hostility she felt in terms suggesting that L. M. was a competitor for her love. 'Really she has persecuted me,' Katherine complained to Murry, 'and if I didn't put up a fight, she'd ruin all our life. . . . 'If there wasn't Jack' – that is what she says – and that I really CANNOT STAND from anybody. . . . What she can't stand is you and I – us. You've taken away her prey – which is me.' The more fervently Katherine dwelt on her future idyllic life with Murry, the more vehemently she railed against the woman whose very presence in Bandol threatened the validity of that dream. It was in terms of food and eating that she most often expressed her revulsion against L. M. As if her companion had become one of the sexually aggressive males in her own stories and she, in her illness, a helpless victim, Katherine wrote that L. M. wanted to devour her: 'She's a revolting hysterical ghoul. She's never content except when she can eat me.' If Katherine could translate L. M.'s appetite for food into an appetite for herself, she could just as readily think of her as having 'pecked her way into my lung to justify her coming'. From being a hen, L. M. became a vulture, and then a vampire. 'She's drawn my furious blood and she knows it. She's made me feel again *weak, exhausted* with rage, and so she's happy. . . . I grant I have an L. M. complex – but to hate any one as I hate this *enemy* . . . of ours', Katherine exclaimed to Murry.

It was out of this particular blend of love and hate that Katherine Mansfield's famous declaration that she had 'two kick-offs' in the writing game emerged. One kick-off was 'real joy', the other was 'an *extremely* deep sense of hopelessness, of everything doomed to disaster, almost wilfully, stupidly . . . *a cry against corruption*'.[1] But whether their inspiration was joy or hopelessness, both kick-offs were invariably set in motion by Katherine's immediate experience of personal suffering. Ironically, her joy at the Villa Pauline had followed the death of her brother; her sense of hopelessness during this return visit to Bandol came from the suppressed knowledge that her vow to follow Leslie in death was being realised.

Because the themes of her stories were so often shaped by her own psychological states, 'Bliss' and 'Je Ne Parle Pas Français' depict the corruption she felt so keenly in terms of sexual perversion. A woman's repressed lesbianism is at the heart of 'Bliss'; 'Je Ne Parle Pas Français' is an extended and psychologically penetrating study of male homosexuality – from a woman's point of view. Both works have been acclaimed. 'Je Ne Parle Pas Français', to an even greater extent than 'Bliss', however, has defied sustained analysis. Reviewing it for the *Athenaeum* in April 1920,

J. N. Sullivan announced that the work 'possesses genius' but is 'quite unanalysable'. Murry speaks of 'something equivocal and mysterious in its suggestion of a haunting and undefined evil lurking near the heart of life'.[2] Edward Wagenknecht commented that, while the author touched on 'sexual hunger and perversion' here, she handled the theme 'so subtly and delicately that, as Mr Murry himself remarks in a wholly different connection, hardly anybody has ever completely understood the story'.[3]

A major obstacle to the understanding of the story is the author's masking of her central theme. In 'Bliss' the background satire diverts attention from the psychological tragedy of Bertha Young; similarly in 'Je Ne Parle Pas Français' the background tale of Mouse and Dick Harmon lessens the impact of the vital homosexual theme. So do the excisions which Katherine Mansfield was forced to make. At first she resisted her publisher's demands. 'No, I certainly won't agree to those excisions', she wrote angrily to Murry. 'Shall I pick the eyes out of a story for £40. I'm furious. No, I'll never agree. . . . The *outline* would be all blurred. It must have those sharp lines.' But, needing the money, she eventually agreed to the work's censorship.[4]

Her first impulse was correct. The excisions, although brief, all serve to heighten our sense of the narrator's depravity. Duquette prides himself on his ability to describe the 'submerged world . . . very naively, with a sort of tender humour and from the inside, as though it were all quite simple, quite natural'; and, playing a part, he adopts just such a deceptive manner in his narration. As he draws the audience into his confidence, commenting on his fellow Parisians, talking nostalgically about 'Mouse' and recalling sadly his friendship with Dick Harmon, he is almost a sympathetic character.

Unless one is aware of the excisions and reads between the lines, it might appear that the focus of the narrative is the story of Mouse and Dick's elopement. Because they have read 'Je Ne Parle Pas Français' too literally, many critics have missed the psychological depth of the work, and its full significance. J. N. Sullivan in his early review was one of these. 'This second [homosexual] theme', he said, 'is almost too interesting; one's attention runs some risk of being diverted from the proper centre of the story. . . . We think this is due to a slight weakening in Miss Mansfield's concentration.' More recently, Marvin

Magalaner has discussed the story chiefly in terms of Mouse and Dick, virtually ignoring the real protagonist.

Part of the problem lies in the very technical skill which exposes us simultaneously to two different viewpoints. There is the narrator's studied presentation of himself as he would like to be seen; and there is the conflicting picture of his character which takes shape in spite of his intentions. Nevertheless, clues to the kind of man Duquette really is are dropped all through his confession. To follow these is to see that the story of Mouse and Dick matters less in its own right than for the way it finally illuminates the true character of the French pimp. In fact, the narrative is at once Duquette's narcissistic confession and a damning exposé of his personality. As he talks, moving backwards and forwards in time, the hidden relationships between his experiences in the past and his behaviour in the present are subtly uncovered. It is the gradual accumulation of detail which eventually throws into relief the contrast between Duquette and Mouse: between sexual perversity and sexual innocence, between sadistic male predator and masochistic female prey.

A psychologically vital key to the understanding of Duquette is the fact that he is a voyeur who feeds on the emotions of others. Thus he describes human beings as 'portmanteaux' and himself as a kind of customs officer who derives a thrill from inspecting their contents and demanding, 'Have you anything to declare?' The spectacle of human unhappiness affords him the greatest enjoyment. He chooses to frequent a 'dirty and sad' little café whose proprietress has an 'air of fatigue and hopelessness'. As the narrative unfolds, it becomes clear that he derives sadistic satisfaction from observing, and contributing to, the humiliation of women. Disliking women, he bitterly calls life 'the old hag', 'the old bitch', and 'a rag-picker on the American cinema, shuffling along wrapped in a filthy shawl with her old claws crooked over a stick'. Later, he cynically imagines a pregnant Virgin Mary riding into the café, before turning his thoughts to the prostitutes who do gather there.

Each scrap of information that the narrator drops, however casually, contributes to the understanding of his true character. The derisive contemplation of female helplessness bolsters his weak ego; equally, his awareness of acting a part in his own story, of being on stage 'at exactly the moment you were expected' makes him feel 'master of the situation'. Just how warped Duquette's personality is, the past which he pretends to have forgotten but cannot resist recounting indicates. As a child, he discloses, he was seduced by an African laundress. 'Ah, those kisses! Especially those kisses inside my ears that nearly deafened me.' Excised from the published version is the revealing sentence, 'And then with a soft growl she tore open her bodice and put me to her.' Introduced to prostitution in youth, he continues the practice in adulthood. His clientèle, 'from little prostitutes and kept women and elderly widows and shop girls and wives of respectable men, and even advanced modern literary ladies', always make the first advances, he boasts. 'Curious, isn't it?' In the uncut version there follows the rhetorical comment, 'Why should I be able to have any woman I want?'

Duquette's reasons for asking the question became clearer as his effeminacy is revealed. A narcissistic admirer of his own 'radiant vision' in the mirror, he collects 'all sorts of little things, like gloves and powder boxes and a manicure set, perfumes, very good soap . . .' And he describes himself as if he were a woman: 'I confess, without my clothes I am rather charming. Plump, almost like a girl, with smooth shoulders, and I wear a thin gold bracelet above my left elbow.' When he talks of his attraction to the English writer, Dick Harmon, his homosexuality becomes explicit. Encouraged by the Englishman's seeming lack of interest in the opposite sex, he attempts to impress, indeed to court the other man by showing him 'both sides of my life' and taking 'immense pains to explain things about my submerged life that really were disgusting and never could possibly see the light of literary day'. Although the question of Dick's real emotional and sexual orientation remains open, we are left in no doubt about Duquette's. When his friend casually announces his return to England, he feels 'as a woman must feel' when a man suddenly remembers an appointment whose claim is stronger. The arrival of a 'charming letter' from Dick causes him to liken himself in his blue kimono to a 'portrait of Madame Butterfly . . . on hearing of the arrival of *ce cher Pinkerton*'.

Declaring that he has been 'insulted – insulted' by Dick, Duquette appears more pathetic than evil as he describes his humiliation. The portrait of his twisted personality takes a new turn, however, with the arrival in Paris of Dick and Mouse. The couple become his prey. Feeding on their unhappiness, he wreaks revenge on Mouse for his pain at the hands of Dick – and for the pain inflicted by all the other women in his life, including the concierge who is demanding rent. In voyeuristic fashion, he 'bathes' in their emotions, pretending commiseration while inwardly exulting. He longs to tell Mouse that 'it was months and months since I had been so entertained'. Offering to help Mouse when it becomes clear that she too has been abandoned by Dick, he leaves inwardly exhilarated by the suffering he has witnessed. 'I have seen two people suffer as I don't suppose I ever shall again', he exults. In the uncut version of the story, an additional sentence underlines the man's sadism: 'And . . . [sic] good night, my little cat, said I, impudently to the fattish old prostitute picking her way home through the slush . . . [sic] I didn't give her time to reply.'

The importance of the sentence is that it again reveals Duquette in the act of mentally defiling a virgin (for it is implied that Mouse is sexually pure) by associating her with prostitution. As if he *had* been wondering whether Mouse, deserted by Dick and unable to return to England unmarried might be forced into prostitution, he is depicted fantasising in the closing section of the story. In imagination he is a little boy playing by the sea with a little girl who might be Mouse. Then the appearance at his table of 'some dirty old gallant' jerks him back to reality. Now the pimp, he says, 'But I've got the little girl for you, *mon vieux*. So little . . . so tiny.' The depth of his depravity is lessened in the published story by the excision of the additional words, 'and a virgin'. Moreover, 'a virgin' is repeated in the original version: 'I kiss the tips of my fingers – a virgin – and lay them upon my heart.'

If the narrator's sadistic toying with Mouse, both in deed and thought, is a kind of homosexual retaliation for his own rejection by Dick, his spiteful closing speculations about 'Madame' remind us of his need to prey upon and debase all women. The final line of the published story – 'No, not yet, Madame' – shows him accepting his present victim's invitation to dinner. The original version had a much stronger ending: 'I'd rather like to dine with her. Even to sleep with her afterwards. Would she be pale like that all over? But no. She'd have large moles. They go with that kind of skin. And I can't bear them. They remind me somehow, disgustingly, of mushrooms.'

To read the version of 'Je Ne Parle Pas Français' that

Katherine Mansfield originally wrote is to see that the story of Mouse and Dick Harmon is important less in its own right than for what it reveals about the narrator. There was no 'weakening' of the author's concentration when she placed Raoul Duquette unequivocally at the centre of the story. He is the agent of the 'mysterious . . . and undefined evil' that Murry found lurking in a work that is full of images of death and destruction. Reflected through the consciousness of the narrator, these suggest the deathly despair that lies behind his self-confident façade. There is his cynical conception of people as 'portmanteaux', thrown around 'until finally the Ultimate Porter swings them on to the Ultimate Train'; his mental picture of the waiter in the café 'waiting to be photographed in connection with some wretched murder'; his likening of a morsel of pink blotting paper to 'the tongue of a little dead kitten'; his conception of the concierge as 'stewing out the hearts and livers of every tenant in the place'; and his imagining of Dick's death when the Englishman fails to return to Mouse: 'Dick has shot himself . . . I rushed in, saw the body, head unharmed, small blue hole over temple, roused hotel, arranged funeral . . .'

Dick and, more importantly, Mouse serve as foils to the protagonist. In his oedipal attachment to his mother and his callous desertion of Mouse, Dick echoes the narrator's obsession with the African laundress and his inability to love women. Mouse is a necessary symbol of innocence, a Desdemona-like figure against whom Duquette (like Iago) can wreak his blind malice. But it is not merely Mouse's fragility and air of virginal helplessness which fascinates Raoul Duquette: there is also a sense in which she is the woman he might have been; and thus she represents his alternate self, or double. As is usual in the literary depiction of doubles or split characters, Duquette and Mouse are psychological and moral opposites. His depraved promiscuity contrasts with her virginal innocence; her almost masochistic resignation complements his sadistic aggression. And yet there are hints of something interchangeable between the pair. Although she is an English woman, and he a French man, Mouse is twice described as 'boyish' while Duquette is 'like a girl'. As if they were in some way opposing sides of the same personality, certain likenesses emerge. Both characters love Dick Harmon and are deserted by him: Dick brings 'real tears' into the narrator's eyes, and causes Mouse to weep, too. Duquette in his kimono thinks of himself as 'Madame Butterfly'; later he sees Mouse as 'a tiny creature, half butterfly, half woman, bowing to you with her hands in her sleeves'. Both are without family ties, moreover. Rootless figures, they are lonely strays: Duquette a stray fox-terrier, and she a mouse without a nest. Finally, there is a suggestion in the text that they each have doubles. The narrator mentions his 'other self . . . chasing up and down', and Mouse he describes as getting 'in the black hole and . . . stroking Mouse II'.

'Je Ne Parle Pas Français' is so different from Katherine Mansfield's other stories that it seems appropriate to comment, as Murry did, on its origins. In his autobiography he talks of 'a moving personal symbolism' in the story, 'which only I can understand. The fate of Mouse, caught in the toils of the world's evil, abandoned by her lover, is Katherine's fate.' Murry did not make a connection between Katherine's almost pathological letters from Bandol about the relationship between herself and Ida Baker, and the theme of the story. But when he gave her his reactions to the first part of her manuscript he told her: 'This is the only writing of yours I know that seems to be *dangerous*. To put it another way. Here you seem to drag the depths of your consciousness. . . . The world is shut out and you are looking into yourself.' The second part of the manuscript, he wrote later, struck him 'dumb and numb' with pain. It hurt too much.'[5]

Possibly, Murry saw the likeness noted by Anthony Alpers between Dick Harmon's abandonment of Mouse and his own early abandonment of the French girl Marguéritte – and perhaps his own abandonment (in Katherine's eyes) of herself, ill, in France. Katherine when she tried to explain the factual basis of the story, told Murry:

> The subject, I mean lui qui parle, is of course taken from Carco and Gertler, and God knows who. . . . I read the fair copy just now and couldn't think where the devil I got the bloody thing from. . . . There is so much less taken from life than anybody would credit. The African laundress I had a bone of – but only a bone – Dick Harmon of course partly is –

A few days later she continued where she left off: 'Boge, haven't I got a *bit of you*? Funny thing is I think you'll always come walking into my stories.'

The truth seems to be that, as with so many of her stories, Katherine Mansfield took from life external details of a situation she knew about, and even the outlines of some of her characters. Onto these she grafted a psychological theme which, as Murry recognised, was dragged from 'the depths of [her] consciousness'. Thus parallels can be found between the arrival of Mouse and Dick in Paris and Francis Carco's description of the similar arrival there of Katherine and Murry in 1913.[6] Carco met the couple at the station and accompanied them to a hotel where, at Murry's request, he had reserved two rooms. Katherine, he says, looked timid – almost like a child – and she told him with a bow, 'Je ne parle pas français.' There the resemblance between real life and the story ends. Far from wanting to desert Katherine, Murry 'seemed drunk with happiness'; Carco himself returned frequently to give Katherine French lessons and escort her around Paris.

Far more interesting is Katherine's assimilation of Dostoevsky's *Letters from the Underworld*. Certain parallels between the Russian story and 'Je Ne Parle Pas Français' suggest that Dostoevsky provided her with some pegs on which to hang her own unique confession. Both writers, for example, employ a mouse image. In Part One of Dostoevsky's story, entitled 'The Mousehole', the narrator describes the man who, having been humiliated, acts like a mouse: 'the downtrodden mouse plunges immediately into a cold, poisonous, and – most important – never-ending hatred'. Now, although there is practically no resemblance between Katherine Mansfield's woman named Mouse and Dostevsky's mouse-man, there is a similarity between the psychological condition of Duquette, whose sensitivity to humiliation makes him seek irrational vengeance on those weaker than himself, and the perverse malice of the Russian narrator. Both narrators are role-players. Duquette asks, 'How can one look the part and not be the part?'; the narrator of *Letters* confesses, 'I made up whole stories about myself and put myself through all sorts of adventures to satisfy, at any price, my need to live.' Neither character is able to feel genuine love, but both toy sentimentally with the idea of it. 'Once or twice,' says Dostoevsky's narrator, 'I tried to make myself fall in love. And believe me . . . I certainly suffered! Deep down, of course, I couldn't quite believe in my suffering and felt like laughing.' Both narrators are haunted by the past and gain satisfaction from recounting their stories. Significantly, Dostoevsky's character is troubled by an old memory 'like an exasperating tune that I can't get out of my head', while Duquette's story is evoked by Mouse's swan-song, 'Je ne parle pas français.'

If a few ideas from Dostoevsky crept into Katherine Mansfield's long story in the confessional mode, it was because of a certain affinity between the two writers. When it came to creating psychologically tortured characters, both were profoundly autobiographical. The unresolved contradictions they perceived in human personalities emerged in their fiction as divided characters, sometimes split into two separate and opposing halves. There is the merest outward hint of doubles in 'Je Ne Parle Pas Français'; only the imagery suggests that Duquette and Mouse might be ego and alter-ego. Still it was with more insight than he understood that Murry told Katherine that she was dragging the depths of her consciousness. For if she put something of herself into the character of Mouse, she equally endowed Duquette, the writer, with traits of her own. She gave him her introspection, her bisexuality, her compulsive need to shape into art aspects of her life, and even the sense of importance she derived from being a writer. Duquette insists that his confession proves 'that I really am important'; Katherine, after sending Murry her story, said: 'but what I felt so curiously as I wrote it was – ah! I am in a way *grown up* as a writer – a sort of authority'.

17 The Nightmare Marriage

In February 1918, Katherine Mansfield privately recorded her first haemorrhage:

> Oh, yes, of course I'm frightened. But for two reasons only. I don't want to be ill, I mean 'seriously', away from Jack. Jack is the first thought. 2nd, I don't want to find this is real consumption, perhaps it's going to gallop – who knows? – and I shan't have my work written. . . . But I feel the first thing to do is to get back to Jack.

It was not until April 1918 that she was able to make the hazardous wartime journey back from France to England. Three weeks later she married the man whose love and support had come to mean as much as life itself. Almost from the moment of her arrival in England, however, Katherine's hopes of love and succour were doomed to disappointment. As Murry himself writes, the reality of their marriage was utterly different from the dream which had sustained her during the first terrible months of illness. 'Our marriage . . . was a painful thing', he says in *Between Two Worlds*. 'It was so different from anything which, in the six thwarted and impatient years since Katherine and I first came together, I had dreamed our marriage would be. In spite of all my efforts of will, a wave of bitterness and dismay welled up and soured my heart.' Murry's trouble was that 'Katherine saw me more or less as I had always been: when I looked upon her, it was hard to discover the Katherine whom I had known. The nightmare was in reality itself.' Explaining his decision to send her to Cornwall and the care of her friend Anne Estelle Rice a bare six weeks after their marriage, he says that his rooms were 'quite unsuited for one in her condition. . . . What Katherine demanded was that I should ignore her illness altogether. It was impossible.'

Katherine's bewildered disappointment at the turn of events is evident in the first, brave letter she wrote Murry from Cornwall. Addressing him as 'My dear husband', she closes with a reference to the sound of the sea, which 'makes me feel what a blind, dreadful, losing and finding affair life has been just lately, with how few golden moments, how little little rest'. A few days later she cried out, 'Oh, Bogey, I think it is *infernal* that we should be apart, and yet I bring you nothing but anxiety and sorrow – so we *must* not be together. What an impasse! Sometimes, I am so bewildered – utterly bewildered. . . .' Even as she clung to her dream of the home they would make together ('We must have our Heron soon'), Katherine was being forced by Murry's attitude to realise that her illness had radically altered their relationship. Only three weeks after their marriage, there came her bitter reaction, entitled 'An idea', to one of his letters: 'Are you really happy when I am not there? . . . You are always pale, exhausted, in a kind of anguish of set fatigue when I am by. Now I feel in your letters this is lifting and you are breathing again.'

It was not only the discrepancy between fantasy and reality which brought forth, a few days later, an even more devastating letter: it was the realisation of her husband's weakness, of his inability to sustain her either emotionally or spiritually:

> I think, reading your three letters this morning, I suffered every atom that you suffered. Nay more, because it was I who inflicted it on you – you who came crying to me and saying 'This is what you have done to me! This!' Even now I can't get calm and I am all torn to pieces by love and hideous remorse and regret. . . . Before I begin to speak – you must know that you're all life to me. God! haven't my letters said just that? Hasn't all my suffering and misery been just because of that – because of my terrible – exhausting – utterly INTENSE love?

Most striking in this letter is Katherine's dependency on Murry's love: the deprivation of this love, she reiterates, 'nearly killed' her; yet 'He will never realize that I am only WELL when we are "together". All else is a mockery of health.' In her almost explicit correlation of her need for love and her ill health, indeed her virtual accusation that Murry's withholding of love was responsible for a kind of drift towards death, Katherine was expressing in her own terms the connection observed by psychiatrists between certain emotional conflicts and tuberculosis.

It has been argued that the predisposition to tuberculosis is established very early in life in a kind of infant despair. As adults, tuberculous patients act like deprived children with an inordinate need for affection. They tend to react disproportionately to rebuffs, to separation from, threat of losing and actual loss of a supporting figure. The last resort of the deprived child is to be very sick without dying – so sick that, as if trying to make up for all the love and attention he has missed, he attracts attention from his parents, his brothers and sisters, and perhaps the community. Such an emotional pattern is evident in Katherine Mansfield's life. So too is a conflict between feelings of love and hate for the persons closest to her. One writer, discussing the psychological traits of individuals predisposed towards tuberculosis, virtually outlines the kind of emotional ambivalence which afflicted Katherine:

> They profess to love persons . . . whom they also hate and whom to love they often have very little justification. . . . Individuals like these are bound to be uneasy in their social relationships. . . . As the borderline between phantasy and reality in their minds becomes obliterated, they are liable to behave as if everybody could guess what they regard as their evil intentions . . . and last but not least, they have to make up or to atone for what they have done, albeit only in their phantasies.[1]

A conflicting mixture of love and hate governed Katherine Mansfield's feelings about nearly all the people who were most important in her life: her mother, father, brother, and such friends as Ottoline Morrell, Dorothy Brett and Virgina Woolf. But the most severe such conflict was occasioned by her ambivalent relationship with Ida Baker and, increasingly, with Murry. In Cornwall, during the first month of her separation from the man she had just married, Katherine's familiar habit of playing off one against the other reasserted itself. Incessantly she complained to Murry about L. M., who once again was trying to rebuild her own independent life. 'I had a nightmare about L. M. last night', she wrote. 'You know she *does* terrify me. I have got a "complex" about her regard for me.' Then, in her next letter, Katherine bitterly accused Murry of using L. M. to stand between them: 'Of course, L. M. would keep us one remove from each other. . . . Did you reckon on that when you were so anxious to keep her?'

Nevertheless, barely a month later, Katherine was again attempting to attach L. M. to her. 'You're not just an agency to which I apply for pills and cigarettes, free of charge, though your whole letter was concerned with trying to make me believe that's what I've brought our "relationship" to', she wrote after a period of silence from her friend. 'However if it pleases you to feel it, my dear, you must feel it. . . .' Jealous now of L. M.'s friends and the life she was making for herself, Katherine told her a few days later:

> I don't know why I write to you so intimately. For you have quite given me up and thrown me over in such a way, too. Walking out of the house without a word. But perhaps there was someone waiting for you at the gate. . . . I don't know and I'm sure I don't care. It's only when you are *in* the house that I love you. I never – as it were recognise you when you're dressed and ready to depart. . . . Yes, I only love you when you're blind to everybody but US.

Towards the end of June, Katherine's rather perfunctory notes beginning 'Dear Jones' changed in tone. Asking L. M. for special favours – and for the extra money (code named 'Tea') which she dared not request from her husband – her mode of address was more affectionate. 'Jones Dear, Have you any Tea to spare?' begins a letter written on 25 June. 'It's like this. I have borrowed £7 from Jack this month and I don't dare to ask for any more. . . . I have thought of you so much these last few days. I was wondering, in bed this morning, if you think of me – often, I mean. Well *do*. I am a little nicer.'

The contrast between letters such as these *to* L. M. and Katherine's letters to Murry *about* L. M. not only underlines the conflict within her personality; it demonstrates that in her selfishness, too, Katherine's behaviour conformed to that of other over-dependent tubercular types. Of these people, Dr Wittkower, a psychiatrist, has observed:

> the choice of their friends, husbands or wives was not infrequently dictated by their utilitarian value. They were much too fond of themselves to be capable of a real and deep attachment to anybody else. Generally, their social relationships were characterised by an utter disregard for other people's interests.[2]

Certainly, it was not her friend's interests which Katherine had in mind when she modified her attitude about L. M. joining their Hampstead household. For, as she acknowledged in a letter to Murry, L. M. was not only useful: she was virtually indispensable. 'If we do not have L. M. one bother will be the moving', Katherine told her husband. 'We shall absolutely need HER for that. . . . It is absolutely impossible for you to attend to this and your work. No strange woman could. She's the only one.' Later, as if L. M. were a commodity they shared, Katherine instructed Murry, 'I am glad L. M. has been decent. Make her *pack* for you and look after you all this week. Use her, dearest.'

Possessive of L. M. yet wanting independence from her, demanding L. M.'s sole care and attention yet unprepared in return to satisfy her emotional needs, Katherine was as neglectful and insensitive of her friend's feelings as she increasingly accused Murry of being towards her own. Coldly demanding, if not critical, when she felt sure of L. M.'s attachment; acting as if L. M. were indeed the all-sacrificing (as well as frustrating) mother, Katherine jealously interfered with L. M.'s other friendships by reminding her of their past happiness together.

If Katherine Mansfield had traits of character which predisposed her towards tuberculosis, she equally had traits which militated against her recovery from the disease. Dr Brice Clarke has written that 'complete inability to accept the fact of tuberculosis and to rearrange her life in accordance with medical advice was the essential cause of her death'. He speaks, too, of her death wish: 'The shock of the loss of her only brother was extremely severe and may have contributed to neglect of her health by accentuating an unconscious death wish.'[3] Other medical experts have described tuberculous patients as being half in love with death and voluntarily or involuntarily indulging in indiscretions which serve to give the disease a better hold.

Half-refusing to accept the fact that she was indeed seriously ill, Katherine Mansfield from the first resisted the idea of entering a sanatorium. To L. M., shortly after her return to England in April 1918, Katherine wrote of having seen a doctor in whose advice she had confidence because he was from New Zealand. '*He* said: Yes there is no doubt I have definitely got consumption. He appreciates that a sanatorium would kill me *much* faster than cure me. (It's a 2nd lunatic asylum to me.)' Later, telling Murry of the 'AGONIES from loneliness and illness combined' that she suffered in her hotel in Cornwall, Katherine reaffirmed her refusal to enter a sanatorium: 'I have discovered the ONLY TREATMENT for consumption. It is not to cut the malade off from life: neither in a sanatorium, nor in a land with milk rivers, butter mountains and cream valleys. . . . DON'T YOU AGREE??? . . . I MUST NOT BE LEFT ALONE.'

Murry, in his autobiography, explains the agony that he in turn experienced when he received such letters. 'Indeed, Katherine's letters at this moment drove me into a kind of delirium', he writes.

> I felt that it was literally true that we were killing one another. . . . This love, which devoured her so, demanded for its fulfilment that she should never leave me, nor I her. . . . The ecstasy of love, which she required, was not health, but only a hectic hastening to death. Yet if I stood my ground against her fatal desire, she tore me to pieces by her suffering and her despair.

And so Murry acceded to his wife's demands that she again live with him. Towards the end of June Katherine returned to London and his rooms at Redcliffe Road; and in August 1918 she, Murry and L.M. moved into their Hampstead home, the Elephant.

For the whole of the following year while she remained in England, Katherine Mansfield wrote virtually no fiction. In the period just after her marriage however, she had produced one notable – although unfinished – story: 'A Married Man's Story'. 'I have started working – another member of the "Je Ne Parle

Pas'' family, I fondly dream – It's a devastating idea', Katherine told her husband in May 1918. 'A Married Man's Story' was written only three months after 'Je Ne Parle Pas Français', and there are certain similarities between the two works. Both are the confessional monologues of self-absorbed men, each of whom is a writer and an admitted role-player; crucial to the psychological situation of both stories is the narrator's inability to relate normally to women; indirectly in 'Je Ne Parle Pas Français', and directly in 'A Married Man's Story', the narrator seeks to explain his adult personality and way of life in terms of his childhood experiences. In each case this delving into the past reveals that a childhood trauma has been responsible for the emotional crippling of the characters.

Nevertheless, the married man who, while pretending to work at his desk in the evening, contemplates his wife and baby unemotionally, is a totally different type from the sexually perverted Raoul Duquette. Duquette's life, both inner and outer, is based upon deception: he deceives himself as well as those around him. The problem of the man who no longer loves his wife is that he understands only too well that their life together is sustained by a tissue of lies. Wondering if she will 'never grow accustomed to these simple – one might say – everyday little lies?' he pictures with detachment the loneliness of his wife, '*a broken-hearted woman*': 'Nobody is going to call her or to wonder what she is doing out there. And she knows it. And yet, being a woman, deep down, deep down, she really does expect the miracle to happen; she really could embrace that dark, dark deceit, rather than live – like this.' The repetition of 'live like this' leads him to take the reader into his confidence and ask the question whose exploration appears central to the story: 'Why do people stay together?' Putting aside all the usual practical answers, he comes to a thought he's often half entertained':

> Which is that human beings, as we know them, don't choose each other at all. It is the owner, the second self inhabiting them, who makes the choice for his own particular purposes, and – this may sound absurdly far-fetched – it's the second self in the other which responds. Dimly . . . we realize this, at any rate to the extent that we realize the hopelessness of trying to escape. So that, what it all

> amounts to is – if the impermanent selves of my wife and me are happy – *tant mieux pour nous* – if miserable – *tant pis*.

The 'second self' is less the narrator's double, here, than a metaphor for the unconscious or repressed determinants in the personality; yet it is these determinants, he believes, which take precedence over, indeed master, the conscious but servile ego. As in the case of Raoul Duquette, the narrator's inner division, his impermanent and uncertain sense of identity, make him play a part. In the early days of his marriage he would teasingly put on a little act and play up to his wife's expectations: 'But now? For some reason I feel it would be crude to stop my performance. It's simplest to play on.' Only when his wife has gone to bed does he relax. And then his study changes too, becoming the companion which his wife can never be: 'It is not only I who recognize that [she will not come back tonight]; the room changes too. It relaxes, like an old actor. Slowly the mask is rubbed off; the look of strained attention changes to an air of heavy sullen brooding.'

Wanting to write 'the plain truth, as only a liar can tell it', he recalls his inability, in the early days of their marriage, to reassure his wife about her lack of physical beauty. Nevertheless, he tells the reader, they were a marvellously, radiantly happy couple until last autumn. With the words 'but . . . to explain what happened . . . I should have to go back and back', he launches into the digressive account of his own childhood which takes up the remainder of the unfinished narrative. The relationship between the narrator's confession of his failed marriage, his uncaring treatment of his wife, and his childhood experiences is left unexplained, indeed puzzling. Only as the story unravels do the missing, psychological links become clear.

We learn that as a boy he was afraid of his father; moreover, his birth had sapped his mother's strength and made her an invalid: 'Bed, sofa, window, she moved between the three.' An only child, he was thus without mothering or companionship in his early years. 'But what has all this to do with my married happiness?' the narrator interrupts himself. 'How can all this affect my wife and me? Why – to tell what happened last autumn – do I run all this way back into the Past?' His answer is that the remembered details of the past 'are a living part of me. Who am I, in fact, as I sit here at this table, but my own past? If I deny that, I am nothing.' With near-Freudian insight he insists, 'if I were to try to divide my life into childhood, youth, early manhood and so on, it would be a kind of affectation. . . . For one thing I have learnt, one thing I do believe is, Nothing Happens Suddenly. Yes, that is my religion, I suppose.'

Seeking to understand himself in the present, then, the narrator returns to the story of his childhood. The crucial event was the death of his mother, apparently poisoned by his father. Hating his father, blaming him for his mother's death (and indirectly himself for being born), the boy became so alienated from human beings that he lost all sense of his own identity. ' "Who am I?" I thought. "What is all this?" ' The only answer he could find was within the confines of his own bedroom. There, after his mother's death, fantasy became a substitute for real life. In imagination the stars and flowers became his friends; and it was they who finally gave him a sense of belonging. One night, the barriers came down with the childish realisation that 'everything lived, everything'. With the disclosure of the depth of his childhood estrangement from ordinary people, the married man's story abruptly ends: 'I had been all my life a little outcast', he confesses; 'but until that moment no one had "accepted" me. . . . I did not consciously turn away from the world of human beings; I had never known it; but I from that night did beyond words consciously turn towards my silent brothers. . . .'

'A Married Man's Story' is the confessional narrative of a character who is made to seem totally self-aware. His inner probing resembles that described by Murry when he told Katherine, 'the world is shut out and you are looking at yourself'. But, although the narrator can assert that he is the sum of his past experiences, that his childhood cannot be separated from his early manhood, he does not, indeed cannot, spell out the precise psychological connection between his early life and his failed marriage. It is left to the reader to infer that the man's alienation from human beings and his secret, continuing preference for the companionship of inanimate or non-human objects has warped him emotionally. The habit of retreating into the security of his private dream-world has made him a writer; but it has also damaged his ability to have normal relations with other people. Indeed, the boy who hated his father has unconsciously identified himself with the aggressor and taken on elements of his personality. Just as the sinister chemist was cold and unfeeling towards *his* wife, so the emotionless narrator detachedly observes – but does nothing to mitigate – his own wife's suffering.

In spite of its unfinished state and unresolved questions, 'A Married Man's Story' is a powerful work, impressive in its insights. There is a noticeable absence of symbolism here, however. Instead of using symbols at once to convey and mask psychologically significant meanings, the narrator is made to reveal himself without dissimulation. Perhaps because of this lack of emotional distancing, Katherine Mansfield found it impossible to complete a story which too nearly exposed her innermost feelings – as well as something of her present situation. Questions are raised by the narrator only to be left unanswered; themes are introduced only to be dropped. Only obliquely, with reference to the unconscious but masterful 'second self', does the narrator explain why unsuitably married people stay together; and the existence of the second self can only be accounted for in terms of the formative influences of the past. Never at any point are these influences directly related to the narrator's present personality or his feelings for his wife: everything must be deduced by the reader.

Although this obliqueness is central to the technique – and fascination – of the story, it surely derives in part from the fact that here, as in 'Je Ne Parle Pas Français', the author wove elements of herself into both male and female characters. At the time of writing, for example, she was indeed 'a broken-hearted woman' given scant comfort by her husband. Like the woman in the story, she preferred to 'embrace that dark, dark deceit' that all was well rather than to face the truth about the effect her illness was having on her personal life and relationships. Significantly, one of the unresolved threads in the story is the event 'last autumn' which, according to the narrator, destroyed the happiness of the previously 'model couple'. It was the previous autumn Katherine had been diagnosed as tuberculous. Apparently unable to work this aspect of her life into the story, the narrator is made to digress and blame the present state of his marriage on his past.

While the married man's detachment from his wife resembles Murry's at this time, the fictional character's deprived childhood is at least as representative of Katherine Mansfield's conception of her own early life as it is of her husband's. Both Katherine and Murry deeply resented, at times hated, their fathers; but it was

Katherine whose mother's health was weakened by childbearing, and it was Katherine who, as well as blaming her father for the mother's repeated pregnancies, probably felt guilty for having been born herself.

Singularly like Katherine's, moreover, are emotional aspects of the narrator's childhood. At primary school in Wellington she was not popular, and her earliest writing shows that she, like the narrator, tended to withdraw from the outside world into the consolation of fantasy – and her own room. The adult Katherine's turning away from the world of human beings is revealed in letter after letter to Murry. 'Bogey, my whole soul waits for the time when you and I shall be withdrawn from everybody', she said in June 1918.

The married man's conscious preference for withdrawal into his private, inner life is related both to his playing a part and his conception of the 'second self'; Katherine's compulsive role-playing caused her to refer to the second self in story after story: it was as though she never quite believed in her own fixed identity – and never really liked the identities she invented.

PART IV

1918–1923

18 'The Man Without a Temperament'

Between June 1918 and October 1919 there are only a handful of published letters from Katherine to Murry. It is Murry himself who best sums up the situation that existed between them during those unhappy months when Katherine was attempting her 'cure' at home in Hampstead. 'Whatever shelter I tried to build for us both came tumbling down', he writes in his autobiography.

> Our marriage was to have been the miracle; it was not. Then the capture of the Elephant, as we called the final taking of the grey Hampstead house (which we entered on July 29th) would be the miracle; it was not. Then the end of the War – Peace – would be the miracle; it was not. And what was not the miracle, was nothing.
>
> In October, shortly before the Armistice, a colleague of mine at the War Office kindly suggested that a friend of hers, a famous specialist in tuberculosis, should examine Katherine. . . . 'There's one chance for her – and only one. If she goes into a *strict* sanatorium immediately. . . . Discipline is everything. If she will go somewhere for a year and submit to discipline, then she has about an even chance. If not, she has two or three years to live – four at the outside.' So that was that. I thanked him, showed him out, and went up to Katherine.
>
> 'He says I must go into a sanatorium', she said. 'I can't. A sanatorium would *kill* me.' . . .
>
> Did I really believe that she would get well? I did not know. What I did know was that I must say so, again and again – for ever.

In 'A Married Man's Story' Katherine had portrayed with prescience the very tissue of lies and pretence which Murry describes; yet, ironically, she appeared unwilling to connect the emotional division which grew up between them with her own intransigence over the question of a sanatorium. As her illness worsened, so did her sense of alienation from Murry, from L.M. and from people in general. Only her dead brother mattered. 'I am hardly alive', she confided to Dorothy Brett in December 1918. 'But apart from that, I feel in my heart as though I have died – as far as personal life goes.'[1] Helping Murry edit the *Athenaeum* in 1919 but doing very little of her own work, Katherine turned increasingly in thought from the personal relationship which was failing her to the consolation of Art. '*Work*', she wrote in her journal in May, 'Shall I be able to express, one day, my love of work – my desire to be a better writer – my longing to take greater pains. And the passion I feel. It takes the place of religion – it *is* my religion – of people – I create my people: of "life" – it *is* Life.'

Writing palliated but did not blot out Katherine's growing resentment of Murry's attitude. Contemplating her ' "private" life – which . . . *would* astonish even those nearest to me', she noted 'how little Jack shares with me'. Her conclusion was now a familiar one: 'I want to see him, and then adjust my ways and go on alone and WORK. Life without *work* – I would commit suicide. Therefore work is more important than life.' By August Katherine had determined to enter a sanatorium after all. But hardly was the decision made when she changed her mind. 'Here's an absurd situation!' she told Ottoline.

> My doctor strongly urges me *not* to put myself away, *not* to go into a sanatorium – he says I would be out of it in 24 hours and it would be a 'highly dangerous experiment'. . . . So it is the Italian Riviera after all. . . . Being ill and bearing all the depression of those round me had, I think, almost made me insane. *I just gave up hope*. Now I am full of hope again, and I'm off the third week in September.[2]

In September 1919 Murry settled Katherine and L. M. in a villa in Ospedaletti on the Italian Riviera, before returning to England and his job as editor of the *Athenaeum*. Katherine's letters to him reveal a pattern of responses to her new situation similar in some respects to those evinced during her previous sojourn in Bandol. At first, while the weather was good and the change of scenery enjoyable, she wrote happy letters full of love for the man whom she had only recently accused of meeting her with 'the gape, the stare – or the silence'. Once again, Murry's love was her salvation, her defence against the onslaughts of all that threatened from the world outside. Resurrecting an old fantasy of the 'Heron' home where their ideal life would be lived, Katherine returned to the idea that she and Murry were indissolubly bound together because they were children, miraculously innocent and different from other people.

A month after their separation, however, Katherine's letters to him began to reveal a greater self-honesty – and doubts about their relationship. 'When I am with you I am furious because you will not see "happiness" in the future', she wrote. 'Well, still, if we're together in our own home, living our own life, I *do see it*. Apart from that there is nothing: I mean, there is just a living death or a dead one: it really don't signify. (Yes, it does.)' While the fantasy of a kind of magical, transcendent partnership with Murry was in force, the inevitable other facet of Katherine's emotional life reasserted itself. L.M., with whom she could live reasonably peacefully when real life with Murry proved disappointing, became once again an enemy, the one against whom all her pent-up frustration and anger was vented. At first in Ospedaletti L.M. was merely an irritant. By the end of October, however, Katherine had so projected her own hostility onto L.M. that she was calling her a 'murderer'. To Murry she wrote:

> This *awful relationship* living on in its secret corrupt way beside my relationship with you is very extraordinary; no one would believe it. I am two selves – one my true self – the other that she creates in me to destroy my true self. . . . But that's what makes my work so hard and *paralyzes my mind*.

Struggle though she might to sustain the fantasy of an eventual, ideal life with Murry, depression and disillusionment with him were setting in again by November. Counting the months until her return to him the next May, Katherine cried out, 'After that don't leave me alone . . . not with an enemey. . . . *Love* me.' The next day she demanded urgently 'HELP ME, HELP ME.' Apparently Murry did not answer his wife's cry for help satisfactorily; and before long Katherine was writing, in a letter calculated to make him feel guilty, 'You almost make me feel it is unpardonable of me to feel better; that having made you suffer so, I should have justified myself by getting worse and worse. . . .' Then, after emphasising that the local doctor 'was urgent about no mental worry', there came Katherine's most terrible outburst against L.M.: an outburst which was a virtual suicide threat:

> Christ! to *hate* like I do. . . . My deadly deadly enemy has got me today and I'm simply a blind force of hatred. Hate is the *other* passion. It has all the opposite effects of Love. It fills you with death and corruption, it makes you feel hideous, degraded and old, it makes you long to DESTROY.

Katherine's emotions were heightened and exacerbated by the disease from which she suffered; but to attribute the outbursts in these letters to Murry primarily to her illness is too easy. At this critical period the obsessive needs (and resultant conflicts) which had developed in childhood, and had been reinforced by later experiences, seem to have reached a climax. Katherine Mansfield's problem as an adult was that she never outgrew her emotional dependency. Every time heterosexual love failed to live up to her needs, she was thrown back upon the substitute love of her own sex which she continually struggled to deny. So a vicious cycle developed in which the depression which followed the loss of love was accompanied by a reckless self-neglect that was at once a form of self-punishment and a means of blackmailing the rejecting lover. Even when tuberculosis had gained a firm hold, she was unable to break away from these unconscious compulsions and take the steps necessary to save her own life. It was as if she had fantasised, romanticised, threatened and virtually willed death for so long that when it actually loomed on the horizon there could be no turning back.

When Katherine wrote to Murry of 'this *awful relationship* living on in its secret corrupt way beside my relationship with you' and of her two selves – 'one my true self – the other that she creates in me to destroy my true self' – she was referring implicitly to her bisexual conflicts. For she did have two selves: there was her feminine, masochistic 'true' self which came to the surface when all was well with Murry; and there was the masculine, sadistic self which, in the absence of a satisfactory emotional and physical relationship with him, used L.M. as a downtrodden wife. Not only did the conflict caused by the emergence of the now despised, masculine self paralyse Katherine Mansfield mentally and prevent her writing: it had a devastating effect upon her physical health. In a sense, both L.M. and Murry *were* unwittingly killing the woman they loved. She tried to express her knowledge of this when she begged Murry to love her, not to leave her alone, in effect to 'HELP' by neutralising the conflict. Not understanding, perhaps not caring to understand, his wife's complex psychological needs, Murry could not help.

Increasingly, Katherine became preoccupied with the need to 'face things'. She wrote to Murry, 'I believe, Bogey, our whole strength depends upon our facing things. I mean without any reservation or restraints. I fail because I don't face things. I almost feel that I have been ill for so long for that reason: we fear for that reason.'

After describing her hatred of L.M., she began to question the validity of her dreams and fantasies. 'Shall we really have such a house?' she asked Murry.

> It's not too late? We don't just make up dreams. . . . It's not 'all over'? I get overwhelmed at times that it *is* all over . . . and that these letters will one day be published and people will read something in them, in their queer finality, that 'ought to have told us'. This feeling runs exactly parallel with the other – the feeling of hope. They are two roads, I can't keep to either.

Nor could she; for, after speaking about death, Katherine immediately embarked upon a new set of defensive dreams about the house they would buy and redecorate. 'But these dreams are so dear that they feel unearthly', she suddenly caught herself up. 'They are dreams of heaven. How could they become reality? *This* is reality – bed, medicine bottle, medicine glass marked with tea and table spoons, guiacol tablets, balimanate of zinc. Come, tell me, tell me *exactly* what I am to do to recover my faith.'

The final realisation that Murry could not help her recover her faith – indeed, that he was completely without faith himself – proved a turning-point in the inner life of Katherine Mansfield. She was forced now into facing the most difficult facts of all: emotional facts. In the lonely villa at Ospedaletti, the fear of death was growing. 'When I am not working, when I'm in pain, and conscious every moment of my body . . . I've no one to turn to. I can't forget my body for a moment. I think of Death: the melancholy fit seizes me', Katherine wrote to Murry. 'I want to keep you happy. But I can't lie and pretend.' True to her word, she sent Murry her poem 'The New Husband', in which she depicts Death as her mate.

The impact of her verses was as shattering as she could have wished: Murry telegraphed instantly that he would come out for Christmas. Katherine wrote three letters to him on the day she received his wire. In the first two she tried to dissuade him from joining her. 'While I'm ill, it's no good', she told him. The third, written in the middle of the night, contained an indictment even more personally devastating than that of 'The New Husband' poem. Determined to face the facts about the man with whom she had lived for so long, Katherine was equally determined that he should face them too. 'I am awake and I have re-read your letter', she told him.

> It is stranger than ever. It is half an account of what I have done to you and the other half is all money. . . . The truth is that until I was ill you were never called upon 'to play the man' to this extent – and it's NOT your rôle. When you said you ought to be kept you spoke the truth. . . . Ever since my illness this crisis, I suppose, has been impending – when suddenly in agony I should turn all woman and lean on you. . . . However ill I am, you are more ill. However weak I am, you are weaker – less able to bear things. . . .

The three major accusations that emerge from this letter are that Murry's obsession with money is stronger than his love for her; that he is fundamentally weak and therefore not a real man; and that in expecting her to make a continual effort to conceal her mental and physical suffering (in the interests of his own equilibrium) he is selfish and has sinned against love, as she understands it. 'The effort to keep perpetually radiant was too great', she continued. 'But you asked it of me. . . . When you wrote: "That's the stuff to keep me happy", I was full of despair. I knew I could not go on giving it you.' Ten days later, Katherine summed up the situation in her journal:

> As I grew depressed, *he* grew depressed, but not for me. He began to write (1) about the suffering I caused him . . . (2) a constant cry about money. . . . We had been for two years drifting into a relationship, different to anything I had ever known. We'd been *children* to each other . . . each depending equally upon the other. Before that I had been the man and he had been the woman and he had been called upon to make no real efforts. . . . When we first met, in fact, it was I who kept him, and afterwards we'd always acted (more or less) like men-friends. Then this illness – getting worse and worse, and turning me into a woman and asking him to put himself away and to *bear* things for me. He stood it marvellously. . . . But we were not *pure*. If we had been, he'd have faced coming away with me. And that he could not do. . . .

In 'A Married Man's Story', Katherine had suggested the mysterious nature of the bonds that hold unhappily married couples together. 'Human beings, as we know them,' the narrator declares, 'don't choose each other at all. It is the owner, the second self inhabiting them, who makes the choice for his own particular purposes, and . . . it's the second self in the other which responds.' In the case of Katherine Mansfield, the second self was predominantly masculine; and she had sought a mate whose second self was correspondingly feminine. When she first became ill, it was comparatively easy to switch from the idea that they were 'men-friends' to the one that they were only, after all, two innocent children who must cling together for protection. But the problem remained that, while the second selves complemented each other, the first selves were not in harmony.

Katherine and Murry were both ambitious for success in the literary world, she as a creative writer, he as a critic and editor. Inevitably the competing claims of each other's work ran counter to their emotional needs. To feel emotionally secure in her relationship with Murry, Katherine needed him to remain dependent on her; but he wanted independence to establish and assert his own self-worth. His emotional need was for a warmth, affection and mothering which Katherine was too self-absorbed to supply. Having fought to prevent his personality being taken over by her, he was too insecure and too inward-looking to be able to love her in the unselfish way she demanded. The second, childlike selves of each still governed their personalities.

If Katherine was bewildered by her illness, it was partly because the unexpected turn of events was forcing her into accepting the very feminine role that she had spent her whole life in emphatically rejecting. Her tragedy was that the illness which turned her into a woman did not (and could not) simultaneously turn Murry into the different kind of man she now required.

Murry's visit to Ospedaletti at the end of December 1919 did nothing to heal the breach which was widening between them. When he returned to England it was agreed that letters between him and Katherine should be limited to two a week. On 10 January, 1920 Katherine thought out the story to be called 'The Man Without a Temperament', and recorded in her journal an 'appalling night of misery, deciding that J. had no more need of our love'. She had once written to Ottoline of being 'in a furious working mood which always happens when the flesh is weak'. Weak now in body and spirit, she was seized by just such a mood. 'Worked from 9.30 a.m. till a quarter after midnight only stopping to eat. Finished the story', she noted in her journal on 11 January.

> Lay awake then until 5.30 too excited to sleep. . . . I thought of everything in my life, and it all came back so vividly – all is connected with this feeling that J. and I are no longer as we were. I love him but he rejects my *living* love. This is anguish. These are the *worst* days of my whole life.

A fictional presentation of the kind of typical day she and Murry might have lived *if* he had sacrificed his London job to join her in Italy during her two years' search for health, 'The Man Without a Temperament' is one of Katherine Mansfield's most devastatingly honest stories. It is also one of her most tightly woven ('I think there is not a word I would change or that can be changed') and artistically accomplished pieces of writing. As in that other deeply personal story, 'Bliss', Katherine

Mansfield relies heavily on the distancing devices of symbolism and caricature; but she enhances the remarkable objectivity of this later work by refusing to probe the mind of either Mr Salesby or his ailing wife. The plight of both characters is all too clearly conveyed through a wealth of significant external detail, rather than through internal analysis.

The most obvious symbolism in the story is that of Salesby's entrapment by his wife's illness, an entrapment suggested by his repeated turning of a signet ring upon his finger and by the image of the hotel life (and, indeed, of the hotel itself) as a cage. Even more pervasive and important, however, are the interwoven motifs of lifelessness, decay and dragging time. Katherine Mansfield conveys a sense of lifelessness partly by her almost Dickensian caricatures of the other hotel guests. Deprived of their personal names, and thus of their individuality, the hotel guests who share the Salesby's surroundings are characterised as 'the Two Topknots', 'the American Woman', 'the Honeymoon Couple' and 'the General and the Countess'. At one level this dehumanising of the other couples (and each member of the pair is indistinguishable from the other) serves to contrast and throw into the foreground the more normal Mr and Mrs Salesby. But it quickly becomes obvious that this is a distorted world, where people are reduced to the level of mouthing puppets and where non-human entities assume a life and significance of their own. The Two Topknots are depicted with 'two coils of knitting, [which] like snakes, slumbered beside the tray'; the American Woman sits

> in the shadow of a great creeping thing with wide open purple eyes that pressed – that flattened itself against the glass, hungrily watching her. . . . She played up to it. . . . Sometimes she even pointed at it, crying: 'Isn't that the most terrible thing you've ever seen! Isn't that ghoulish!'

Indeed, ghoulish overtones echo throughout this story, in which the nameless, caricatured guests are either associated with, or implicitly likened to, animals. Besides the Two Topknots with their snakes, the American Woman converses with her cat, Klaymongso; the Honeymoon Couple, dripping with perspiration and wetness, are virtually identified with the fish they catch; and the General with his 'Caw! Caw! Caw!' is likened to a crow.

Imparting a Circe-like atmosphere to this bizarre world is the 'scarlet plush and gilt furniture – conjuror's furniture' in the hotel hall; and an impression of grotesqueness is heightened by the story's repeated images of dilapidation, decay and lifelessness. The lifeless interior of the hotel reflects the stagnation of the world without. 'Every leaf, every flower in the garden lay open, motionless, as if exhausted.' On his 'constitutional' walk into the town, Salesby passes 'the public gardens with the carved grottoes and statues and stone animals drinking at the fountain'. Further on is a valley 'with a dried-up river bed at the bottom. This side and that was covered with small dilapidated houses that had broken stone verandahs.' Against this background of death-in-life, of desiccation and decay, the invalidism of Mrs Salesby is projected.

Katherine Mansfield's handling of time subtly serves to convey Mr Salesby's sense of bondage. Like the wife, who walks with 'dragging steps', time is shown to drag interminably for Robert Salesby. Neither he, nor we, are ever allowed to forget the slow revolutions of the clock and the sun. A 'huge "Presentation" clock that struck the hours at the half-hours' stands in the hall; also marking off the hours in the guests' day are the customary intervals at which they take food and drink. When the Salesbys go for their brief walk, time is indicated by reference to the sun, which is 'still high'. Before setting off alone Robert Salesby remarks 'It's just after half-past four. I'll be back at a quarter-past five'; and he hands his watch to his wife. With the striking of a clock his daydream of a happier past is interrupted: 'What time was it. Five? A quarter past?' Greeted by his wife with 'You're three minutes late', he escorts her back to their room coughing. While they sit there, waiting for dinner, 'the sky flamed, paled. . . . "Oh, what time is it?" ' Mrs Salesby exclaims. After dinner, his wife now in bed, Robert sits on the balcony looking at the night sky. And so the day closes.

Serving as a contrast to this portrayal of the Salesbys' seemingly repetitive and endless present are three flashbacks into the very different past of the couple. A mention of snow in one of his wife's letters brings back to Salesby's mind the gaiety with which, at home in London, they had once welcomed an early snowfall. During his walk, he imagines momentarily that he is returning across the English fields to the prospect of Jinnie at home by the fire and supper with their friends. The final flashback, which occurs as he lies in bed waiting for sleep, brings together the various threads of the narrative and discloses their significance. 'Well, my dear chap, that's the whole story', he remembers being told in his study in late summer.

> 'If she can't cut away for the next two years and give a decent climate a chance she don't stand a dog's – h'm – show. Better be frank about these things.' . . . 'And hang it all, old man, what's to prevent you going with her? It isn't as though you've got a regular job like us wage earners. You can do what you do wherever you are –' 'Two years.' 'Yes, I should give it two years. . . .'
>
> . . .He is with her. 'Robert, the awful thing is – I suppose it's my illness – I simply feel I could not go alone. You see – you're everything. You're bread and wine, Robert, bread and wine. Oh, my darling – what am I saying? Of course I could, of course I won't take you away. . . .'

Time is a dominant motif in the story because two years must be filled in before the invalid wife either regains her health – or dies. Since the pattern of imagery suggest that she is in fact dying, future time hardly exists: there is only an endless present punctuated by fleeting memories of the past.

Katherine Mansfield provides an outward contrast between the Salesbys, whom she portrays sympathetically, and the other, puppetlike stylised characters. The bitter irony of the comparison is that, while Mrs Salesby is almost dead physically, her husband is dead spiritually and emotionally. So lacking is any real communication between the couple that their relationship is as inert, their actions are as automatic, as those of the people who surround them. 'You're bread and wine, Robert, bread and wine', Mrs Salesby had said when she pleaded for her husband's company abroad. Aware that she feeds off him emotionally, Salesby's unspoken resentment is expressed in his refusal to eat. Truly a man without a temperament, he evinces neither interest in, nor response to, their daily existence. He 'pursed his lips . . . but he did not whistle'; ignoring his wife's invitation to draw his chair closer to hers, he does not respond to her appreciation of the trees. She eagerly reads – and shares – her letters: he puts his away, unopened. Answering her remarks perfunctorily, he initiates no conversation but stares in front, 'blinking, vacant'. Even the guests notice that he 'just covered a yawn' as he took her arm for an afternoon stroll.

While the brilliant, tropical colours of the wilting plants reinforce the idea of over-ripeness, rankness and decay, the imagery of snow, moonlight and whiteness underlines the coldness of Salesby's personality. In the last section of the story the physical whiteness of Mrs Salesby as she lies asleep in 'the room . . . painted white with moonlight . . . her white hands crossed on the sheet. Her white cheeks, her fair hair pressed against the pillow . . .' resembles nothing so much as the whiteness of a corpse. As if echoing her hopeless struggle against death, the lightning in the evening sky 'flutters – flutters like a wing – flutters like a broken bird that tries to fly and sinks again and again struggles'.

An even grimmer repetition of the death motif brings the story to a climax. Salesby gets out of bed to catch and kill the mosquito which is inside his wife's net; as if the act were symbolic of killing her, too, he now bends and kisses her, whispering the final monstrous word: 'Rot!'

19 Mother, Father and 'Daughters of the Late Colonel'

The writing of 'The Man Without a Temperament' may have clarified Katherine's feelings; for her attitude towards Murry underwent a further change in the following month. Whereas in the past she had resisted asking him for any financial support ('borrowing' from L.M. instead), she now wrote more and more urgently about her need for money. Murry's response to his wife's problem appears to have remained casual. At the end of January 1920 Katherine was telling him that his failure to offer £10 a month towards her and L.M.'s keep had hurt dreadfully. Detailing her medical expenses, she concluded, 'Therefore I ask you to contribute £10 a month towards my expenses. . . . It is so bitter to have to ask you this – terribly bitter.' A few days later, Katherine was openly equating Murry's withholding of money with his withholding of love. 'Curse money!' she cried out. 'It's not really a question of money. It was the question of sympathy, of understanding, of being in the least *interested*, of asking me JUST ONCE how I was. . . .'

Another change since Murry's visit in December 1919 had been the influence upon Katherine of a distant relative, Connie Beauchamp, and of Connie's friend Jinnie Fullerton. These kindly religious women persuaded Katherine to leave Ospedaletti for a nursing home near them in Menton. Before long they took her to live in their own comfortable villa. '*Why* should they do that?' Katherine wondered aloud to Murry. 'It's as though my *Mother* were here again. I miss her so. I often long to lean against Mother and know she understands things . . . that can't be told . . . that would fade at a breath. . . .' Along with this veiled comparison between Murry's lack of loving, practical concern and the care freely given by the two women, there is a resurgence of Katherine's nostalgia for her own family. Especially, she was beginning to feel close in spirit to her mother.

Her mother's early rejection had contributed to Katherine's own repudiation, not only of her mother and her way of life, but also of the traditional female role. That repudiation had never been entire, however. Again and again from Katherine Mansfield's writing there emerges a belief that Mrs Beauchamp herself had resented certain aspects of the feminine role. 'If Father hadn't died I should have travelled and then ten to one I shouldn't have married', Katherine records her mother as saying. Convinced, apparently, that her mother would have preferred her (and the other children) not to have been born, Katherine's own adult revulsion against pregnancy and childbirth was in itself a kind of identification with the unwilling mother.

Thus, one of the most consistent patterns in Katherine Mansfield's personal life, her fiction and her private writing is a rebellion against the biological demands made upon women: the unfinished fragment 'Elena' suggests that her own miscarriage may not have been accidental, and she is thought to have undergone an abortion; the *German Pension* stories repudiate male sexuality and childbirth alike; and even her later, celebrated stories of family life revolve around the mother's rejection of children and of physical relations between husband and wife. It was only after she had become so ill that there was little chance of her having children that Katherine expressed any desire for them. This, pathetically, appears to have been less a genuine wish for motherhood than a further, desperate attempt to retain Murry's love and physical interest at a time when they were all too obviously waning.

In 1920, when her strength was failing, her faith in Murry's love shaken, and her jealousy of his attraction to other women aroused, Katherine's attitude towards sex became increasingly conservative, even puritanical. A certain distaste for the open discussion or portrayal of sexual matters, however, had been evident as early as 1915. Murry's comment in *Between Two Worlds* suggests that this was in part a reaction against her own adventures with the 'demi-monde'. 'She wanted me to remain an innocent lover', he wrote resentfully. 'And then she got bored with me for being an unexciting one. Hence her stupid and deeply disappointing affair with Carco. . . . From the Carco folly she reacted violently; and I was made a paradigm of innocence and fidelity.' More revealing of Katherine's feelings about female sexuality is Murry's account of her reaction, in October 1915, to Lawrence's novel *The Rainbow*.

> We neither of us liked *The Rainbow*, and Katherine quite hated parts of it – in particular the scene where Anna, pregnant, dances naked before the mirror. That, Katherine said to me, was 'female' – her most damning adjective – and an apotheosis of the 'female': a sort of glorification of the secret, intimate talk between women, the sexual understanding of the female confraternity, which Katherine could not abide.

The same inherent revulsion from the processes of childbearing is exhibited in an amusing letter to Ottoline in 1917. 'I had to go down to the city today and found Baby Week in the fullest of full blasts', Katherine told her friend.

> Really, I believe I was the only woman with her quiver empty between Charing X and Victoria Station. I walked along crossing myself and saying the Spanish Nun's Hail Mary terrified lest this fruitfulness should be contagious. And the horrible thing was that I didn't see one couple who weren't more or less revolting – flushed untidy women with their hats on one side, carrying home miniature Queen Victorias – ugh! What an appalling bad job human beings have made of themselves. I kept wondering if they were all like this all over the world, or if it was only in England that we breed such monsters – but I am afraid not.

Since for all her youthful bohemianism Katherine had always recoiled from adult sexuality and its biological consequences, it was quite easy for her in 1920 to ignore her own past and to express moral outrage at the attitudes of others. Complaining about a letter in which Brett wrote 'all about the "orgies" and "drink" and the parties etc.', Katherine told Murry,

> These people's minds are about 1894 – not a day later. They still talk of . . . whether one can or can't (*Oh ye Gods*!) have a platonic friendship with a man and (Oh ye Gods!) agree that

> you can't while the male is male and the female female!!!! I 'shock' them, but if they knew how they shock me. – talks as I've never heard a prostitute talk – or a woman in a brothel. Her mind is a *sink*. She's sex mad. . . . Oh, how pure artists are – how clean and fruitful. . . . Dearest love, let us remain chaste and youthful with our work and our life and our poetry. One can't afford to MIX with people. One must keep clear of all the worldly world.

It was apparently Murry's failure to keep clear of 'the worldly world', however, that was now on Katherine's mind. Unable to have any part in it herself, withdrawn from normal sexual life, she was unwilling that Murry should act differently. A remark of his about Beatrice Hastings drew forth the indignant response,

> Yes, it is true, I *did* love B.H. but have you utterly forgotten what I told you of her behaviour in Paris – of the last time I saw her and how, because I refused to stay the night with her, she bawled at me and called me a *femme publique* in front of those filthy Frenchmen? She is loathsome and corrupt and I remember very very well telling you I had done with her.

In the same letter Katherine drew attention to Murry's own behaviour: 'Love, you are too lenient. Is it much to ask you to be yourself and to condemn what you don't approve of? Those horrible parties of Ottoline when you were gloomy with wine. . . . Oh, I am so deeply truly anxious that we shall be an example and in our small way hand on a torch.'

As the year wore on and Katherine's correspondence with Murry became less intensely personal, more philosophical and literary, it was the sexual licence shown by other writers that called forth her indignation. Of James Joyce's *Ulysses* she had earlier written to Ottoline,

> I am infinitely grateful to you for these chapters of Ulysses. Heaven send the drain that will soon receive them. I think they are loathsome and if that is Art – never shall I drink to it again. But it *is* not Art; it *is* not even a new thing. . . . In Joyce there is a peculiar male arrogance that revolts me more than I can say – it sickens me.

In October 1920, Katherine told Murry,

> I don't know whether it's I that have 'fallen behind' in this procession but truly the books I read nowadays astound me. Female writers discovering a freedom, a frankness, a licence, to speak their hearts, reveal themselves as . . . sex maniacs. There's not a relationship between a man and woman that isn't the one sexual relationship – at its lowest. Intimacy is the sexual act.

Then, in December, there came an outburst over Lawrence's *The Lost Girl*. 'Lawrence denies his humanity', Katherine wrote in a terse note to Murry.

> He denies Life – I mean *human* life. His hero and heroine are non-human. They are animals on the prowl. They do not feel: they scarcely speak. . . . They submit to the physical response and for the rest go veiled – blind – *faceless* – *mindless*. This is the doctrine of mindlessness. . . .
>
> Am I prejudiced? Be careful. I feel privately as though Lawrence had possessed an animal and fallen under a curse. But I can't say that. All I know is, this is bad and ought not be allowed.

All too obviously, Katherine *was* prejudiced. Whether she was aware of the fact or not, there is at the heart of her own most psychologically profound stories an emphasis – however subtle – upon human sexual relations. The notable difference between her treatment of the subject and that of the people she criticised is her point of view: she wrote as a woman who, having rebelled against femininity and instinctively adopted a bisexual orientation, appeared to find heterosexual relations threatening. Nothing illustrates this better than a passage from Dostoevsky's *The Possessed* which she copied into her journal in 1916: ' "Surely you must see that I am in the agonies of childbirth", she said, sitting up and gazing at him with a terrible, hysterical vindictiveness that distorted her whole face. "I curse him before he is born, this child!" ' Katherine added her own revealing comment: 'This vindictiveness is *profoundly* true.'

Although she resented her mother, who after the birth of the next baby 'did not want to kiss me', Katherine Mansfield was deeply influenced by her. Mrs Beauchamp had a weak heart and was something of an invalid. If Katherine's sexual ambivalence reflected an unconscious identification with her mother, so did her tendency to retreat into illness. Katherine always imagined that she, like mother, had a weak heart; and from childhood onwards she fantasised her own illness and the attention it would bring her. The ominous thing about such fantasies is that in such stories as 'His Ideal' and 'My Potplants' the protagonist finally achieves union with a loving mother-figure – but only in death.

In July 1918, when Katherine was firmly in the grip of tuberculosis, Mrs Beauchamp died. 'Yes, it is an immense blow'. Katherine wrote to Dorothy Brett.[1] 'Ever since I heard of her death my memories of her come flying back into my heart – and there are moments when it is unbearable to receive them. But it has made me realise more fully than ever before that I love *courage* – spirit – poise . . . more than anything.' The death of her mother, like the earlier death of Leslie, cancelled out many of the daughter's resentments and left in their place a renewed sense of kinship. Increasingly, as her health worsened and her relations with Murry became more difficult, Katherine turned in thought to the mother who no longer had power to hurt. In May 1919, for instance, she wrote in her journal,

> I am sitting in my room thinking of Mother: I want to cry. But my thoughts are beautiful and full of gaiety. I think of *our* house, *our* garden, *us* children – the lawn, the gate, and Mother coming in. 'Children! Children!' I really only ask for time to write it all – time to write my books. Then I don't mind dying. . . . My little Mother, my star, my courage, my *own*. I seem to dwell in her now. We live in *the same world*. Not quite this world, not quite another.

Katherine's desire to make restitution through writing is like her resolve after the death of Leslie: in fiction, if not in reality, all is to be left 'fair'. Just as she had formerly felt at one with her dead brother – and vowed to join him, moreover – so Katherine now experienced a sense of unity with her mother and in so doing accepted the idea of her own death. A dream recorded six months later at Ospedaletti reveals the extent of this new identification with her mother. Guided by a little girl, the dreamer who is searching for a midwife explains to an old hag,

> She was to come to mother. Mother was very delicate: her eldest daughter was thirty-one and she had heart disease. 'So please come at once.' 'Has she any adhesions?' muttered the old hag. . . . 'Oh, yes' – I put my hands on my breast – 'many, many plural adhesions.' 'Ah, that's bad. . . . But I can't come.'

The dream ends with the little girl running after the dreamer and handing her a black bag. ' "Mrs Nightingale says you forgot this." So I was the midwife. I walked on, thinking: "I'll go and have a look at the poor little soul. But it won't be for a long time yet." ' In the dream, the daughter and her mother have become the same person: both are in danger of dying and need medical assistance. But none is to be had. What Katherine Mansfield realises when she is handed the black bag is that she must officiate at her own birth – and death. The only note of comfort in the dream is that 'it won't be for a long time yet'. This combination of birth and death symbolism suggest that, in the dreamer's mind, death is viewed as a kind of rebirth. Far more pessimistic is Katherine Mansfield's vivid account of a dream of her own death:

> And suddenly I felt my whole body *breaking up*. . . . I shall go on living now – it may be for months, or for weeks or days or hours. Time is not. In that dream I died. The *spirit* that is the enemy of death and quakes so and is so tenacious was shaken out of me. I am (December 15, 1919) a dead woman, and *I don't care*.

In the same journal entry, Katherine Mansfield announced, 'I am become – Mother.' To 'become Mother' was to accept in her more depressed moods an essentially feminine, passive, masochistic identity; it was also to accept illness and the inevitability of death. So Katherine could write to Murry in October 1920, 'If I am to be what I wish to be I must not be rescued.'

Once she was able to put herself in the place of her dead mother, Katherine's attitude to her father also underwent a change. Long ago, in 'Die Einsame', she had conjured up a vision of herself at sea, calling for help to a fatherlike figure in a passing boat. In the story he had left her to drown. But, when Harold Beauchamp came to England in August 1919, only the positive aspects of her father's personality occupied Katherine's thoughts. Still appearing overwhelmingly powerful to her, he seemed a kind of saviour, godlike in his ability to control life and death. 'My Pa arrives tomorrow and my plans are still rather en l'air until I have seen him', she told Anne Estelle Rice. 'Why I don't know. But he seems to me a kind of vast symbolic chapeau out of which I shall draw a little piece of paper that will decide my Fate.'[2] Always conscious of the vast difference between her father and Murry – indeed, marrying Murry partly because he was her father's opposite – Katherine found her appreciation of the older man growing as she became increasingly disillusioned with her husband.

Writing to Murry in November 1919, Katherine implicitly compared her father's warm, outgoing personality with *his* emotional reserve. 'Father at the last was wonderfully dear to me', she said of his visit to Ospedaletti.

> I mean, to be held and kissed and called my precious child was almost too much – to feel someone's arms round me and someone saying, 'Get better, you little wonder. You're your mother over again.' It's not being called a wonder, it's having *love* present, close warm, to be felt and returned.

Feeling the similarity between herself and Mother, being accepted as Mother by her father, Katherine's thoughts inevitably turned towards the difference between her situation as an invalid and her mother's. Murry was not spared her conclusions. 'Once the defences are fallen between you and Death they are not built up again', Katherine told him. 'Mother, of course, lived in this state for years. Ah, but she lived *surrounded*. She had her husband, her children, her home, her friends, physical presences, darling treasures to be cherished – and I've not one of these things. I have only my work.'

By the end of 1919, then, a combination of circumstances seems to have reversed in Katherine's conscious mind, at least, her longstanding resentment towards her parents. Her own illness had led to an increasing sense of union with her mother; and Mrs Beauchamp's death (like the death of her brother) had removed a further rival for her father's affection. Now that he had accepted her as 'your mother over again', she was outwardly prepared to understand and even forgive his faults, just as 'Mother' had done.

Affection for her father helped to fill the emotional gap left by Murry in Katherine's life; so did her renewed acceptance of L.M. For there was a sense in which Katherine Mansfield was emotionally married to two people. She had once told Ottoline, 'I am always renewing a marriage with Murry'. When that marriage was in spiritual abeyance or awaiting renewal, she invariably received back into favour the woman whose love never wavered. The day after sending Murry 'The Man Without a Temperament', Katherine wrote to him,

> Ever since you left here this time . . . my feelings towards Lesley are absolutely changed. It is not only that the hatred is gone. Something positive is there which is very like love for her. She has convinced me at last, against all my opposition, that she is trying to do all in her power for me. . . . I confess now that I do lean on her. . . . It was only when I refused to acknowledge this – to acknowledge her importance to me – that I hated her.

Even after Katherine moved in with Connie and Jinnie at Menton, this closeness with L.M. continued. Planning to return to Murry and their London house for the summer months of 1920, Katherine made clear to him the permanent place of L.M. in their combined lives. 'If I do come abroad,' she wrote, looking ahead, 'L.M. must be with me. She would not let me come alone and she says she dare not. I think she is right.'

Of the months Katherine actually spent with her husband in Hampstead in 1920 there is little record. But a letter to her friends Sydney and Violet Schiff, shortly after her return home, indicates that relations with him remained strained. 'Why does one rebel so at isolation?' Katherine asked.

> It must be. . . . But here's a woman who has been ill for over two years, who instead of looking after the other has made demands upon a man who confesses he has very little vitality

> to spare and doesn't ultimately care for people except as symbols. . . . Oh how well I understand this jealous passionate love of himself.[3]

Shortly before she and L.M. left once again for Menton, Katherine recorded in her journal what must have become a common-enough occurrence:

> I cough and cough. . . . Life is – getting a new breath: nothing else counts. And J. is silent, hangs his head, hides his face with his fingers *as though* it were unendurable. . . . At such times I feel I never could get well with him. It's like having a cannon-ball tied to one's feet when one is trying not to drown.

In September 1920, Katherine returned with L.M. to Menton. As had happened previously when illness forced her to live away from Murry, Katherine's letters to him in the early stages of their separation were loving and happy. Some of the familiar complaints against L.M. were voiced, and in November she told Murry, 'As to L.M. we have just had a fearful fight on the subject of MEN and I think she must be frozen.'

Regardless of what she might say in her letters, however, Katherine Mansfield's truest expression of what she felt for the people close to her appears in her stories. Not needing to solicit love or help or money here, she could say under the guise of fiction what she could never say to people's faces. It is a measure of her inward reconciliation with L.M., then, that in December 1920 Katherine wrote two stories in which L.M. is a central character. In 'Daughters of the Late Colonel' (the story she always thought her best) she interwove a deeply sympathetic portrayal of some aspects of L.M.'s personality with her own knowledge of the overwhelming influence a dominating father can have on his daughters' lives. Preceding this work is 'The Lady's Maid', a shorter story whose genesis may well lie in Katherine's realisation of the sacrifice L.M. had made for her.

In her memoirs, L.M. admits that she had 'hesitated just a little' about giving up her own life and friends to join Katherine in 1918. But 'of course there was no real question in my own mind. Nothing else would have been possible for us.' Certainly any other intimate association was not possible for L.M., once she was living in Katherine's house. When Robert Gibson, a man of whom L.M. was becoming fond, visited, the atmosphere was so strained that he fled. 'I never saw or heard from Gibson again', L.M. writes.

> We had met several times since the voyage home from Rhodesia, and we had been drawn to one another. In a different situation, I might have married him and gone to Africa with him. But I was really leading a double life, my own and Katherine's, and I should not have dreamt of leaving her. She must have understood that that afternoon . . .

'The Lady's Maid', a dramatic monologue in prose, is a moving but straightforward account of how a motherless girl, sent to be a lady's maid at the age of thirteen, continues as an adult to submit to the emotional exploitation of her employer. Outwardly, Katherine seems to have modelled the saintly religious lady, who spends so much time at night kneeling 'on the hard carpet' praying for the list of people in her little red book, not on herself but on Jinnie Fullerton. (Of her she had written to Murry, 'J[innie] is a saint . . . she works like mad for the glory of God . . . refers everything to God or his saints. . . . But it has warped her.')

What becomes apparent from the story, however, is that the devotion which the lady exacts from her maid is remarkably like that which Katherine required and accepted from L.M. Like L.M., the lady's maid had the chance of a life of her own when Harry, who kept a flower shop, proposed marriage. But the day he came to call for her to choose their furniture,

> My lady wasn't quite herself. . . . I didn't like leaving her. . . . Oh, it was all I could do not to burst out crying . . . and I asked her if she'd rather I . . . didn't get married. 'No, Ellen,' she said . . . 'not for the *wide world*!' But while she said it, madam – I was looking in her glass . . . she put her little hand on her heart just like her dear mother used to, and lifted her eyes . . .

And so when Harry arrived, Ellen told him, 'it's all over. I'm not going to marry you . . . I can't leave my lady.' The story ends with the maid admitting that now she has no one but her lady:

'Oh dear, I sometimes think . . . whatever should I do if anything were to. . . . But, there, thinking's no good to anyone. . . .' Katherine Mansfield was surely foreseeing the effect of her own death on L.M.'s life.

'Had a long talk with Ida and suddenly saw her again as a figure in a story', Katherine wrote in her journal in 1922. 'She resolves into so many. I could write *books* about her alone!' Ida Constance Baker is, as critics have noted, the model for the indecisive Con in 'Daughters of the Late Colonel'. L.M. describes the narrative as 'that gentle caricature of [Katherine's] cousin Sylvia Payne and me' and remarks that Sylvia, like Josephine in the story, was nicknamed 'Jug'. The character of the 'late' Colonel, moreover, was to some extent based on that of Ida's widower father whom Anthony Alpers describes as a 'former Indian Army doctor . . . a moody, unsociable, lonely man with a hot temper'.[4] Katherine Mansfield's use of L.M. and her father as models in the story is in no way surprising; but it is significant that onto the consciousness of her two female characters she grafted attitudes towards the dominating father which could only have been her own.

As the title of 'Daughters of the Late Colonel' suggests, the relationship between father and daughters is crucial in the story. And yet most commentators have chosen to emphasise the author's thematic and technical handling of time. Unquestionably, time is an important motif in 'Daughters', as well as a linking device which enables Katherine Mansfield to slip easily from each of the story's twelve sections to the other. But it is not (as in 'The Man Without a Temperament') at the emotional heart of the work. Thematically central to the narrative, and determining its psychological complexity, are the ambivalent feelings of the two middle-aged daughters about the death of their father. From the opening sentence – 'The week after was one of the busiest weeks of their lives' – it is obvious that grief is not their dominant reaction to the death. Caught up in the ritual of mourning, the two women are for the first time in their lives enjoying a sense of importance; and their efforts are concentrated on making what they consider to be the expected, outwardly correct gestures. The mounting humour and pathos of the story arises from the reader's gradual realisation that in the context of the daughters' confined existence, such concern is unjustified. Nobody, not even the vicar who comes to offer 'a little Communion' and, parrotlike, reiterates his desire to be 'helpful', really cares about the two old maids or their father. In terms of their own inner compulsions, however, the ritual is clearly essential: for both sisters need to convince themselves that they do indeed mourn father's death.

Josephine, who fights down a giggle at the thought of the porter wearing father's top-hat, gives the first indication that the sisters' formal reactions are not deeply felt. Much more real are the instinctive feelings which such outward observances as wearing black clothes, asking Nurse Andrews to stay as their guest, replying to letters and disposing of father's watch, are designed to disguise. Dutifully, Josephine cries over all twenty-three letters when she writes the words 'We miss our dear father so much'; but the imagery which expresses the sisters' uncensored thoughts conveys how little they have to miss. If they are haunted, for example, by the memory of father on his death-bed – 'a dark, angry purple in the face' – suddenly opening one eye and glaring at them, it is because he resembles nothing so much as a one-eyed giant. Like the Cyclops who kept his victims imprisoned in a dark cave while he waited to devour them, the Colonel has held his daughters virtual captives in the house, selfishly devouring their lives.

Regretting their decision to ask Nurse Andrews to stay on, the sisters console themselves with the thought that 'it was not long now, and then she'd be gone for good'. What the middle sections of the story reveal is that, while it is possible to get rid of the living, the dead are less easily disposed of 'for good'. Father, in fact, has so terrorised the daughters with his authoritarian personality that his image lives on in their minds. Superficially humorous, their guilt at having buried father 'without asking his permission' expresses the deeper psychological truth that they have secretly wished him dead. It is because of these murderous (although repressed) thoughts that they believe he will 'never forgive them'. For the same reason the two women, terrified of retribution, dread entering the dead man's room. When they act as if father's very bedroom furniture had become alive and taken on his fearsome attributes, Constantia and Josephine are projecting onto the outer world their own sense of guilt. Constantia's 'awful callous smile' as they leave the room reinforces the idea that a dreadful crime has been committed – as does Josephine's sudden recollection of an attempted childhood murder when 'Constantia had pushed [their brother] Benny into the round pond'.

Submission to father's tyranny and his rules has kept the two sisters in a state of childish retardation. Never allowed to become adults and establish their own independent identities, they fear virtually everything: the objects within their own house, the people with whom they come in contact, the unknown outside world and, worst of all, their own repressed emotions. Years of holding back their hostility toward father have caused them habitually to avoid facing things – in effect, to evade reality. To this habit of inner dishonesty, of constant evasion of the truth, the indecisiveness of the women is partly attributable. In a life which has been spent 'looking after father, and at the same time keeping out of father's way', the daughters have replaced an awareness of present time with the opiate of fantasy and day-dream: 'it all seemed to have happened in a kind of tunnel', Constantia finally reflects. 'It wasn't real.' It is this unreality as well as their childlike sense of timelessness that Katherine Mansfield is expressing when, disregarding the boundaries of past, present and future, she moves backwards and forwards within the minds of her characters.

Indecisiveness and an inability to deal firmly with bullies such as Nurse Andrews and the servant girl are related to the daughters' unconscious fear of their own aggressive impulses. In fact, it is partly because they have had to suppress, over the years, almost all their natural impulses that Constantia and Josephine lack strength of character. The Colonel's stamping out of their spontaneity is symbolised by his angry insistence that the music of the barrel-organ be silenced. Significantly, it is the free sound of the music after his death – 'A perfect fountain of bubbling notes . . . round, bright notes, carelessly scattered' – that introduces the sexual fantasies of the two women. The presence of such fantasies is first hinted at in the glimpse of the sisters mentally watching

> a black man in white linen drawers running through the pale fields for dear life. . . . Josephine's black man was tiny; he scurried along glistening like an ant. But there was something blind and tireless about Constantia's tall, thin fellow, which made him, she decided, a very unpleasant person indeed.

Virtually imprisoned by their father in a state of obedient, child-like dependence, the sisters have had no chance of meeting marriageable men. For Josephine, now that he is dead, the gentle touch of the sun might almost be that of a suitor. Constantia's surge of longing, as the barrel-organ plays unchecked, recalls

> the times she had come in here, crept out of bed in her night-gown when the moon was full, and lain on the floor with her arms outstretched, as though she was crucified. Why? The big, pale moon had made her do it. The horrible dancing figures on the carved screen had leered at her and she hadn't minded.

While the sun is traditionally a male symbol, that of the moon is female; and it is the influence of the moon on Constantia which makes her fantasy sexually ambiguous. In 'Prelude' Linda Burnell's longing for escape with her mother in the aloe-become-boat takes place in 'bright moonlight'; Beryl Fairfield, in the same story, has an ambivalent fantasy about a young man as she undresses 'in a pool of moonlight'; and Bertha Young's moment of fantasised union with Pearl Fulton occurs when both women are 'caught in that circle of unearthly light'. Constantia's feelings about men are less sharply defined than are those of Linda, Beryl or Bertha; but they are equally ambivalent. It was Constantia who as a child pushed Benny into the pond; she who, in 'one of those amazingly bold things that she'd done about twice before in their lives', symbolically got rid of father by firmly locking his wardrobe door; and she whose fantasised black man was 'a very unpleasant person indeed'. Her longing, as she lies outstretched on the floor seeing the apparently male figures on the screen as 'horrible' and leering, is not for intimacy with a man; it is for some form of communion with a woman or with the mother (killed by a snake in Ceylon) whom she has never known. The image of crucifixion, with its implication of punishment for a crime, is peculiarly appropriate in a story where guilt over wishing father dead is so central to the theme. Yet as Constantia lies in her crucifixion pose, the similarity of her fantasies to Katherine's girlhood description of how she lay awake in Edie's arms imagining that the post outside was a figure which 'was crucified, hung lifeless . . . yet sneering', suggests that she is also seeking atonement for inadmissable sexual desires.

The ending of 'The Daughters of the Late Colonel' leaves unresolved the emotional themes raised in the story. Wondering 'what did it mean? What was it she was always wanting? What did it all lead to? Now? Now?' Constantia's vague attempt to distinguish the real from the unreal aspects of her life fades into nothingness, like the sun which fades from Josephine's face. Just as surely as Linda Burnell, Beryl Fairfield and Bertha Young, the two sisters are becalmed.

Unlike those younger female characters who were primarily the victims of their own continuing emotional conflicts, however, the two elderly sisters are depicted as being the victims of their past. The themes of this story are those which Katherine Mansfield had used many times before: the ambivalent feelings of daughters for their father, and by extension for men in general; the immaturity of adult women who are fixated upon childhood; the recourse to fantasy-living as an escape from reality; and the destructive effect upon the personality of feelings strongly repressed. But the author's handling of these ideas is different. Less obviously than in 'Je Ne Parle Pas Français' and 'A Married Man's Story', Katherine Mansfield systematically unravels her characters' past lives in an attempt to throw light upon their behaviour and personality in the present. Past and present time are revealed as inextricably interwoven in the minds of these women who can contemplate no future.

Time, as a formal device woven into the very fabric of the narrative, serves to deflect attention from the anxiety-laden emotional themes. Even more important than time for this purpose is Katherine Mansfield's use of humour. Perhaps her supreme achievement in the story is the way in which she manages to contain, within the reassuring framework of comedy, the terrifying inner world of Constantia and Josephine. As in 'Bliss', 'Marriage à la Mode' and 'The Man Without a Temperament', Katherine Mansfield presents a contrast between the sympathetic central characters in the story and the less important characters who, hovering in the background, act as foils to her protagonists. Poking gentle fun at the apparently inconsequential thought processes of the sisters, she caricatures Nurse Andrews with her artificially genteel speech ('When I was with Lady Tukes . . . she had such a dainty little contrayvance for the buttah'); the unctuously helpful parson, and the sisters' embarrassed nephew, Cyril, yelling of meringues to Grandfather Pinner. All this leavens with comedy the inherent tragedy of the narrative.

'Daughters of the Late Colonel' is Katherine Mansfield's funniest story at the same time as it is thematically one of her most serious. In this work she finally enclosed in an acceptable fictional form her own deep wish to be rid of the father whom for so long she had hated irrationally. She also made her peace, as it were, with the other person who had born the brunt of a hatred equally irrational and ungenerous: L.M. In the last year of her life, 1922, Katherine was still obsessed by her conflicting feelings for these two people who, in spite of all her complaints, had done the most to help her materially. 'The Fly', written in 1922, suggests that, whatever she may have said in her letters, she never really came to terms with her dislike of her father. But a passage in her journal (written the same month as 'The Fly') shows an understanding of L.M.s predicament – and an appreciation of her – very like the one implicit in 'Daughters of the Late Colonel':

> I must not forget the long talk Ida and I had the other evening about *hate*. . . . Why do I feel it for her? She says: 'It is because I am nothing, I have suppressed all my desires to such an extent that now I have none. I don't think. I don't feel.' I reply: 'If you were cherished and loved for a week, you would recover.' And that is true, and I would like to do it. It seems I ought to do it. But I don't. The marvel is that she understands. No one else on earth could understand.

20 More Thrilling than Love – Honesty

The most tragic thing about Katherine Mansfield's final years was that she needed one person above all others to understand her emotional needs, and that person was Murry. From him the kind of intimate sharing that she sought was not forthcoming. As the truth dawned on her, she began reacting in a variety of ways. There was the familiar ploy of attempting to switch her allegiance from Murry to L.M. and other women friends; there was the search for some philosophical adjustment to the changing relationship between herself and Murry; and there was the punishment of Murry (in her more negative moods) by addressing him as if he were a child, or a woman – but not a man. Thus in February 1920, the day after writing, 'Don't make an effort to love me – my silly darling', she called him 'Isabel' and 'Betsy' in a letter which ridiculed him for his niggardliness with money:

> I'll repay you for the overcoat when Constable pays me. Thank you enormously for the figgers. They frighten me. You never mentioned your new suit. I don't know what colour it is or shape or anything – or whether there is any fringe on the trousers. . . . When I am rich, you will have such lovely clothes – all real lace and silk velvet.

Shortly afterwards she told him, 'You're the very last man on this earth to have to do with an "invalid wife". I know that so well. I know that the springs of our life together will be poisoned if I am not well.' And, indeed, they were poisoned. Adopting the pose of mother or playmate in her letters, she now called Murry by such childlike pet-names as 'My precious little mate', 'My little King of Broomy Castle', 'Mr Absurdity', 'My own explorer', 'my darling little Follower', 'my silly little Trot', 'Darling little Fellow'. In response to one letter from him complaining that his salary of £1000 a year was insufficient to cover his expenses, she mocked, 'Poor little boy with the pudding! Everybody seems to have a spoon except the child with the plate.'

Murry's response to her demands – and her derision – was to withdraw into himself on the one hand, and on the other to seek more congenial female company. His flirtation with their mutual friend Dorothy Brett drew forth Katherine's scornful analysis as much as her jealousy. 'Whatever he may feel about it now the truth is she flattered him and got him!' she wrote in her journal. Perhaps because she had foreseen such an eventuality, Katherine wrote calmly to Murry in December 1920 about his affair with the Princess Bibesco:

> You're very attractive to women, as you know. . . . And you always can escape, darling, for though you are so tender-hearted, you're ruthless, too. I mean if it was a question of a woman or your work, there wouldn't *be* a question, would there?

Katherine might hide her pain from Murry and write philosophically; but she could not conceal her real feelings from herself. 'I should like this to be accepted as my confession', she wrote in her journal, 'There is no limit to human suffering. . . . I do not want to die without leaving a record of my belief that suffering can be overcome. . . . What must one do? . . . I must turn to *work*. I must put my agony into something, change it . . .'

Katherine's propensity for self-dramatisation had caused her emotional life, in one sense or other, always to seem at the point of crisis. But now a succession of real physical and mental crises was forcing her to 'face things' in a way she had not done earlier. In December 1919 she concluded a long, bitter survey in her journal of the changing relationship between her and Murry with the declaration, 'Honesty (why?) is the only thing one seems to prize beyond life, love, death, everything. It alone remaineth. O those that come after me, will you believe it? At the end *truth* is the only thing *worth having* . . .' Nearly a year afterwards Katherine announced that she had begun a 'journal book'. 'It ought to be rather special', she told Murry. '*Dead* true – and by dead true I mean like one takes a sounding . . .' Later, quoting Marie Bashkirtseff's 'one must tell everything – everything', she added, 'That is more and more real to me each day. It is, after all, the only treasure, heirloom we have to leave – our own little grain of truth.'

Although she gave up the idea of writing a 'journal book' to be published, Katherine continued privately to examine herself. 'Is my love of rêverie greater than my love of action?' she asked in February 1921. 'Treacherous habit! . . . After supper I must start my Journal and keep it day by day. But *can* I be honest? If I lie, it's no use.' Fantasy and reverie had helped to make Katherine Mansfield an artist but, as she was coming to recognise, her tendency to blur the borderlines between fantasy and reality had been damaging. Now, striving to acquire more self-discipline, she became increasingly preoccupied with honesty and, by impliction, with reality. In enunciating her belief in honesty she was adopting no radical new credo. It had been the urge to tell the truth about the human mind that from the very first inspired her stories. But Katherine Mansfield had a divided personality in which fantasy and reality overlapped. Her problem had always been that, while in fiction she told the truth, in real life she acted a role, put on a mask to disguise that truth.

By 1921 the harsh fact of imminent death was a truth which no role-playing could disguise. As she felt mortal existence (with all its disappointments) slipping away from her, her attitude to fantasy and reality gradually changed. Fantasy she allowed to soften, even transform, the psychological realism of her stories; but, in actual life, reality – no matter how cruel – she determined to face. 'How marvellous life is, if only one gives oneself up to it!' she wrote to her brother-in-law, Richard Murry. 'It seems to me that the *secret* of life is to *accept* life. Question it as much as you like after, but first accept it.'[1]

In the second-to-last year of her life, Katherine Mansfield had many things to face and accept. First and foremost was the approach of death. The father whom in 1919 she thought of as 'a kind of vast symbolic chapeau' able to decide her fate had no power to save her. By 1920 she knew with equal certainty that Murry could offer neither physical nor spiritual salvation. But she had been warned by a dream that she was to be her own midwife at her rebirth – or death; and in October 1920 Katherine told her husband, 'If I am to be what I wish to be I must not be rescued.' Later she asked him,

> Is it right to resist such suffering? Do you know I feel it has been an immense privilege. . . . And if someone rebels and says, Life isn't good enough on those terms, one can only say: 'It *is*!'. . . It has taken me three years to understand this – to come to see this. We resist, we are terribly frightened. The little boat enters the dark fearful gulf and our only cry is to escape – 'put me on land again'. But it's useless. Nobody listens. The shadowy figure rows on. One ought to sit still and uncover one's eyes.

Uncovering one's eyes, for Katherine Mansfield, meant not only living with a sense of the inevitability of death: it meant entering into a process of prolonged self-scrutiny. She wrote to Murry near the end of 1920:

> Only since I came away this time have I . . . confronted myself as it were, looked squarely at the extraordinary 'conditions' of my existence. . . . It wasn't flattering or pleasant or easy. . . . I've *acted* my sins, and then excused them or put them away with 'it doesn't do to think about these things' or (more often) 'it was all experience'. But it hasn't ALL been experience. There IS waste – destruction, too,

Two dreams reported in a letter to him the very next day indicate that the 'sins' troubling Katherine were related to the early bohemian life which was so alien to her family background. In the first dream she

> was living at home again in the room with the fire escape. It was night: Father and Mother in bed. Vile people came into my room. They were drunk. B[eatrice] H[astings] led them. 'You don't take me in, old dear' said she. 'You've played the lady once too often. . . .' And she shouted, screamed *Femme marquée*. . . .

From this scene the dreamer finds herself in Piccadilly Circus awaiting the Day of Judgement. 'A cart drawn by two small black horses appeared. Inside there were Salvation Army women doling tracts out of huge marked boxes. They gave me one! "Are you corrupted?" ' Overshadowing Katherine's guilt about various episodes in her life is the symbolism of death, and of the punishment for which as a 'marked' or stained woman she is picked out. The image of corruption, suggesting moral degradation as well as the physical disintegration of the body, hints at the nature both of her crime and her punishment.

The second dream began in a café where Gertler introduced Katherine to Oscar Wilde. Finding him a fascinating talker, she asked him home and he replied, 'would 12.30 to-night do? When I arrived home it seemed madness to have asked him. Father and Mother were in bed. What if Father came down and found that chap Wilde in one of the chintz armchairs?' When Wilde arrived, with Ottoline Morrell, Katherine found him 'fatuous *and* brilliant' as he told how he was haunted by the memory of a cake when he was '*in that dreadful place*'. This dream, although less fearful than the first, is conflict-ridden. Divided between her fascination for the infamous Wilde and her fear of father's disapproval, Katherine mentally transforms the writer who so shaped her adolescent attitudes (and indirectly brought her into the company of such artistic people as Gertler and Ottoline) into the infinitely more respectable Proust.

If Katherine Mansfield now felt an affinity with Proust rather than with Wilde, it was because the remembrance of things past was becoming an increasingly important part of her own inner life. The consolations of fantasy she had virtually outgrown; and, like the daughters of the late colonel, she had no future worth contemplating. Amid the wreckage of the present there were only memories. 'It is all memories now – radiant, marvellous, far-away memories of happiness', Katherine had told Murry during their separation in 1919. Later she privately confessed that her life with him she was 'not inclined to relive'. What mattered now was the childhood she had once depicted so resentfully. The past, like her knowledge of death, her incomplete relationship with Murry, and her need for L.M., was something that had to be accepted and transformed. 'We only live by somehow absorbing the past – changing it', she wrote to Murry in October 1920. 'I mean really examining it and dividing what is important from what is not (for there IS waste) and transforming it so that it becomes part of the life of the spirit and we are *free of it*.'

As her guilt-ridden dreams indicate, one aspect of the past that Katherine Mansfield considered waste and wanted to be free from was the excesses of her youth. Ever since her brother's death she had been moving away from bohemianism towards more conservative, even moralistic attitudes. But, repudiate her earlier self though she might, Katherine continued to be haunted by that self. In January 1922, for example, a journal entry records,

> Heard from Mimi. Her letter was almost frightening. It brought back the inexplicable past. It flashed into my mind too that she must have a large number of letters of mine which don't bear thinking about. In some way I fear her. . . . At the same time, of course, one is fascinated.

The same month Katherine noted in her journal a talk with her cousin, Elizabeth. 'A strange fate overtakes me with her. We seem to be always talking of physical subjects. They bore and disgust me, for I feel it is a waste of time, and yet we always revert to them . . .'

Feeling as she did about 'physical subjects', it is no wonder that Katherine Mansfield should try to prevent, in May 1922, a reprinting of her *German Pension* stories. These exposed and indeed perpetuated, the personality and the past which she wanted buried. 'About *In a German Pension*', she wrote to her literary agent:

> I think it would be very unwise to republish it. Not only because it is a most inferior book (which it is) but I have with my last book, begun to persuade the reviewers that I don't like ugliness for ugliness' sake. The intelligentsia might be kind enough to forgive youthful extravagance of expression and youthful disgust. But I don't want to write for them. And I really can't say to every ordinary reader 'please excuse these horrid stories. I was only twenty at the time!'[2]

Murry, writing to a prospective American biographer in 1947, confirms Katherine's desire to obliterate from memory the period of her life about which she felt ashamed:

> My instinct is against the effort to dig up or into Katherine Mansfield's past; mainly because she herself wanted it buried, and did her best to do so. . . . I personally was present on two occasions when she made a great burning of letters she had

> written to people, and which she had recovered by great pains.[3]

Nevertheless, Katherine asserted again and again in 1921 and 1922 that the only way to bear life was by 'living in the past'. Not inclined to relive her past with Murry, wanting to bury most recollections of her adolescence and young adulthood, the only past that could be contemplated with any equanimity was her early childhood. About this, at least, she felt no guilt. 'Ah, Jeanne,' she wrote to her sister, 'anyone who says to me, "Do you remember?" simply has my heart. . . . I remember everything, and perhaps the great joy of Life to me is playing just that game.'[4] The 'visionary consciousness' of the artist, she believed, could somehow shape and transmute the influence of the past. To Richard Murry she explained the process as 'almost a case of living *into* one's ideal world – the world that one desires to express. . . . There is *this* world, and there is the world that the artist creates in this world, which is nevertheless *his* world, and subject to *his* laws – his "vision".'[5]

And so the woman who had spent much of her early writing life blaming her parents (implicitly, if not explicitly) could instruct her brother-in-law in 1921,

> Don't blame your parents too much! We *all* had parents. There is only one way of escaping from their influence and that is by going into the matter with yourself – scanning yourself and making perfectly sure of their share. . . . Don't think I underestimate the enormous power parents can have. I don't. It's staggering, it's titanic. After all, they are real giants when we are only table high and they act according. But like everything else in life . . . we have to get over it . . . to grin and bear it and to hide the wounds. . . . What I mean is, *Everything must be accepted*.[6]

The period from July 1921 to January 1922, when Katherine was living with Murry at Montana in Switzerland, has been recognised as one of the most fruitful in her writing life. And, of the stories which she wrote then, those in which she once again recreated her New Zealand childhood are the most admired. Although the relationship between 'At the Bay' and the earlier

'Prelude' is immediately evident, the links between 'The Voyage', 'Her First Ball', 'The Doll's House' and such immature works as 'New Dresses', 'How Pearl Button was Kidnapped', 'The Little Girl' and 'At Lehmann's' are less obvious. Yet Katherine's own remarks towards the end of her life suggest that it is not so much the themes of the later stories which set them apart from the earlier ones: it is the artistic ordering of their content. When she was a young writer, aggressively determined 'to tell all', she had indulged unduly in self-revelation. Often ambiguously involved with her heroines, she had depicted with a minimum of disguise and control the emotional conflicts which preoccupied her. Because she recognised a certain need for concealment, she had from the first experimented with symbolism; but time and again the images which were meant to cloak only reinforced an all too obvious innuendo. It was Katherine Mansfield's ability (won at such cost) to detach and distance herself from the pain of her experiences which made possible the artistic achievement of her last years. The actual physical details of remembered events, as well as her feelings about them, continued to form the basis of her stories. But the real world with its power to hurt she transformed into an ideal fictional world, subject to her laws, her vision; the raw material of personal confession she transmuted into the more universal truths of art. Like Wordsworth, who in his Preface to the *Lyrical Ballads* determined to depict 'incidents and situations from common life . . . and at the same time to throw over them a certain colouring of imagination', Katherine Mansfield selected ordinary, remembered scenes from her own childhood and having polished and coloured them in imagination, brought them into what she called the 'uncommon light of day'. The results of this visionary process in 'The Voyage', 'Her First Ball' and, to a lesser extent, 'The Doll's House', are works of almost limpid clarity: without any confusing ambiguity of plot, construction, or inner motivation, they share the fresh beauty of lyric poems.

Notable as these stories are for the absence of unconscious 'sediment' they retain the emotional tension which is so vital to fiction. But, whereas the young Katherine Mansfield had written openly and bitterly of the childhood traumas which obsessed her, the mature writer who had come to accept her past was concerned less with the exposure of inner conflict than with its resolution. Whereas tension or anxiety had tended to dominate the earlier stories by remaining insufficiently resolved, it is here allowed to develop and subside within a framework of reassurance and order. Thus the child's fear of abandonment becomes in 'The Voyage' a little girl's journey, tinged with sadness after the death of her mother. The themes of parental misunderstanding and sibling rivalry, once described so resentfully, are presented in muted form in 'The Doll's House'. In this story adult injustice is softened by the pity of one child for another. A young girl's initiation into the physical realities of adult life informs both 'At Lehmann's' and 'Her First Ball'; but, while Sabina echoes the shriek of Frau Lehmann in childbirth, Leila is allowed to forget the unpleasant words of the fat old man as she whirls away in the arms of yet another partner.

In 'The Voyage' the death of Fenella's mother is the immediate cause of the little girl's journey by ship from Wellington to Picton; and it is death, with all its connotations of loss, abandonment and change that creates the tension in the story. Only with the lightest of strokes, however, does Katherine Mansfield convey the presence of anxiety. Fenella's father hurries her and Grandma along the wharf 'with quick, nervous strides'; Grandma sobs when she bids her 'own brave son' goodbye; and Fenella finds this farewell 'so awful that [she] . . . swallowed once, twice, and frowned terribly'. The child's own moment of crisis comes when Father finally kisses her: ' "How long am I going to stay?" she whispered anxiously.' His answering 'we'll see about that', and his unaccustomed gift of a shilling, only add to her distress at the separation. 'A shilling! She must be going away for ever! "Father!" cried Fenella. But he was gone.' 'The Voyage' is one of Katherine Mansfield's most intensely pictorial stories and it is through visual images that she first conveys the sadness which hangs over the little girl's life. Not until half-way through the narrative does it become clear that Fenella's mother has died, yet in the opening paragraph the circumstances and feelings of the characters are suggested by an emphasis on blackness and darkness. Objects on the wharf 'all seemed carved out of solid darkness'; the woodpile was 'like the stalk of a huge black mushroom' and even the lantern 'seemed afraid to unfurl its timid, quivering light in all that blackness'. The link between darkness and the child's sense of loss and anxiety recurs when Father leaves the ship: straining for a last glimpse of him,

Fenella only sees 'the dark rope', the 'dark wharf', the strip of water between them growing 'broader, darker', and finally the 'dark hills'. Down in the coffinlike cabin it is the stewardess who makes explicit the association between darkness and death. Taking 'a long mournful look at grandma's blackness and at Fenella's black coat and skirt, black blouse, and hat with a crape rose', she announces, 'sooner or later each of us has to go, and that's a certingty'.

In spite of these images, death and darkness remain in the background of the narrative. In the foreground is the consciousness of Fenella, who is interested in the present moment rather than in the past or the future. Alone with grandma, she is keenly aware of every movement the old woman makes; and her mixture of childish shyness and fascination before the mysteries of age continually lightens the mood of the story. More gently and subtly than in 'Daughters of the Late Colonel', Katherine Mansfield employs humour to counteract anxiety. The sight of grandma sitting on the luggage praying as the ship pulls out, for example, offers a certain comfort; but, when grandma stops a second time on the way to the cabin, 'Fenella was rather afraid she was going to pray again'. In the salon, the embarrassed Fenella 'wished her grandma would go on', but the old woman, stopping to inspect a ham sandwich 'delicately with her finger', is 'bawled' at by a 'rude steward'. We smile at, and with, the child – as we do at the sight and sound of grandma undoing her stays before hopping into the top bunk with 'three little spider-like steps'. 'If everything had been different, Fenella might have got the giggles.' As it is, she listens to the 'long, soft, whispering, as though some one was gently, gently rustling among tissue paper to find something', which is the sound of grandma saying her prayers.

The old woman's emphasis on prayers – 'Our dear Lord is with us when we are at sea even more than when we are on dry land' – is outwardly reassuring. Equally reassuring, is the structure of the story. For the voyage which begins in darkness and ends in daylight has the mythic resonance of rebirth rather than death. Fenella hardly has time to think, on awakening, 'Oh, it had all been so sad lately. Was it going to change?' before land appears out of the morning mists. The return to land, safe and familiar in comparison with the sea, parallels the movement from darkness to light and heralds the change from sadness to cheerful acceptance of life, from loss of parents to gain of grandparents.

There are no dominating symbols in this story, as there are in the works where Katherine Mansfield focuses upon the inner conflict of her characters. Instead, Fenella's mind registers a succession of images whose cumulative effect is to convey an affirmation of life in the face of death. To the child, there is no real disjunction between the human and the non-human world: everything is potentially alive. The lamp on the wharf had 'burned softly, as if for itself'; the handle of Grandma's umbrella, 'which was a swan's head, kept giving her shoulder a sharp little peck as if it too wanted her to hurry'; the cabin porthole is a 'dark round eye' which 'gleamed at them dully'. At the end of the journey, the 'landing stage came out to meet them . . . it swam towards the Picton boat, and a man holding a coil of rope . . . came too'. When Fenella and her grandmother bowl away in a little cart, 'the sea still sounded asleep', just as Grandpa is still asleep when the travellers arrive. To the child, who has observed how the 'big, trembling dewdrops soaked through her glovetips', who has looked at the 'drenched sleeping flowers' on either side of the path leading to the house, Grandpa might almost belong to the natural world too. 'He was like a very old, wide-awake bird', a bird who 'ruffled his white tuft and looked at Fenella so merrily she almost thought he winked at her'. Fenella's unconscious perception that she is part of a living universe thus effectively counteracts her discovery of death.

The external details of 'The Voyage' Katherine Mansfield undoubtedly based upon her own recollections of visits to her paternal grandparents in Picton. Similarly, she appears to have drawn from her own experiences the setting for 'Her First Ball'. Indeed Maude Morris, a Wellington contemporary, expressed 'no doubt that the dance described is the 1907 Garrison Ball and that it was Katherine Mansfield's first grown-up dance'.[7] Katherine returned to New Zealand from boarding school in England in December 1906 and the only ball in Wellington before her return to England in 1908 was the Garrison Ball. 'The description of every part of the dance hall is photographic, the stage with the chaperones and orchestra', said Mrs Morris, who was also present. 'The decorations were the same. . . . The programmes with their pretty pencils, of which I still have some, the dressing room with its attendants, the benches, passages and double doors were all there.' Even the Bells and the Neaves, mentioned in the story as having recently given dances, were actual nearby residents.

Using these real-life details as the basis of her story, Katherine Mansfield recaptures briefly the fairy-tale quality of youth. Riding with the sophisticated Sheridan girls to her first ball, Leila, the country cousin, might almost be Cinderella miraculously transformed by a fairy godmother. Just as the inexperienced Leila finds herself transformed for one evening, so does the world which she perceives appear magically changed. Even in the cab 'the bolster on which her hand rested felt like the sleeve of an unknown young man's dress suit; and away they bowled, past waltzing lamp-posts'. In the dreamlike atmosphere conjured up by the ball, magic is constantly asserting itself as objects take on human qualities and people merge with the non-human world. Thus, while 'gay couples seemed to float through the air; little satin shoes chased each other like birds'; the 'great quivering jet of gas lighted the ladies' room. It couldn't wait; it was dancing already'.

Caught up in a spell which is partly visual, partly musical, Leila registers her partners merely as voices. In contrast to the 'faint voice' and the 'new voice', who are uninterested in Leila as a person, is the fat, rather shabby older man who recognises that this is her first ball. Hitherto the world of the dance had been timeless: 'Her first ball! She was only at the beginning of everything.' But, for Leila as for Cinderella, time is the enemy of magic just as reality is the destroyer of illusion. When the man who has been dancing for thirty years cruelly tells the girl that she 'can't hope to last anything like as long as that', the spell is broken. The notion that she too would grow old and fat like the chaperones 'sounded terribly true'. Suddenly the happiness of youth is spoiled by the knowledge of age; ugliness is juxtaposed to beauty, and the beginning is seen in terms of its end: 'Was this first ball only the beginning of her last ball after all?' But, just as Katherine Mansfield counteracted the anxiety of separation and death in 'The Voyage' by enclosing her story in a mythic framework of darkness and light, death and rebirth, so here she softens Leila's initiation into adulthood by returning her to the world of magic. If happiness like life is finite, magic is both timeless and irresistible. Back on the dance floor, 'in one minute, in one turn, her feet glided, glided. The lights, the azaleas, the dresses, the pink faces, the velvet chairs, all became one beautiful flying wheel.'

Two entries in Katherine Mansfield's journal indicate that 'The Doll's House', completed on 30 October, 1921, had its genesis at least as far back as February 1916. Then, in the aftermath of Leslie's death, Katherine was gathering together her memories of the country where she and her brother had been born. 'I begin to think of an unfinished memory which has been with me for years', Katherine wrote. 'It is a very good story if only I can tell it right, and it is called "Lena". It plays in New Zealand and would go in the book.' While she was working on 'The Aloe' during those months in Bandol, recollections of her childhood came flooding back. One of them involved the doll's house which had been given to the Beauchamp children by a Mrs Heywood, just before the birth of the sickly baby, Gwen. Although Katherine was only two at the time she remembered that

> Meg and Tadpole had gone away . . . and they had gone before the new doll's house arrived, so that was why I so longed to have somebody to show it to. I had gone all through it myself, from the kitchen to the dining room, up into the bedrooms with the doll's lamp on the table, heaps and heaps of times. But there was nobody to show it to.

What was worse, 'all day, all night grandmother's arms were full, I had no lap to climb into, no pillow to rest against. All belonged to Gwen.' Even 'old Mrs McElvie came to the door', to ask about the baby. Then one day grandmother and Gwen were photographed: 'the picture was hung over the nursery fire. . . . The doll's house was in it – verandah, balcony and all. Gran held me up to kiss my little sister.'

Confused though Katherine's recollections of herself at the age of two may well have been, the external details of 'The Doll's House', like those of her other New Zealand stories, are remarkably true to life. Mrs Heywood is merely changed to 'Mrs Hay', and Vera, Charlotte and Kathleen Beauchamp become the same Isabel, Lottie and Kezia Burnell who appear in 'Prelude' and

'At the Bay'. The Mrs McElvie of Katherine's recollections is transformed into the mother of the 'Kelvey' children. Mrs MacKelvey, according to Ruth Mantz, was the well-liked village washerwoman in Karori, although her husband was not in prison but a gardener. Of the three MacKelvey children, Ruth Mantz writes, 'Lil, the eldest, was the only normal one. . . . "Our Else", the artistic one, was the mother's favourite. . . . They all looked after her. . . . This "pathetic little wish-bone of a child" cared only for the one thing: she loved to paint.'[8]

There was only one primary school in Karori, which the children of rich and poor alike attended. Amongst Kathleen Beauchamp's schoolfellows were the little MacKelveys, who every day trailed to and fro past the gate of her house. Kathleen shared a desk with Lena Monaghan. Ruth Mantz quotes Katherine Mansfield's later unpleasant memory of the Monaghan children: 'To me it's just as though I'd been going home from school and the Monaghans had called after me, and you – about the size of a sixpence – had defended me and p'raps helped me to pick up my pencils and put them back in the pencil box.'[9] According to Maude Morris, who like Katherine Mansfield was tormented as a child by the Monaghans, Lena Monaghan was the model for the spiteful Lena Logan, who cruelly taunts the Kelvey girls. The Monaghans, like the Logans in the story, even kept cows. Yet another contemporary confirms the accuracy of Katherine's portrayal of the teacher who 'had a special voice for [the Kelveys] and a special smile for the other children when Lil Kelvey came up to her desk with a bunch of dreadfully common-looking flowers'. The real-life teacher, apparently, was a snob who favoured the rich children and harassed the poor.

Thus virtually all the characters in Katherine Mansfield's most famous story of childhood injustice existed in reality. What Katherine's association of the doll's house with the birth of a rival for grandmother's love suggests is that the emotions which inform the story were also true to life. The central incident in the narrative – the incident which appeals to the surviving child in every reader – is the rejection, indeed the victimisation, of the Kelvey children by those more socially favoured. Suffering a sense of rejection since the birth of Gwen, Katherine displaced onto the washerwoman's children her own deep sense of being less attractive than her sisters, less loved by her parents and peers. In memory it was the author who longed to have someone to show the doll's house to; in the story Isabel, the dominant older sister, exults over the new possession at school. Kezia's resentment of Isabel is never openly expressed in 'The Doll's House'. But here, as in all the stories in which Katherine Mansfield depicts her childhood self along with her sisters, she is contrasted favourably with the eldest sister.

The differences in temperament and attitude between Isabel and Kezia are sharply defined in 'The Doll's House'. In this story, where the child's world is shown to be a microcosm of the adult's, the bossy eldest sister who 'was always right' is ranged alongside the heartless Aunt Beryl and the mother who forbids the washerwoman's children to see the doll's house. Imitating the adults in their snobbish ways, Isabel uses the acquisition of the elegant doll's house to court popularity at school. It is she who points out the beauties of the house and chooses 'who's to come and see it first'. Later, it is Isabel who encourages Lena Logan to bait the Kelvey children. While the Kelveys' social difference places them at the end of the pecking order, Kezia suffers from being overshadowed by her sister. At school 'nobody paid any attention' to Kezia's opinion that 'the lamp's best of all'; and at home Mother sharply dismisses her plea for the Kelveys with, 'Run away, Kezia.' Her action in inviting the outcast children to see the house is therefore one of rebellion – against the mother who would not listen, and against the sister who had 'the powers that went with being eldest'. Kezia's generous deed is also her own brief bid for a share of the gratification which the doll's house had afforded Isabel.

Rivalry among the sisters, although never emphasised by the author, underlies the thematic structure of 'The Doll's House'. Heightening the work's emotional impact are echoes of that archetypal story of childhood maltreatment, 'Hansel and Gretel'. In her 1910 'Fairy Story' Katherine had surely drawn on 'Hansel and Gretel' in her depiction of the woodcutter. Here, the 'spinach green' doll's house with its door gleaming like a 'slab of toffee' is reminiscent of the edible house which enticed Hansel and Gretel. Just as the hungry children in the fairy tale are driven away by their wicked stepmother, so Kezia is told to 'run away' by her mother, while the poorly fed Kelveys are commanded by Aunt Beryl, 'run away, children, run away at once. And don't come back again.'

As in her other mature stories, Katherine Mansfield softens the anxiety inherent in her theme. Overlaying the work's psychological meaning is the obvious moral indignation at class discrimination. But even more important in terms of the story's overall effect is the symbol of the 'little lamp'. Its beauties appreciated only by Kezia and the Kelveys, the lamp is at once a symbol of the three children's separateness – and their innate superiority. Kezia shares with the Kelveys a sense of being underprivileged. The appreciation of the washerwoman's children for the little lamp suggests that they, like her, have a compensatory gift of vision.

The lamp, with its ability to irradiate and transform the darkness, represents the imagination of the artist who has the power to transform reality, to creat an ideal world 'subject to *his* laws – his "vision" '. Katherine Mansfield modelled Our Else, who with her sister looks dreamily over the hay paddock at the end of the story, on the real Else MacKelvey, who in fact cared only to paint. Possession of artistic imagination, the author seems to be saying, transcends more than the hurts of reality. It transcends all social distinctions.

21 'At the Bay'

The major work of Katherine Mansfield's last years – indeed, arguably her greatest story – is 'At the Bay'. Frank O'Connor, one of her more severe critics, has given his verdict that 'At the Bay' and 'Prelude' are Katherine Mansfield's 'masterpieces and in their own way comparable with Proust's breakthrough into the subconscious world'.[1]

Apart from the length of these works, which makes them more nearly novellas than short stories, and their unusually large cast of characters, they are different thematically from her other stories. The loneliness and emotional apartness which separates one human being from another is in some way central to virtually every story she wrote; and it is central also in 'Prelude' and 'At the Bay'. But in these longer works there is an attempt to counteract existential loneliness by presenting characters as they live together within the companionable structure of the family and, in 'At the Bay', of the universe. As a consequence, the narratives operate on two different levels. There is the surface level, which shows us the comings and goings of family members in the course of an ordinary day; and there is a deeper level which, probing the isolation of individual minds, constantly questions (by implication) the security offered by the family. 'At the Bay' is both gentler and profounder than 'Prelude' because here Katherine Mansfield achieves a philosophic resolution to the emotional contradictions of family life.

In another sense, too, these stories stand apart from her other writing. Both were written in response to the certain knowledge of death. Distraught by her brother's death in 1915, Katherine quickly linked his fate with her own death, which she felt must follow. 'Prelude' became a conscious act of reparation, an attempt to expunge the bitterness she harboured towards her family. By the time she came to write 'At the Bay' in 1921, the death she had wished so dramatically for herself was looming closer. One doctor had finally admitted that her case was hopeless, and she wrote in her journal, 'Why am I haunted every single day of my life by the nearness of death and its inevitability?' As a healthy young writer, Katherine Mansfield had savoured death in countless romantic, literary gestures. Dying in 1921, she wanted to celebrate life. 'What can one say of the afternoons? Of the evening? The rose, the gold on the mountains, the quick mounting shadows?' she wondered in her journal. 'But the late evening is the time – of times. . . . To write something that will be worthy of that rising moon, that pale light.' With its affirmation of the oneness of the world of nature and the world of man, 'At the Bay' is surely that story. For what Katherine Mansfield needed to plumb now was not so much the mysterious depths of human relationships: it was the mysterious ebb and flow of life itself. The death which she faced alone had to be seen in the wider, universal perspective of the death – and renewal – of all natural forms. Thus individual suffering, individual regret, give way in this story to a greater but shared pain at the knowledge of life's shortness.

The relationship of death to life is therefore central to the thematic structure of 'At the Bay', and critics have given it due weight. They have perceived other thematic patterns in the work as well. Saralyn Daly emphasises an inherent contrast between the principles of order and disorder; Marvin Magalaner stresses the significance of freedom versus imprisonment. But, while Magalaner finds that 'as an artistic representation of what life is about ['At the Bay'] is masterful', he says that it 'lacks the complexity of imagery and association of "Prelude" '. For him, 'the relevance of each episode to the others is not always clear . . . for the good reason that it is not there except in a nebulous, hazy fashion'.[2]

The problem with understanding and evaluating 'At the Bay' is that no critic has fully explored the rich thematic texture of the narrative, or the wealth of imagery which gives it both power and coherence. Indeed, to analyse the story closely is to see that everything *is* relevant and interconnected and that, if anything, 'At the Bay' is a more complex work than 'Prelude'. In the latter, Katherine Mansfield was primarily concerned with the emotional tensions underlying family life. In 'At the Bay' these tensions are still present, but intertwined with them is an anxiety about death.

What has partly confused readers of these two major stories is Katherine Mansfield's continual refinement of a technique reflecting her early immersion in symbolism. In her adolescent 'Vignettes' she had struggled to find ways at once to represent and disguise 'the forbidden'; when she came to write the *German Pension* stories she gave both objects and actions symbolic meaning that was sometimes obtrusive; but by the time she wrote her last, great New Zealand stories she had learned to handle symbolism so delicately that it virtually defies detection. In 'At the Bay' there are no such concrete and identifiable symbols as the swelling bird and the thorny aloe tree. Her technique here is a logical extension of her earlier methods, but it is different. With the utmost subtlety she endows the impersonal forces of nature with some of the psychological attributes which in 'Prelude' were invested in male and female characters, especially in Linda and Stanley Burnell. The most prominent vehicles of symbolic meaning in 'At the Bay' are the pervasive motifs of the sun as it marks the time, and the sea. Associated with the fiery heat of the sun is forceful masculinity; the sea, which both gives and destroys life, is linked with women in her various guises.

While the cast of characters in 'At the Bay' is almost the same as in 'Prelude', the emphasis has changed, then. Although Linda and Jonathan Trout dream of what might have been, and Beryl at night again conjures up a lover, Katherine Mansfield does not attempt to explore deeply the frightening fantasies of individual minds. The characters' thoughts are revealed to us, but not the workings of their subconscious. And so the symbols which in 'Prelude' expose the subconscious are no longer prominent. Instead, Katherine Mansfield weaves into her narrative motifs whose universality suggests something very like the Jungian collective unconscious.

As if representing this, the omniscient author quietly uncovers for us the world of nature in its least observed moods, interprets the universal significance of these moods, and shows us the instinctive closeness of human beings to their natural surroundings. 'Very early morning. The sun was not yet risen', the story opens. The voice of the author describing the natural world blends into the background of the narrative. Part of the background also, and at the same time central to the meaning of almost every episode, are the motifs of the sun and the sea.

Inseparable from the sun in its movement through the sky is the idea of time. Time is a structural device which emphasises the limitation of the action to one day and unifies the separate sections of the work. But it also conveys a sense of the unity of all living beings. Time is integral to the author's thematic concern with life's shortness; and it thus bears a weight of meaning which is primarily philosophical. The sun, on the other hand, is frequently associated with psychological themes. Both the patterning of incidents and the attitudes of the characters suggest a correlation between the power and potential destructiveness of the sun, and masculinity.[3] Significantly, Stanley Burnell's daily movements parallel the sun's: he rises with the sun and returns home when the sun sets. And, just as the presence of the sun is felt in virtually every episode of the story, so does the figure of Stanley Burnell, whether present or absent, command more attention than any other character.

The complexity of meaning and patterning in 'At the Bay' derives partly from the portrayal of some characters' instinctive avoidance of the sun (and heat) and others' conscious association with these forces. Mrs Harry Kember's perverse unnaturalness is characterised by her deliberate and excessive exposure to the sun's heat. Unlike the wholesome and motherly Mrs Fairfield, who protects herself with 'a black hat tied under the chin', Mrs Harry Kember has allowed herself to become 'burnt out and withered. . . . When she was not playing bridge . . . she spent her time lying in the full glare of the sun. She could stand any amount of it; she never had enough. All the same, it did not seem to warm her.' Always known by her husband's forename, 'Harry', Mrs Kember appears to have identified herself with the male element: childless, lacking in femininity, insinuatingly lesbian, she seems to Beryl 'like a horrible caricature of her husband'.

Unlike Mrs Kember, the little Burnell girls go down to the beach wearing sunbonnets; and their mother, in episode VI, is depicted remaining out of the sun in the shady garden. Linda's exposure to the male element in the form of Stanley Burnell (with whom living was like being 'in a house that couldn't be cured of the habit of catching on fire') has left her broken and chilled. Linda, in her fruitfulness, should seem the opposite of Mrs Kember: the archetype of natural woman. But she is not.

She is a mother who 'did not love her children. . . . No, it was as though a cold breath had chilled her through and through on each of those awful journeys; she had no warmth left to give them.'

The sun of which Linda will have no part – just as she wants no part of her husband's life-giving potency – is in the next episode depicted as oppressive. 'The sun beat down, beat down hot and fiery on the fine sand, baking the . . . pebbles. It sucked up the little drop of water . . . it bleached the pink convolvulus . . . At this point in the narrative, when the sun is at its hottest and most destructive and Kezia and her grandmother are taking their siesta, the theme of death is raised openly. The fate of Uncle William, who, the old woman says, 'went to the mines, and . . . got a sunstroke there and died', underlines the sun's power to kill and maim. As the afternoon wears on and the sun's heat diminishes, the intensity of emotion associated with it abates. Even so, the association between heat and masculinity lingers on in episode VIII when Alice, the servant girl, who carries 'a very dashed-looking sunshade', walks out to visit Mrs Stubbs, the local storekeeper. Mrs Stubbs, with her long bacon knife and her photographs of herself beside such suggestively phallic objects as a Grecian pillar, a giant fern tree and a towering mountain, is another woman with the attributes of a man. Her primus stove exudes heat and, as she talks cheerfully of Mr Stubbs's death, Alice uneasily wishes that she was back home.

The symbolic connotations of the sun in 'At the Bay' have escaped critical notice, but the complementary motif of the sea has not. Saralyn Daly points out that the sea dominates the entire story, although she does not probe its symbolic meaning. Marvin Magalaner recognises such a meaning and suggests that 'the Jungian idea of water as an ever-moving feminine flow, the archetype of fecund woman . . . may be applicable here'. Water, he says, 'bears a heavy weight of historical, mythical, and psychological meaning'.[4] But he chooses not to pursue the idea of the sea-as-woman. Instead he links the sea-as-life with the theme of freedom versus escape.

One difficulty in coming to grips with the weight of meaning carried by the sea in 'At the Bay' is that this motif, like that of the sun, embodies meanings that are both philosophical and psychological. Philosophically, the time–sun motif is associated with the theme of death; the sea carries the contrary mythic resonance of birth. In the opening paragraph, the voice of the author describing the gradual awakening of life at the bay hints at the mysteries of creation: 'Perhaps if you had waked up in the middle of the night you might have seen a big fish flicking in at the window and gone again.' The reassuring, mythic overtones of this section give way to something different, however, when Stanley Burnell and Jonathan Trout come out for their morning swim. Possessive of the water, Stanley in his resentment of Jonathan's presence there first acts as if the sea were feminine: part wife, part mother. To be immersed in its depths is to partake of its life-giving qualities – to be reborn and revitalised. But to remain too long in its womblike embrace (as does Jonathan) is dangerous.

There is a sense, then, in which the sea in 'At the Bay' is symbolically invested with some of the psychological attributes of woman, especially in her role of mother.[5] In 'Prelude' there were two mothers: Mrs Fairfield, whose presence was reassuring and unifying, and Linda, the reluctant mother, whose rejection of her role provoked anxiety and divisiveness in the family. While both mothers are present in the later story, their functions have subtly changed. The sea, not Mrs Fairfield, is the presiding mother-deity, the unifying force around which all the characters gather; and the sea (or water) acquires also the negative attributes of Linda in her rejecting, emotionally destructive moods. It is significant that water is especially inimical to men. Both Stanley and Jonathan are left unfulfilled – 'cheated' – by their early morning swim. After Stanley leaves for work, Alice underlines the dangers that water holds for the opposite sex. Exclaiming, 'Oh, these men', she holds the teapot 'under the water even after it had stopped bubbling, as if it too was a man and drowning was too good for them'. The idea of water as destructive to men is later picked up comically when Mrs Stubbs reveals to Alice the cause of her husband's death: 'it was dropsy that carried him off at the larst. Many's the time they drawn one and a half pints from 'im at the 'ospital.'

The pervasive motifs of the sun and sea (or water) provide a unifying framework for 'At the Bay' and very subtly reinforce the emotional tensions in the work. If the sun's heat has the strength and potential destructiveness of a man, water, the opposing element, has a woman's power to deny as well as to bestow life. Revealed with deceptive casualness, an inherent hostility of female towards male imparts emotional relevance to the separate episodes. The first hint of such an antagonism is provided in the opening section by Florrie, the female cat. 'What a coarse, revolting creature!' she thinks as the male sheep-dog passes by. In episode III, after the blustering, bullying Stanley Burnell has left the house, there is a sense of conspiracy among the women: 'Oh, the relief, the difference it made to have the man out of the house. Their very voices were changed as they called to one another; they sounded warm and loving and as if they shared a secret.' As if aware of this feeling, Stanley overreacts to the loss of his walking-stick: 'The heartlessness of women! The way they took it for granted it was your job to slave away for them.' Alice's thought that drowning is too good for a man sums up the latent hostility of this early-morning scene – the only scene where all the family are shown together.

Later, at the beach in mid-morning, the battle between the sexes is portrayed openly. The Samuel Josephs boys and girls continually have to be restrained from fighting one another; and we learn that Mrs Harry Kember is so alienated from her husband that 'some of the women at the Bay privately thought he'd commit a murder one day'. Halfway through the story the theme of sexual hostility reaches an emotional climax. Linda, sitting meditatively apart from the others, makes the admission (paralleling her admission of sexual hatred for Stanley in 'Prelude') that the time not spent in calming her husband and listening to his story is 'spent in the dread of having children . . . that was her real grudge against life'. Nor is the theme dropped at this point. In a lighter vein, Mrs Stubbs that afternoon revels in her freedom from married life, enigmatically calling the death of her husband 'a judgmint'. And the frightened turning away of a woman from a man's sexual advances dominates the ending of the story. Beryl, in the closing episode of 'At the Bay', wrenches herself free from Mr Harry Kember. Frozen with horror by his 'bright, blind, terrifying smile', she runs from him calling, 'You are vile, vile.'

In 'At the Bay', as in 'Prelude', there is another side to a woman's resentment and fear of male sexuality: a mother's rejection of her children. Linda's dread of having children is conveyed quite explicitly in the central episode of 'At the Bay'. She decides that it is 'useless pretending' to love her children and that, as for the baby boy, 'he was mother's, or Beryl's, or anybody's who wanted him.' Linda's unexpected surge of feeling for the smiling infant does not cancel out her earlier expressions of indifference towards her children, and Kezia seems instinctively to understand her mother's attitude. As in 'Prelude', she turns to the grandmother for maternal care and is fearful at the prospect of abandonment. 'You couldn't leave me. You couldn't not be there', she agonises, at the thought of her grandmother's death.

It is not only Kezia who exhibits a degree of emotional insecurity, however. Nearly all other members of the family demonstrate, in one way or another, that they, too, yearn for love and suffer from anxiety about separation. Lottie, for instance, is afraid that the two older sisters will hurry to the beach leaving her behind; at the end of the day the children playing in the wash-house are fearful that the grown-ups have forgotten – or abandoned them. 'No, not really forgotten. That was what their smile meant. They had decided to leave them there all by themselves.' But the grown-ups themselves are emotionally anxious. There is Jonathan Trout, who goes about with 'a look like hunger in his black eyes' and whimsically asks Linda for 'a little love, a little kindness'. Beryl, in the closing scene, wants a lover because 'it's so frightfully difficult when you've nobody'. Perhaps Stanley, more than all the adults, suffers from his dependence on being loved and a sense that his needs are constantly thwarted. Trying to punish his wife for her lack of concern over him, he calls out as he goes to work, 'No time to say good-bye!' But Linda, as if she had never noticed, replies to his request for forgiveness at the end of the day with a cutting 'what must I forgive you for?'

There is, then, a clear psychological patterning in 'At the Bay' which is reinforced by the motifs of the sun and the sea. Less important thematically, yet helping connect the different episodes of the story, is Katherine Mansfield's use of animal imagery. In 'Prelude', the repeated bird motif had emphasised a common bond among the female characters: their childbearing function and its ramifications in their emotional lives. Animal imagery in 'At the Bay' serves several purposes. It adds to the impression that human beings are hardly separable from the natural world in which they live; it introduces a note of humour into the story; and, more significantly, it links the characters and conveys some essential aspects of their personalities. Thus the likening of Mrs Harry Kember with her 'strange neighing laugh' first to a horse and later, when she swims, to a turtle and a rat, underlines her physical perverseness. In this grotesque presentation of the woman there is an implied condemnation of the mannish lesbian who would poison some such vulnerable person as Beryl. The quite different comparison of Alice and Mrs Stubbs to cats is a humorous way of suggesting the common ground they share, and it is a means of reducing the anxiety caused by the appearance of yet another masculine woman in the form of Mrs Stubbs. Animal imagery has sexually ambiguous overtones when Linda, musing in the garden during the morning, fleetingly thinks of her husband as looking like 'a trapped beast'. At the end of the day Jonathan Trout walks with Linda in the same garden and philosophically likens himself to an insect, feeble in its entrapment.

A more light-hearted use of animal imagery occurs in episode IX which is devoted to the children. Earlier, the grandmother's affectionate understanding of Kezia's personality had been expressed when she called her 'my squirrel' and 'my wild pony'. Playing animal snap in the wash-house, the children assume animal names which suggest their own characters. Pip, the dominant boy cousin, indentifies himself with the strong, masculine bull; Rags, who follows his brother obediently, becomes a sheep; Lottie, whose personality is still fluid, changes from a donkey (which she behaves like) to a dog, whose part she cannot play. Isabel, a conceited boaster, appropriately becomes a crowing rooster; and Kezia, who is sensitive but able to hit back, is given the role of a bee with power to sting.

The qualities of a masterpiece resist definition. 'At the Bay' is especially difficult to explicate because the story which appears so simple on the surface is in fact extraordinarily complex. Thematically, it encompasses a whole range of feelings about human life. Woven into the texture of the narrative is a sense of the psychological conflicts between men and women, parents and children. These are the problems of youth, and in the natural course of things give way to the pressing problem of age: anxiety about death. Katherine Mansfield's achievement in this story is to weave into one tapestry the preoccupations of youth and age, and so to balance psychological truths against philosophical truths that they seem indistinguishable. Thus life, death and sexuality are intertwined; and the same motifs which convey a mystical sense of man's continuing life in the endless round of creation are linked with a woman's fear of the hazardous process of giving birth.

But it is not just with the beginning and end of life that the author is philosophically concerned: it is with how best to use the interval between birth and death. There is a choice, Katherine Mansfield implies, between safety and danger: between existing in a kind of inertia or waking sleep (and failing to realise one's potential); and extending life's boundaries through exploration or active discovery.

The contrast between inertia and exploration, like that between death and life, is conveyed through a sequence of motifs which runs through the entire narrative. References to sleep recur in the first half of 'At the Bay'. In the opening section we hear the soothing sounds of 'the sleepy sea'; then the re-emergence of human life is signalled when 'the first sleeper turned over and lifted a drowsy head'. Taking his morning swim with Stanley, Jonathan Trout is preoccupied with the 'extraordinary dream' he had last night. Later in the morning, Mr Harry Kember with his 'slow, sleepy smile' is compared to 'a man walking in his sleep', while his wife is shown lifting 'her sleepy face . . . above the water'. In the garden, Linda Burnell 'dreamed the morning away', the baby boy 'sound asleep' at her side. Not until episode VII when Kezia and her grandmother are taking their siesta together, does the motif of sleep give way to the more sombre one of death.

Katherine Mansfield conveys her sense that exploration, with all its dangers, is preferable to inertia – indeed, necessary, if life is to be experienced to the full – through the characters themselves. In the second episode she implicitly compares the attitudes to life of Stanley and Jonathan Trout. Stanley, who exults as he enters the sea that he was 'first man in as usual! He'd beaten them all again', reacts like an explorer beaten to his goal when he discovers that Jonathan is already swimming. In contrast to Stanley's energy and competitiveness is the other man's lassitude, his preference to 'take things easy, not to fight against the ebb and flow of life, but to give way to it'. The suggestion that life is something to be explored, and that there are discoveries to be made, recurs in the fourth episode. The little Burnell girls look like 'minute puzzled explorers' as they hurry to join their boy cousins searching for 'treasure' in the sand. 'Look what I've discovered', cries Pip.

In the following episode Beryl, on another part of the beach, explores a new and potentially dangerous relationship with Mrs Harry Kember while Linda, lying inactive under the manuka tree, muses about her youthful dreams of exploring with her father 'up a river in China'. Marriage has limited her opportunities, forced on her a different role: 'It was always Stanley who was in the thick of the danger. Her whole time was spent in rescuing him.' As the day wears on, the motif of exploration persists. Kezia's uncle William 'went to the mines' in Australia in search of adventure. On a smaller scale, Alice, timidly venturing along a deserted road to visit Mrs Stubbs, is testing out something new. And later the children playing in the darkening wash-house continue their exploration of life's possibilities: 'You were frightened to look in the corners . . . and yet you had to look with all your might.' Similarly frightened but courageous, Beryl, in the final episode, follows through to its conclusion her thought, 'If I go on living here . . . anything may happen to me.' Foregoing the safety of her bedroom, she responds to Harry Kember's mocking challenge, 'you're not frightened, are you? You're not frightened?' by stepping out into the darkness to meet him.

Linda's discussion with Jonathan Trout in episode X brings this theme to a climax and draws together the different threads of the story. 'I've only one night or one day, and there's this vast dangerous garden, waiting out there, undiscovered, unexplored', he laments. Jonathan acquiesces in his entrapment: 'Weak . . . weak. No stamina', he confesses. Linda shares with her brother-in-law a sense of life's shortness, a frustration at the ties of marriage and a passivity which precludes change. But his admission of inertia and defeat is for her an emotional turning-point – and a moment of discovery. The circumstances of Linda's life prevent her from extending the limits of her physical existence, from exploring space: yet she is able to make discoveries of another kind. In the morning she had discovered in spite of herself a new feeling for her baby boy; now, as Jonathan bemoans his helplessness, she inwardly compares him with her husband. The recognition that Jonathan is 'not resolute, not gallant, not careless' causes her to see Stanley in an altered light. She makes her second major affirmation that day when he returns home from work. 'Enfolded in that familiar, eager, strong embrace', Linda rediscovers her love for him as she smiles at, and accepts, his foibles.

Such an affirmation of life is essential to the resolution of the philosophical problem which is raised in 'At the Bay'. The question, 'Why be born at all?' is implicit in Linda's meditation in the garden that morning. All through the narrative, however, the interpreting voice of the author suggests her own answer to the problem of life's dualisms – to the fact that human beings must live with the knowledge of their own inevitable end; that they are divided between a longing to explore the dimensions of life, and a fear to leave the known and familiar; that they aspire to freedom from family ties yet are emotionally dependent on each other; and that some are forced to accept sexual roles that they would rather be without.

Katherine Mansfield's answer, so subtly conveyed that it is hardly noticeable, is that there is a 'mysterious fitness' and unity in the natural order. Involving the reader with her inclusive 'you', she so merges the world of nature and the human world that they are barely distinguishable. In the mythic opening section where 'you could not see where [the hills] ended and the paddocks and bungalows began', the sea, the little streams and the vegetation not only seem timeless: they seem consciously alive. The awakening animal and human life partakes of nature's timelessness. With his 'velvet trousers tied under the knee', the old shepherd might be appearing from an earlier century, while his sheep which 'seemed to be always on the same piece of ground' are virtually interchangeable with the 'ghostly flocks and herds' which answer them from under the sea.

As we watch the mists lift on yet another morning, we sense an implied reassurance that everything is constantly reborn, that nothing really dies. Another such reassurance about the continuity of life in nature occurs midway through the story. In episode VII, when human beings have withdrawn from the sun's heat, the natural world is again seen to reassert its own life. The voice of the author compares the weed-hung rocks to 'shaggy beasts come down to the water to drink' and each pool to 'a lake with pink and blue houses clustered on the shores'. The voice asks, 'Who made that sound? What was going on down there?'

Against the backdrop of this interchangeable, perpetual life there is an intrinsic rightness to the grandmother's acceptance that death 'happens to all of us sooner or later'. The philosophical problem of death is raised for the third and last time in episode X, when Jonathan and Linda talk in the garden. Earlier in the day, Linda had reflected on the cruel paradox that the petals which 'shone as if each was the careful work of a loving hand' were destined to be wasted. Now, the voice of the author seems to merge with Linda's thoughts in one possible, negative explanation of the wastage inherent in creation: the beams in the sky 'remind you that up there sits Jehovah, the jealous God, the Almighty. . . . You remember that at His coming the whole earth will shake into one ruined graveyard.' And yet all the time counteracting this notion of a tyrannical, Old Testament God is the beauty of nature: the 'rose-coloured clouds', the blue sky overhead which faded and 'turned a pale gold', and the beams which finally seem to Linda 'infinitely joyful and loving'.

From Tolstoy, Katherine Mansfield copied into her journal in 1921, 'Life is everything. Life is God. All is changing and moving and that motion is God.' Imperceptibly, in 'At the Bay', she resolves the paradox of life and death by fusing a Wordsworthian concept of the oneness of nature and man with her perception that nature itself shares in the attributes of a loving Christian God. And so at the end of this story which juxtaposes a woman's dread of childbearing with the necessity for birth and renewal, we are prepared to return to the beginning – and the continuance of life: 'A cloud, small, serene, floated across the moon . . . and the sound of the sea was a vague murmur, as though it waked out of a dark dream.'

22 Haunted by Death

In the months following her brother's death, Katherine Mansfield had dedicated the remainder of her life to recreating and immortalising both him and the world they had shared. 'The next book will be yours and mine', she had promised in February 1916. No longer 'concerned with the same appearance of things', her writing would be 'changed utterly' in form. It would be changed because writing had become an almost religious mission, and changed because she at last had someone to write to and for: 'It is the idea . . . that I do not write alone. That in every word I write and every place I visit I carry you with me.'

In fact, it was not until her own death was imminent that the sister finally made good her promise. For, with the exception of 'The Aloe', revised as 'Prelude', Katherine Mansfield wrote almost nothing between 1916 and 1921 which centred either on her brother or their life at home in New Zealand. In the period generally reckoned as the most fruitful of her life, however, between July 1921 and February 1922, she wrote the group of stories based on her memories of New Zealand which at once fulfilled her vow and established her literary reputation. In over half of them the idea of death is of crucial importance, and in over half Katherine Mansfield included, virtually for the first time, a character who was modelled on her brother. Leslie Beauchamp appears as the baby boy in 'At the Bay', as Leila's cousin Laurie in 'Her First Ball', as the favoured son 'Harold' in 'An Ideal Family', as Laura's brother Laurie in 'The Garden Party' and as the boss's dead soldier son in 'The Fly'.

Katherine Mansfield completed 'At the Bay' in September 1921. A month later she wrote the story for which she is probably best known, 'The Garden Party'. A journal entry dated March 1916 indicates that the genesis of this work lay in the trains of thought and recollection which had preoccupied her in the months following Leslie's death. 'Tinakori Road was not fashionable; it was very mixed', Katherine wrote about the Wellington neighbourhood in which she had lived. 'There was no doubt that the land would become extremely valuable, as Father said. . . . But it was a little trying to have one's own washerwoman living next door . . . and further along there lived an endless family of half-castes . . . and below . . . in a hollow . . . was Saunders Lane.'

Hardly bothering to change names, Katherine Mansfield recreates in 'The Garden Party' the physical location of her late girlhood: the 'big, white-painted square house', the lily-pond in the garden, and Saunders Lane, the street which was a direct continuation of the Beauchamp's front path. In this street there actually did live a carrier named Scott who had a fatal accident; next door to the Beauchamps was Kitty Marchant (called Kitty Maitland in the story); and Godbers was a well-known Wellington catering firm. This much of 'The Garden Party' and certain characteristics of the Beauchamp family, Katherine Mansfield drew from life. One important alteration is the change made in the age of the brother. Leslie Beauchamp was six years younger than Katherine: in the narrative he is transformed into Laurie and made to appear so close in age and sensibility to Laura that, as the name suggests, he might almost be her twin.

'The Garden Party' and 'The Fly' are Katherine Mansfield's most anthologised stories, and dozens of interpretative articles have been written about them. It is a tribute to the complexity and appeal of these works that critics continue to be fascinated by their meaning and form. Most commentators have concentrated upon the philosophical significance of 'The Garden Party'. They have variously discussed it from the mythic point of view, seeing echoes of the Garden of Eden as well as the Classical myth of Demeter and Persephone; they have seen it as a story of initiation from youth into adulthood; they have examined the thematic juxtapositions of innocence and experience, of beauty and ugliness, of life and death. But, while they have noted, too, the work's social implications, they have not seen that these are central to an understanding of 'The Garden Party'.

Katherine Mansfield's journal entry suggests that her initial idea for the story developed out of the close proximity she had observed between the houses of the rich and the poor. The paradox that she presents us with is that, in spite of this physical closeness, the two social groups inhabit quite distinct and separate worlds. Laura's progress in the course of the narrative may be the philosophical one from innocence to experience; but in a very real sense it is the girl's instinctive attempt to find out for herself the extent and validity of the differences separating people like the Sheridans from people like the Scotts. The idea of class distinction, then, provides the thematic framework for 'The Garden Party' as well as informing its verbal structure and patterning.

Into her narrative, Katherine Mansfield weaves a series of contrasts and parallels which unobtrusively carry forward her theme at the same time as they unify the different elements of the story. 'The Garden Party' is a great story and a complex one because in it, as in 'At the Bay', we are presented simultaneously with several distinct yet interlocking levels of meaning. There is the social meaning provided by the real-life framework; the emotional and psychological overtones of the events in which Laura plays a central part; and the broader, philosophical significance of the total experience Katherine Mansfield lays before us.

The fact that the rich can avoid (or attempt to avoid) the unpleasant realities of human existence, even summon up beauty and elegance at will, is conveyed in the very first paragraph of the story. This opening paragraph is redolent of the fullness and richness of life, indeed of birth, since the rose bushes are bowed down as if 'visited by archangels' in the night. At the same time, there is an unreal, artificial quality to this beauty which the personification of the roses underlines. And so the scene is set for the contrast which is integral to the patterning of the narrative: the contrast between the essentially artificial, almost unreal world of the Sheridans and the quite different but real world of the Scotts. While the Sheridans' money brings them life in its fullness, the Scotts' lack of money confers on them only hardship and death.

The world of the Scotts dominates the ending of the story, the world of the Sheridans the first part. Rich and poor alike have their social rituals, and the ritual being celebrated by the Sheridans is the garden party, which at once allows them to display their wealth and fulfil the obligations of hospitality. Convention governs the attitudes, the behaviour and even the voices of the Sheridan women. Laura's conscious attempt to copy her mother's voice, followed by her realisation that she sounds 'so fearfully affected', indicates the artificiality of the Sheridan manner of talking. Laura, who despises 'stupid conventions', cannot act a role; but her mother and sisters do. Jose, for example, delights in the artificial. She loves 'giving orders to the servants' and making them feel that 'they were taking part in some drama'. Emotion is something she simulates but does not feel. Practising her song, 'This Life is *Wee*-ary, /Hope comes to Die', Jose sings of a tragic feeling only to break into a 'brilliant, dreadfully unsympathetic smile'. Behaviour is learned, not something spontaneous, in this sheltered world of wealth; and the Sheridan reaction to events taking place outside the family circle is dictated by what is expected. Thus Laura's instinctive feeling that the garden party should be cancelled because a death is being mourned nearby is rejected by her mother and sister in virtually identical words. Jose tells Laura, 'nobody expects us to', and this is echoed by Mrs Sheridan: 'People like that don't expect sacrifices from us.'

It is principally through Laura's perceptions that we glimpse the quite different world of the workmen. The distinguishing characteristic of these ordinary people is their naturalness and spontaneity. Whereas feelings are assumed, disguised, or restrained by the Sheridan women, they are expressed freely by the working class. Instinctively, Laura is attracted to the warmth and friendliness of the working men who come to erect the marquee; and the sensitivity shown by the man who smells a sprig of lavender makes her compare these men and the boys of her own social class. 'How many men that she knew would have done such a thing', she thinks. 'Why couldn't she have workmen for friends rather than the silly boys she danced with and who came to Sunday night supper?' Laura is searching for an identity of her own when she inwardly voices her dislike of the 'absurd class distinctions' and 'stupid conventions' which pervade the Sheridan world and prevent her from having friendships with such men. She tries to legitimise her attraction to the workmen by pretending to be 'just like a work-girl'. But the class barriers cannot be broken down, and it is with her brother, Laurie, that she shares her own warmth. 'Suddenly she couldn't stop herself. She ran at Laurie and gave him a small, quick squeeze.' Responding in a 'warm, boyish voice', Laurie echoes the warm voices of the workmen.

Tension in the story is generated by the underlying conflict between Laura, who cannot fully accept the artificial Sheridan conventions, and her mother. Because she is close to the natural world, the girl empathises with the feelings of the working people who are themselves part of that world. With Laurie, Laura had explored the forbidden territory where 'washerwomen lived in the lane. . . . It was disgusting and sordid. . . . But still one must go everywhere; one must see everything.' If Laura is something of a rebel, out of tune with her mother and sisters because she needs to include knowledge of the real, outside world in her perception of life, she is also set apart because she is 'the artistic one'. So long as her imagination functions usefully in the context of the Sheridan life-style, all is well. But when she imaginatively experiences the horror of the working man's death and, forgetting the distinctions between the different social worlds, wants to stop the garden party, she is condemned as 'extravagant'.

Laura's inner division is central to the working out of 'The Garden Party'. On the one hand her naturalness draws her to find out about life as it is lived outside the confines of the Sheridan household; on the other her artistic temperament causes her not only to respond to beauty but to cast over it a special imaginative colouring. The world of illusion is as precious to her, although for different reasons, as it is to her mother and sisters. It seems to be Laura who feels that roses 'understood that [they] are the only flowers that impress people at garden-parties', who registers the noise of the piano being moved as a 'long, chuckling, absurd sound', who imagines that 'little faint winds were playing chase' and that 'two tiny spots of sun . . . [were] playing too'. Knowingly, Mrs Sheridan appeals to the imaginative side of her daughter's personality when she cleverly distracts the girl by placing her own hat on her head. 'I have never seen you look such a picture', she says admiringly. As Laura gazes at her own beauty in the mirror and decides to forget the death until after the party, the attractions of illusion triumph over the demands of reality. And for the duration of the party, illusion holds sway.

But the magical perfection of the garden party, indeed the whole story, is enclosed within a philosophic framework which reminds us that everything has its opposite. There is a hint of birth in the opening paragraph; in the final section death asserts its presence. In contrast to the frivolous party given by the

Sheridans, the gathering at the Scotts' is for the funeral rite of death. Instead of the artificial drama enjoyed by Jose, a real-life drama must be endured in Saunders Lane. And, while sadness and deeply-felt emotion are kept at bay by the Sheridan women, the dead man's wife mourns, her face 'puffed up, red, with swollen eyes and swollen lips'.

Emphasising the gulf between the rich and the poor is the descriptive language of the story. Words such as 'perfect', 'delicious', 'beautiful', 'splendour', 'radiant', 'exquisite', 'brilliant', 'rapturous', 'charming', 'delightful', 'stunning' convey the outward beauty of the Sheridans' life – and its artificiality. In striking contrast are words describing the working people and Saunders Lane: 'haggard', 'mean', 'poverty-stricken', 'revolting', 'disgusting', 'sordid', 'crab-like', 'wretched'. In the domain of the Sheridans, mutability can be warded off so long as the outwardly beautiful appearance of things is preserved. This unattainable ideal of permanence, or stasis, is symbolised by the word 'picture'. In their ordered perfection, the garden, the roses and the canna lilies resemble pictures. When Mrs Sheridan places her hat on Laura's head and says, 'I have never seen you look such a picture', she is in effect framing the young girl's beauty, giving it the semblance of permanence. There is a different kind of picture which Laura briefly visualises: that of the poor woman in the lane and her dead husband. 'But it all seemed blurred, unreal, like a picture in the newspaper.'

Laura is the central character in 'The Garden Party', from whose point of view the story is essentially told; and it is she who bridges the contrasting worlds of the Sheridans and the Scotts. Her personal dilemma is that she must reconcile a sympathetic understanding of the poor, and an awareness of reality, with an imaginative attachment to the almost unreal, magical beauty which sweetens the lives of the rich. Her ordeal comes at the end of the story when she must physically cross the boundaries between her house and Saunders Lane, and in doing so face up to that other, 'blurred, unreal' picture. When she enters the cottage of the dead man, the story comes full circle. Just as she had done previously, the girl emphathises emotionally with the working people and echoes their grief with a sob. Earlier in the day, her emotional identification with the workmen had been deflected towards her brother: again, it is Laurie who 'put his arm round her shoulder. "Don't cry", he said in his warm, loving voice.'

Laurie, whose warmth links him with the workmen, helps his sister emotionally to transcend the barriers between the classes. The unchanging love of brother and sister, moreover, makes bearable the cruelty of life, the heartlessness of human beings, the 'Love that Changes' of Jose's song, and the knowledge of mutability – of the inevitable ending of a 'perfect afternoon', and the ending of life.

But the crucial philosophical problem in 'The Garden Party', the problem that Laura shares with all sensitive human beings, is how to encounter ugliness and death yet retain a personal vision of beauty and hope. In this closing scene, Katherine Mansfield contrives an answer. She brings together the contrasting pictures of beauty and ugliness in a picture whose beauty appears truly permanent, 'a marvel'. The sister-in-law of the dead man tells Laura that ' 'e looks a picture'; and Laura, the artistic one, agrees that he is indeed 'wonderful, beautiful'. Imaginatively, she is able to forget the suffering inflicted by his death and think only that, 'while they were laughing and while the band was playing, this marvel had come to the lane'. In her writing, Katherine Mansfield, too, has come full circle. Nothing, in her youthful stories, tempered a young girl's initiation into the harshness of adult life. At the ending of 'The Garden Party' she allows Laura to retain her illusions. If we are left with the uneasy feeling that she has let her character off too lightly, we nevertheless accept the emotional rightness of the ending. For there is a sense in which Katherine Mansfield has granted us, too, a reprieve; has assuaged both our guilt about social inequalities and our haunting anxiety about death.

The subject that had burdened Katherine Mansfield's memory all her life – her ambivalent feelings towards her family – drew forth her best writing. In her last great story, 'The Fly', she turned yet again to the portrayal of the person who more than anyone else had haunted her emotional life: her father.

'The Fly' was written in February 1922 while she was in Paris undergoing Dr Manhoukhin's new treatment for tuberculosis. Into this work she put her renewed sense of self-division, her knowledge of irrational hate and her own despairing hopelessness. Now she could summon neither fantasy nor her own special 'magic' to help temper the reality of death; not even her feeling about the continuity of life in nature offered consolation. The outcome of this final battle with physical and spiritual suffering is a great short story, one whose ambiguity and universality has provoked numerous critical commentaries.

As Marvin Magalaner puts it,

> from R.W. Stallman's view that the theme of 'The Fly' is that 'Time conquers grief', expressed in *The Explicator* in 1945, to Ted E. Boyle's 'The Death of the Boss: Another Look at Katherine Mansfield's "The Fly" ' in *Modern Fiction Studies* in 1965, which sees the story as the 'spiritual death of the boss', conflicting views have proliferated.[1]

Clearly, 'The Fly' is a work which can be approached from a variety of angles. One can focus on the symbolism, especially the symbol of the fly; one can examine the verbal patterning of the story; and one can dissect the character and the motives of the central character before passing moral judgement upon him. Saralyn Daly has combined all these approaches in her admirable discussion of the work. She argues convincingly that the boss is a bully and a sadist who 'no doubt bullied the boy as he now bullies Macey and Woodifield'.[2]

A slightly different interpretation of the story's significance emerges if one focuses on the central importance of the theme of death. Images suggestive of both the aging process and death pervade the narrative. Mr Woodifield is characterised as 'old' in the first line and practically every subsequent reference to him is prefixed by that word. As some critics have pointed out, Woodifield, who has suffered a stroke and is kept 'boxed up' in his house every day of the week except one, is virtually in his coffin already. The first reference to the boss's dead son is to a photograph of 'a grave-looking boy . . . standing in one of those spectral photographers' parks'; Woodifield's difficulty in remembering what he wants to say causes the boss to think, 'he's on his last pins'; and when the old man does remember it is that his daughters have visited the grave of his son and the boss's son in Belgium. He is pleased to report that the war cemetery is beautifully looked after, with 'flowers growing on all the graves'. After Woodifield has left, we learn that his reference to the grave came as a 'terrible shock' to the boss, who 'never thought of the boy except as lying unchanged, unblemished in his uniform, asleep forever'. The boss recalls the moment when he first heard of the boy's death and reflects 'how quickly time passed'. Immediately after this, he sees the fly in the inkpot and begins systematically dunking it with ink: 'Never say die', the boss thinks as he watches the fly's struggle for survival. It is after he has flung the 'corpse' of the dead fly into the wastepaper basket that a 'grinding feeling of wretchedness' seizes him.

References to youth and life are less prominent than those to death, but they are an integral part of the story's thematic patterning. Old Woodifield is grotesquely likened to a baby peering out of its pram; the boss offers him whisky that 'wouldn't hurt a child'; like a child, Woodifield speaks in a piping voice and looks as if he were 'going to cry'. The significance of this portrayal of Woodifield is the contrast in the boss's mind between himself and Woodifield: although he is five years older than his visitor, the boss pretends he is still in his prime. He has redecorated his office expensively, as if in anticipation of future use. Confidently he flips the *Financial Times*, serves his guest whisky and tosses off his own drink. He walks with 'firm heavy steps' before he sits down and thinks about his son. The first indication that the boss has even contemplated the prospect of his own decline and death is when he asks himself how he ever could have 'kept going all those years without the promise for ever before him of the boy's stepping into his shoes and carrying on where he left off?' Except for the boy, he tells himself, 'life . . . had . . . no other meaning'; and the boy's death has left 'his life in ruins'. With the words, 'For the life of him he could not remember', the story ends.

The fact that the story is told chiefly from the boss's point of view is vital to an understanding of 'The Fly'. For the way in which the protagonist views himself in relation to other people is central to the work's meaning. Whatever the moral implications of the story, the author is less concerned to pass judgement upon her principal character than very subtly to explore his inner state. Katherine Mansfield presents us with a profound psychological portrait in 'The Fly'; but, instead of encoding her meaning in symbols, she sprinkles clues with deceptive casualness throughout the narrative. These clues are the repeated references to life and death, to youth and age. What the author is concerned to show us is the confused emotional state of an aging man who secretly fears death but cannot bring himself to accept, or even admit, that he too must die. The important thing about the boss's character, as it is gradually revealed to us, is less that he is a bully and a sadist than that he is a consummate self-deceiver. Such is his self-deception that a tension is created by the ironic contrast between the protagonist's view of himself and the very different insight into his mental processes that the reader is permitted.

At first, the visit of the near-senile Woodifield is a source of satisfaction to the boss; it makes him feel younger. But the reference to the boy's grave upsets him because he is forced to think about the death that he fears for himself. This fear he has warded off by refusing to contemplate the physical decay of his son's corpse. He is not a total hypocrite in telling himself that his own life had been sustained by the thought of his son 'carrying on where he left off': in a sense the boy's continuing life had been an assurance of his own continuance. With the realisation that six years have passed since his son's death, the boss is reminded that his male line will not carry on after him and that time is running out for him, too. Wanting not to die, wanting to feel himself resistant to death (if not immortal), the boss begins to test out his hopes on the fly. Just as to some extent he emotionally identifies with his son and his son's fate, so he identifies himself with the fly in its struggles. If the fly can perform the miracle and against all odds survive the forces of destruction, so might he. Thus it is with the words 'Never say die' that the boss urges the insect on. The significance of the 'grinding feeling of wretchedness' which leaves him 'positively frightened' after the death of the fly has been much debated by critics. And, indeed, encapsulated in this ending is the entire meaning of the story. Everything that has gone before points to the truth that the boss, for all his outward show of strength and command, is an inwardly weak man, lacking in spiritual resources and terrified by the repressed knowledge that he has no power to stave off death. The emotion that he cannot feel at the thought of his son's death, he feels only too keenly at the prospect of his own. There is a double-edged ironic twist to the concluding sentence: 'For the life of him he could not remember.' The boss is shown pushing his fears back into his subconscious in yet another act of self-deception; and, as he too loses his ability to concentrate, he is shown following Woodifield into advancing age. In his perverse assertion of a false youthfulness, the difference between the boss and the childlike Woodifield is seen to be more apparent than real. Read in this way, the final effect of 'The Fly' is not so much to make the reader pass moral judgement upon the central character as to pity him.

Like the other great stories written in Katherine Mansfield's last years, 'The Fly' needs no heavy reference to the author's biography for its meaning to be understood. And yet into this, as into her other stories, Katherine Mansfield wove some of her own emotional attitudes – and her memories. Certain parallels between details in 'The Fly' and actual facts indicate that the character of the boss was based upon her father, and that his dead son was her brother, Leslie. In a letter, Katherine described the fictional boss as a bank manager; Harold Beauchamp was himself a businessman and the director of a bank. At the time of writing, in 1922, Leslie Beauchamp had been dead six years: in the story it is six years since the boss's only son was killed in the war. 'The Fly' reveals that, in the very last year of her life, Katherine Mansfield remained obsessed by the two male family members who in different ways had so influenced her writing career.

A notebook fragment, entitled 'Six Years After' and dated 1922 by Ian Gordon,[3] throws light on Katherine's feelings about her dead brother. In the fragment, a middle-aged woman on a sea-voyage with her self-centred husband sits alone on the deck and thinks about her dead son. As she gazes out at the water, her son seems to her a presence who calls accusingly, 'Don't forget me! You are forgetting me, you know you are!' In memory, the mother recalls a dreadful dream her little boy once had, a dream which seemed to be of his own death: 'I dreamed I was in a wood – somewhere far away from everybody – and I was lying down and a great blackberry vine grew over me. And I called and called to you – and you wouldn't come – you wouldn't come – so I had to lie there for ever.' Now, the mother 'was never off her guard for a moment but she heard him. He wanted her. "I am coming as fast as I can! As fast as I can!" ' she answers his ghost. 'This is anguish! . . . Still, it is not the idea of her suffering which is unbearable – it is his. Can one do nothing for the dead?' When her brother was killed in 1915, Katherine promised that she would join him in death once she had immortalised him in her writing. Into the mind of the mother in 'Six Years After' Katherine Mansfield put her own emotions: her own guilt-stricken feelings that she had perhaps been forgetting her brother, after all; her premonition of the impending death which would reunite her with Leslie; and her renewed desire to atone, to do something for the dead in the only way she could. There would seem to be a direct link, then, between the guilt about forgetting her brother suggested in this fragment and Katherine's transformation of the idea in 'The Fly".

Yet, it is significant that it is not the character of the dead son which is central to 'The Fly' but that of his father. The boss who sadistically, selfishly, kills the fly is the descendant of a long line of insensitive male figures who dominate and bully those weaker than themselves. A first, halting portrayal of such a figure appears in the childish story 'Les Deux Étrangères'; in 'Die Einsame' a seemingly omnipotent male figure sails away, leaving the helpless female protagonist to drown; the dominating Rudolf in 'Juliet' forces himself on the heroine and causes her death. Several gross, unfeeling bullies appear in the *German Pension* stories; and, if Herr Brechenmacher is an extreme example of the type, aspects of his character are still present in the father in 'The Little Girl' and 'New Dresses', in Stanley Burnell of 'Prelude' and in the late colonel in 'Daughters of the Late Colonel'.

Katherine Mansfield could never entirely erase from her mind bitter memories of her father. Even so, in her mature stories she depicted him as a man with two sides to his personality. Stanley Burnell in 'Prelude' and 'At the Bay' is a man whose bluff, materialistic exterior conceals emotional insecurity and a childlike need to be loved. Mr Hammond in 'The Stranger' is similarly demanding emotionally, similarly without inner strength. Outwardly self-satisfied and conscious of his power, the boss in 'The Fly' is shown to be inwardly insecure. In ranging the boss alongside Woodifield, Katherine Mansfield was doing more than providing a foil for her central character: she was in a sense providing him with a double and thus expressing her own ambivalent feelings about the two sides of her father's nature. Childlike, grateful for any attention and unable to hurt a fly, old Woodifield represents the awesome father-figure stripped of his power. The boss who systematically destroys the fly, is the personification of the male character traits the author feared most.

Katherine Mansfield had been creating doubles in her fiction (or characters so alike that they might almost be aspects of the same personality) ever since girlhood. In the process she gave concrete form to her own acute sense of self-division: 'All is disunited. Half boos, half cheers.' Perhaps nothing illustrates better this continuing division – and the extent to which her fiction tells one story, and her letters another – than a letter she wrote to her father a month after completing 'The Fly'. Here, in effect, she asked him for forgiveness:

> My darling Father,
>
> . . . How you can possibly find it in your heart to write like that to your undeserving little black sheep of a child only God knows. It wrings my heart to think of my ungrateful behaviour and I cannot understand how I have been the victim of my fearfulness and dread of misunderstanding. You have been – you are – the soul of generosity to us all. Then how – loving you as I do – feeling your sensitiveness and sympathy as I do – can I have made you suffer? It is a mystery.[4]

23 Postscript

As her life drew to its end, Katherine Mansfield turned increasingly in her letters and in her journal away from the criticism of others to criticism of herself. From being preoccupied with the past, with the 'memories . . . that one cannot without pain remember', she became obsessed with the future and with the idea of remaking herself so as to achieve a kind of rebirth. She had already faced the facts about the kind of man Murry was and the inadequacy of her relationship with him: now she began facing the facts about her own personality. 'I am glad that you criticised me', she wrote to Koteliansky in November 1921. 'It is right that you should have hated much in me. I was false in many things and *careless* – untrue in many ways. But I would like you to know that I recognise this and for a long time I have been trying "to squeeze the slave out of my soul".'[1]

Having just finished 'The Garden Party', Katherine castigated herself in her journal for a wrong attitude to writing.

> When I have finished a story . . . I catch myself *preening* my feathers. . . . There seems to be some bad old pride in my heart. . . . This interferes very much with work. . . . One must learn, one must practise, to *forget* oneself. . . . Oh God! I am divided still.

Since girlhood, Katherine had chided, pitied and exhorted herself in the pages of her notebooks or journal. In November 1921 she decided, 'It is time I started a new journal. Come, my unseen, my unknown, let us talk together.' Her talking in the journal was partly a confession of sinfulness, partly an attempt at self-analysis: 'I have been idle; I have *failed*. Why? Many reasons. There has been a kind of confusion in my consciousness. . . . I have not felt pure in heart, not humble, not good.

There's been a stirring up of sediment.'

The 'sediment' which left Katherine depressed and self-critical was partly a continuing ambivalence about her relations with others, especially her relations with Murry and L. M. After her first appointment with Doctor Manhoukhin in Paris she noted privately, 'But on the way there . . . I realised my heart was not in it. I feel divided in myself and angry and without virtue. Then L. M. and I had one of our famous quarrels. . . .' Katherine was quarrelling with L. M. because she was not Murry, who had stayed behind in Montana. Irrationally, Katherine blamed L. M. for making the sacrifices Murry was unwilling to make; at the same time she took herself to task for her callous attitude to L. M.'s devotion. 'Nothing of any worth can come from a disunited being', she said in a journal entry dated February 1922.

> If, combined with M.'s treatment, I treated myself – worked out of this slough of despond – lived an honourable life – and, above all, made straight my relations with L. M. – I am a *sham*. I am also an egoist of the deepest dye – such a one that it was very difficult to confess to it in case this book should be found.

By 9 February, Murry had changed his mind about remaining alone in Montana and joined Katherine in Paris. L. M.'s lot was to return to Switzerland and look after the empty chalet. A familiar emotional pattern now reasserted itself: again living with Murry in stressful circumstances, she wrote bitter comments about him in her journal; to L. M. she wrote letters which were demanding yet affectionate. Ever more conscious of her divided personality, Katherine ironically made L. M. a proposition that would formalise that division. Admitting in a March letter 'I take advantage of you – demand perfection of you – crush you', she nevertheless said: 'No, we can't simply live apart for all our lives from now on.'[2] Her plan was that, when she was well, she would spend six months of every year in England with Murry; the other months would be her free months. 'Now my *idea* is that we should spend the foreign months together, you and I.' Perhaps recognising that this attempt to solve her emotional conflicts by dividing herself between Murry and L. M. was only another fantasy, she added towards the end of her letter, 'I'm only talking in the dark – trying to keep you – yes, I will own to that. . . But I know any form of life for Jack and you and me is impossible and wrong.' In a later letter to L. M. that month Katherine added, 'The irony is I should never get well with you who wish me well more than any other being could.'

But by the end of May, when L. M. was preparing once more to take up a life of her own in England, the pendulum had swung again. Katherine wooed her friend with a loving letter. 'The old feeling is coming back – an ache, a longing – a feeling that I can't be satisfied unless I know you are *near*. Not on my account; not because I need you – but because in my horrid odious, intolerable way I love you and am yours for ever.' In June, Katherine broke off the Manhoukhin treatment and returned to Switzerland with Murry. Then she was more honest about her need of L. M. Too ill to cope with the practical details of life and receiving little help from Murry, she had to beg L. M. to come back.

> *Don't* take advantage of me because I have begged you to come and say I can't do without you. I haven't turned into a grateful angel. I'm at heart a distraught creature with *no time* for anything for the moment. . . . But try and believe and keep on believing without signs from me that I do love you and want you for my wife.

The return of Katherine and Murry to Switzerland in June 1922 brought about their final estrangement. Katherine moved with L. M. to Sierre while Murry remained in Randogne. Although they kept in contact until Katherine's death in January 1923, the Murrys never lived together again.

For all her self-castigation, Katherine in the last year of her life was unable to put straight her conflict-ridden relationship with the two people whom she had loved so ambivalently for so long. Separation from them both seemed the only solution. When all three went back to London in August, therefore, Katherine chose to live in Dorothy Brett's house, although she still depended on L. M. for practical help. Later, after she had entered the Gurdjieff Institute at Fontainebleau, Katherine's letters to L. M. became impersonal. 'Why are you so tragic?' she asked in one November letter. 'The part of you that lived through me had to die – then *you* will be born. . . . But you do see that our relationship was absolutely wrong now? You were identified with me. I prevented you from living at all.' A couple of days later, in a postscript, there came her solution to the problem of L. M. and Murry. 'What a pity you and Jack could not start a small farm together', she told L. M. 'Why don't you suggest it if you like him enough.' Incredibly, this idea that the two people she loved best should live together (or marry) while she herself experienced death and rebirth was precisely what as an adolescent she had fantasised in 'Juliet': 'David and Pearl were married as soon as [they] reasonably could be after Juliet's death, and a year and a half later, when a girl child was born, they both decided she should be christened after "poor Juliet".'

It was with some truth, then, that Katherine could write to Murry from Fontainebleau and tell him that L. M. had, in effect, no further place in her life: 'I have almost forgotten her. And only two months ago it seemed I could not have lived without her care.' Until the very end, Murry took precedence over L. M. in Katherine's emotions. From the time of their last separation in Switzerland, however, Katherine had been recording a hopeless sense that she must break finally from him too. Reviewing her relationship with Murry in October 1922, she wondered in her journal, 'What remains of all those years together? It is difficult to say. If they were so important, how could they have come to nothing. Who *gave up* and *why*?' To Murry himself Katherine wrote just as frankly about their earlier life. 'Looking back, my boat is almost swamped sometimes by seas of sentiment', she told him.

> And I think of the garden at the Isola Bella and the furry bees and the house-wall so warm. But then I remember what we really felt there – the blanks, the silences, the anguish of continual misunderstanding. Were we positive, eager, real, alive? No, we were not. We were a nothingness shot with gleams of what might be. But no more.

In his own brief explanation of their separation before Katherine's death, Murry says, 'We agreed that we now had a depressing effect upon one another, and that we ought not to live together until one or other of us had found a faith to live by.'[3] The inner resources which Murry calls 'faith', Katherine entered the Gurdjieff Institute to find. This much-criticised act at the end of her life did not, however, constitute the escape into mysticism that so many people assert. Her reasons for joining the group living at Gurdjieff's Institute for the Harmonious Development of Man were as complex as her own personality.

As such stories as 'At the Bay' show, Katherine had thought deeply about the spiritual aspect of life and about the individual's links with the universe as well as with other human beings. But her letters indicate that, however much she might wish to believe in God, intellectually she could not. In July 1921 she told Dorothy Brett,

> It seems to me there is a great change come over the world since people like us believed in God. God is now gone for all of us. Yet we must believe and not only that we must carry our weakness and our sin and our devilishness to somebody. I don't mean in a bad, abasing way. But we must feel that we are *known*, that our hearts are known as God knew us. Therefore love today between 'lovers' has to be not only human, but divine.[4]

Unable to believe in the Christian God, unable to pretend that a substitute for divine love could be found in the love between lovers, and so weakened by illness that art was almost beyond her, Katherine was looking for some source of inner strength in 1922. *Cosmic Anatomy*, a book sent to her by A. R. Orage in January that year, seems to have helped. 'Something has been built, a raft, frail and not very seaworthy; but it will serve', she said of it in her journal. One of the attractions of *Cosmic Anatomy* was that it combined philosophical and psychological ideas. 'To get even a glimpse of the relations of things – to follow that relation and find it remains true through the ages enlarges my little mind as nothing else does. It's only a greater view of psychology', she noted. Concerned though she had become about the spiritual side of existence by the end of her life, Katherine Mansfield remained intensely interested in psychology. As her physical health worsened, she began to scrutinise more fiercely her inner condition. It was less mysticism than self-honesty that caused her to ponder the effect of her mind on her body and declare in January 1922, 'But I have a suspicion like a certainty that the real cause of my illness is not my lungs at all, but something else. And if this were found and cured, all the rest would heal.'

Katherine's tragedy was that by the time she came to the conclusion that 'the weakness was not only physical. I *must heal my Self* before I will be well', it was far too late. With characteristic courage, however, she accepted the blame for the state she had been reduced to. She even wrote about her condition as if it were a punishment she had earned. 'Let me take the case of K. M. She has led, ever since she can remember, a very typically false life.' A few days later Katherine added in her journal 'I feel a bit of a sham. . . . And so I am. One of the K. M.'s is so sorry. But of course she is. She has to die. *Don't* feed her.' Then, in a separate entry, headed '*Important*', she wrote: 'Haven't I been saying, all along, that the fault lies in trying to cure the body and paying no heed whatever to the sick psyche? Gurdjieff claims to do just what I have always dreamed might be done.'

Although she may have been attracted by Gurdjieff's mysterious Russian background and his semi-mystical ideas, it was not because she had embraced mysticism that Katherine entered his Institute in October 1922. She had become utterly convinced of the interrelationship of mind and body; and on 14 October, her thirty-fourth birthday, she was forced to make the terrible admission, 'I can no more cure my psyche than my body. . . . 'Someone has got to help me to get out.' Gurdjieff seemed to offer the kind of help she sought. 'I am going to Fontainebleau next week to see Gurdjieff', she wrote to Murry. 'From all I hear he is the only man who understands there is no division between body and spirit, who believes how they are related. You remember how I have always said doctors only treat *half*.' Like the protagonists of her own childhood stories who found at the point of death that they wanted to live, Katherine Mansfield wanted more than anything else a reprieve from her fatal disease. Yet she was admitting there could be no such reprieve when she told Murry, 'No treatment on earth is any good to me, really. It's all pretence.' The best she could hope for, in the time remaining, was relief from her emotional conflicts and peace of mind.

Katherine Mansfield's last letters are full of her determination to attain a kind of inner wholeness or harmony – to die a good death. On 18 October she wrote to Murry:

> I have been through a little revolution since my last letter. I suddenly made up my mind . . . to try and learn to live by what I believed in, no less, and not as in all my life up till now

> to live one way and think another. . . . I don't mean superficially, of course, but in the deepest sense I've always been disunited. And this, which has been my 'secret sorrow' for years, has become everything to me just now. I really can't go on pretending to be one person and being another any more, Boge. It is a living death. . . . I have been through a horrible deadly time coming to this. . . . It doesn't show much, outwardly, but one is simply chaos within!

The next day Katherine explained herself similarly to Koteliansky:

> I am a divided being with a bias towards what I want to be, but no more. And this it seems I cannot improve. . . . I have tried. If you knew how many notebooks there are of these trials, but they never succeed. So I am always conscious of this secret disruption in me – and . . . I mean to change my whole way of life entirely. . . . I do not want to write any stories until I am a less terribly poor human being.[5]

Early in October 1922, just before she entered the Institute, Katherine wrote to Dorothy Brett about rebirth. 'Life is a mystery', she said. 'We can never get over that. Is it a series of deaths and series of killings? It is that too. But who shall say where death ends and resurrection begins. That's what one must do. Give it, the idea of *resurrection*, the power that death would like to have. Be born again and born again faster than we die.'[6] Whatever her thoughts were about the soul, the only kind of rebirth that Katherine could contemplate with any certainty was the rebirth of the self. It was about this that she spoke again in the last long letter she ever wrote, to Murry on 26 December:

> You see, my love, the question is always: '*Who am I*?' and until that is answered I don't see how one can really direct anything in oneself. . . . You see, Bogey, if I were allowed one single cry to God, that cry would be: *I want to be REAL*.

Murry was among those who felt that Katherine Mansfield made a terribly mistaken decision in choosing to spend her last months at the Gurdjieff Institute. But, however dubious the teachings and practices of Gurdjieff and his friends, the dying

Katherine seems to have found at Fontainebleau the peace she sought. She had been there a month when she told Murry, 'I know I shall never grow strong anywhere in the world except here. This *is* the place, and here at least one is understood entirely, mentally and physically.' Earlier, she had confided to Dorothy Brett that 'we must carry our weakness and our sin and devilishness to somebody.' Gurdjieff, in his self-appointed role of priest, if not psychotherapist, was that somebody.

Indeed, there was a strange sense in which Katherine's life had come full circle at the Institute. All her life she had longed to be known and accepted 'entirely, mentally and physically'. Part of her feelings of resentment and self-division as an adult, as well as her compulsion to return again and again in fiction to the traumas of childhood, were because she had felt denied such understanding as a child. In submitting to the rule of Gurdjieff, a man at least as dominating as Harold Beauchamp, Katherine was symbolically returning to childhood and accepting without fear and resentment a surrogate father. In so doing she was not only exorcising the dislike of her own father which had warped her emotional life; she also was accepting, and being received back into, the family group she had criticised, had fled from – and had subconsciously pined for ever since.

Although Katherine Mansfield wrote bravely about regaining her health when she entered the Institute, everything points to her knowledge that the only kind of health she might regain was her emotional health. Those who saw her in the days preceding her death on 3 January 1923, speak of her radiance and inner peace; it seems entirely possible that emotionally, at least, she did achieve a kind of rebirth.

Inevitably, one speculates about the kind of writer Katherine Mansfield might have become if she *had* regained her physical health and lived. In 1916, after her brother's death, she had said, 'I want to write about my own country till I simply exhaust my store.' She had in fact been writing stories set in the New Zealand of her childhood since at least 1911; and the unburdening of memories about her early life, at first resentfully, later nostalgically, provided the impetus and the themes of a great deal of her writing. The philosophical and emotional maturity of the stories Katherine wrote towards the end of her life, when she had become reconciled to so much, suggests that she might have come close to exhausting her store. She herself noted in January 1922 that her cousin, Elizabeth, 'suggested that if I did become cured, I might no longer write'. It is hard to think of Katherine Mansfield without a pen in her hand, without somehow still wanting to 'tell all'. Yet if she had lived – and resolved her psychological conflicts – it is likely that she would have written a different type of fiction.

In conversation with Orage[7] shortly before her death, she intimated something of the sort. She had stopped writing, Katherine told her friend, in the realisation 'that it is not writing as writing that needs criticism, correction, and perfection as much as the mind, character and personality of the writer. One must become more to write better.' Moreover she admitted:

> I've been a selective camera, and it has been my attitude that has determined the selection; with the result that my slices of life . . . have been partial, misleading, and a little malicious. Further, they have no other purpose than to record my attitude, which in itself was in need of change if it was to become active instead of passive. . . . And like everything unconscious, the result has been evil.

Her new plan, Orage reports, was to widen the scope of her camera and then to employ it for a conscious purpose. This was her understanding of the problem:

> Life can be made to appear anything by presenting only one aspect of it; and every attitude in us sees only one aspect. Assuming that this attitude is more or less permanent in any given writer and insusceptible of being changed by his own will, he is bound to present only the correspondent aspect of life, and, at the same time, to do no more than present it. . . . Could we change our attitude, we should not only see life differently, but life itself would come to *be* different. . . . I'm aware, for example, of a change of attitude in myself: and at once not only my old stories have come to look different to me, but life itself looks different. I could not write my old stories again, or any more like them: and not because I do not see the same detail as before, but because somehow or other the pattern is different.

'Only a few weeks later,' Orage concludes, 'Katherine Mansfield was dead. I saw her a few minutes before her death, and she was still radiant in her new attitude.'

Notes

I have followed C. K. Stead and Anthony Alpers in accepting the *Journal of Katherine Mansfield* (1954) as an important and generally accurate source of biographical information. A study of Katherine Mansfield's original notebooks in the Alexander Turnbull Library (A. T. L.) does show that the *Journal* is a compilation, that Murry omitted some material, misread some words and possibly misdated some entries. Given the difficulty of the material he had to work with, however, I do not think that Murry was an irresponsible editor. Whatever the minor inaccuracies in his transcription and arrangement of the private notes Katherine Mansfield left, the fact remains that the published extracts do throw valuable light on her inner life. In the absence of a revised, definitive *Journal*, it would be ill-judged not to use the material that is at present available. Mrs. Margaret Scott has generously shared with me her transcriptions of some of the material omitted from the *Journal*. When quoting, therefore, I have sometimes corrected the published *Journal*; other extracts I have cited as unpublished.

An effort has been made to minimise the number of reference figures in the text. Because of the frequent quotations from Katherine Mansfield's stories, *Journal* entries and *Letters to John Middleton Murry*, individual page numbers have not been cited. As far as possible, the source of the quotation and approximate date are implied in the text. Where specific reference is not made to the *Journal*, phrases such as 'Katherine Mansfield admitted privately' indicate that the source is the *Journal*. Similarly, references to her 'telling Murry', or 'writing to Murry', indicate that the source is her *Letters to John Middleton Murry*.

A similar method has been used with quotations from Murry and Ida Baker. Unless otherwise indicated, all quotations attributed to Murry are from *Between Two Worlds*; Ida Baker's comments, and Katherine Mansfield's letters to her, are from *The Memories of L. M.*

NOTES TO THE PREFACE

1. Conrad Aiken, 'The Short Story as Confession', *Nation and Athenaeum,* 14 July, 1923, p. 490.
2. Katherine Mansfield, *Novels and Novelists*, ed. J. M. Murry (London, 1930) p. 236.
3. Virginia Woolf, *The Diary of Virginia Woolf*, ed. Anne Olivier Bell (London, 1977) pp. 226–7.
4. *The Journal of Katherine Mansfield* (London, 1954) p. 205 (hereafter cited as *Journal*).

NOTES TO CHAPTER ONE: CHILDHOOD FANTASIES

1. 'Two Little Girls', in 'Extracts from a Notebook', *Adelphi*, 1931, p. 288.
2. Letter from Tom Mills in the Morris Collection, Alexander Turnbull Library (hereafter cited as A. T. L.).
3. Margaret Woodhouse (née Wishart), 'Notes re K. M.' in A. T. L.
4. *Journal*, p. 102.
5. Ibid, p. 43.
6. MS. papers 119, A. T. L.
7. Ibid.
8. *Queen's College Magazine*, XXII (Mar 1904) 129–31.
9. MS. papers 119, A. T. L.

NOTES TO CHAPTER TWO: THE PAINS OF ADOLESCENCE

1. All letters quoted from Katherine Mansfield to Sylvia Payne are in MS. papers 119 at the A. T. L.
2. Ibid.
3. R. E. Mantz and J. M. Murry, *The Life of Katherine Mansfield* (London, 1933) p. 198.
4. MS. papers 119, A. T. L.
5. Ibid. Fragmentary juvenilia hereafter cited are in MS. papers 119 at the A. T. L. unless otherwise identified.

NOTE TO CHAPTER THREE: 'JULIET'

1. *Turnbull Library Record*, III, no. 1 (Mar 1970) 4–28.

NOTES TO CHAPTER FOUR: FORBIDDEN LOVE

1. MS. papers 119, A. T. L.; quoted in Philip Waldron, 'Katherine Mansfield's *Journal*', *Twentieth Century Literature* (1974) p. 13.
2. *Turnbull Library Record*, III, no. 3 (Nov 1970) 133–6.

NOTES TO CHAPTER FIVE: THE CONSOLATION OF ART

1. 'Vignette', *Native Companion*, Oct 1907.
2. Marie Bashkirtseff, *The Journal of a Young Artist, 1860–1884*, trs. Mary J. Serrano (New York, 1899).
3. *Turnbull Library Record*, IV, no. 1 (May 1971) 10–11.
4. Typescript in Morris Collection, A. T. L.
5. MS. papers 119, A. T. L.
6. Ibid.
7. Quoted in Anthony Alpers, *Katherine Mansfield: A Biography* (New York, 1954) p. 84.
8. 'Vignettes' and 'Silhouettes' were published in *Native Companion* in October and November 1907 respectively. They are reprinted in Jean E. Stone, *Katherine Mansfield: Publications in Australia, 1907–09* (Sydney, 1977).
9. *Native Companion*, Dec 1907.

NOTES TO CHAPTER SIX: EMOTION VERSUS WILL

1. 'Katherine Mansfield: How Kathleen Beauchamp Came into her Own', *New Zealand Railways Magazine*, Sep 1933, pp. 6–7. See also Mantz and Murry, *Life*, pp. 269–71.
2. Typescript in MS. papers 119, A. T. L. (Published in the Wellington *Evening Post*, 13 Jan 1909.)

NOTES TO CHAPTER SEVEN: LONDON AND A DUAL EXISTENCE

1. *Katherine Mansfield: The Memories of L. M.* (London, 1971) p. 54.
2. *Turnbull Library Record*, IV, no. 1 (May 1972) 19–25.

NOTES TO CHAPTER NINE: LONELINESS AND ITS DANGERS

1. William Orton, *The Last Romantic* (New York, 1937). Katherine Mansfield's references to her life with Orton, quoted by Murry in the *Journal*, are taken from *The Last Romantic*.
2. See *The Urewera Notebook of Katherine Mansfield*, ed. I. A. Gordon (New York, 1978).

NOTES TO CHAPTER TEN: MURRY AND THE THEME OF CHILDHOOD

1. 'A Biographical Note on Katherine Mansfield' (1948), copy in A. T. L.
2. 'Mary', uncollected story published in the *Idler*, Mar 1910.

NOTE TO CHAPTER ELEVEN: REALITY VERSUS DREAM

1. 'The House', uncollected story published in *Hearth and Home*, Nov 1912.

NOTES TO CHAPTER TWELVE: ROLE-PLAYING

1. Ruth Herrick in 'They Were at School Together', *New Zealand Listener*, 25 Sep 1942.
2. 'A Biographical Note on Katherine Mansfield'.
3. *The Scrapbook of Katherine Mansfield,* ed. J. M. Murry (London, 1937) pp. 28–37.
4. Letter of Katherine Mansfield to Koteliansky in British Museum.

NOTES TO CHAPTER THIRTEEN: DEATH OF LITTLE BROTHER

1. Letter from Margaret Woodhouse to G. N. Morris in Morris Collection, A. T. L.
2. Letter from Frieda Lawrence to Sylvia Berkman, Nov 1939. Copy in Morris Collection, A. T. L.
3. 'The Wind Blows' and 'The Apple Tree' were published in *Signature*, Oct 1915.
4. Copy in MS. papers 119, A. T. L.
5. *Journal*, p. 95.

NOTES TO CHAPTER FOURTEEN: 'PRELUDE'

1. In October 1917 Katherine described to Dorothy Brett the feeling of

'identification' with a duck which Kezia experiences in 'Prelude': 'When I write about ducks I swear that I am a white duck. . . . In fact this whole process of becoming the duck (what Lawrence would, perhaps, call this "consummation with the duck or apple") is so thrilling that I can hardly breathe, only to think about it. For although that is as far as most people can get, it is really only the "prelude". There follows the moment when you are *more* duck, *more* apple or *more* Natasha than any of these objects could ever possibly be, and so you create anew.'

2. Beryl and Juliet both gaze at themselves in the mirror. Beryl sees her face as 'wide at the brows', her eyes 'a strange uncommon colour – greeny blue with little gold points in them'. Her mouth is 'rather large. . . . Her underlip protruded a little.' She has a mass of 'lovely, lovely hair . . . brown and red, with a glint of yellow'. Juliet's features are similar: 'Her hair . . . fell in long straight masses of pale gold to her waist. Her forehead was high and square while there was an unusual fullness over her brows. Her eyes were a peculiar colour, almost approaching green. . . . Her mouth was full of sensitive curves – the underlip decidedly too full for regular beauty.' Moreover, both Beryl and Juliet are described as having distinctively beautiful hands.

NOTES TO CHAPTER FIFTEEN: GARSINGTON AS FICTION

1. Vera Brittain, *Radclyffe Hall: A Case of Obscenity* (London, 1968) p. 95.
2. Parts of Katherine Mansfield's letters to Ottoline Morrell were published in *The Letters of Katherine Mansfield*, ed. J. M. Murry (London, 1928). All the letters to Ottoline Morrell quoted here are held at the Humanities Research Centre, University of Texas at Austin, Texas.
3. Murry's unpublished letters to Ottoline Morrell are held at the Humanities Research Centre, Austin, Texas.
4. *Ottoline at Garsington: The Memoirs of Lady Ottoline Morrell, 1915–1918*, ed. Robert Gathorne Hardy (London, 1974) pp. 190–2.
5. Ibid., p. 150.
6. *The Autobiography of Bertrand Russell* (London, 1968) II, p. 21.
7. *Ottoline at Garsington*, pp. 166–7.
8. Dorothy Brett and John Manchester, 'Reminiscences of Katherine Mansfield', *Adam International Review*, 1972 pp. 85–6.
9. *Ottoline at Garsington*, p. 149.
10. Ibid., pp. 186–7.
11. *Ottoline: The Early Memoirs*, ed. Robert Gathorne Hardy (London, 1963) p. 62.
12. The 'translation', so to speak, of people into symbols was a game played at Garsington on at least one occasion when Katherine was present. Ottoline writes in *Ottoline at Garsington* (p. 150), 'We were playing a game after dinner describing people by symbols, such as pictures, flowers, scents; unfortunately Katherine was described by some rather exotic scent such as stephanotis or patchouli, and although her name was not mentioned, we all knew and she knew what was meant. It was dreadful. The spite that was in the company maliciously flared out against her and hurt her.'
13. The link in Katherine Mansfield's mind between 'Marriage à la Mode'

and Garsington is further confirmed by a letter she wrote to Ottoline in August 1919: 'I long to see these pictures: they *sound* so radiant. But there is always something fascinating, captivating, about the *names* of pictures: "Woman Drying Herself"; "Woman in a Hammock"; "Lady on the Terrace".'

14. *Ottoline at Garsington*, pp. 166–7.

NOTES TO CHAPTER SIXTEEN: 'JE NE PARLE PAS FRANÇAIS'

1. *Katherine Mansfield's Letters to John Middleton Murry, 1913–1922* (London, 1951) p. 149.
2. *Katherine Mansfield and Other Literary Portraits* (London, 1949) p. 12.
3. Edward Wagenknecht, 'Katherine Mansfield', *English Journal*, 1920, p. 274.
4. 'Je Ne Parle Pas Français' was published in its original form by the Heron Press, Hampstead, 1920.
5. *Between Two Worlds* (London, 1935) p. 465.
6. Francis Carco, *Bohème d'Artiste* (Paris, 1940).

NOTES TO CHAPTER SEVENTEEN: THE NIGHTMARE MARRIAGE

1. E. D. Wittkower, *A Psychiatrist Looks at Tuberculosis* (London, 1949) p. 103.
2. Ibid.
3. Brice Clarke, M.D., 'Katherine Mansfield's Illness', *Proceedings of the Royal Society of Medicine*, XLVIII, no. 12 (1955) 1029–32.

NOTES TO CHAPTER EIGHTEEN: 'THE MAN WITHOUT A TEMPERAMENT'

1. *Letters of Katherine Mansfield*, p. 192.
2. Ibid., p. 214.

NOTES TO CHAPTER NINETEEN: 'DAUGHTERS OF THE LATE COLONEL'

1. *Letters of Katherine Mansfield*, p. 187.
2. Ibid., p. 213.
3. Unpublished letter to Sydney and Violet Schiff, British Museum.
4. Alpers, *Katherine Mansfield* (London, 1954) p. 58.

NOTES TO CHAPTER TWENTY: MORE THRILLING THAN LOVE – HONESTY

1. *Letters of Katherine Mansfield*, p. 294.
2. Copy of letter to J. B. Pinker, 3 May 1922, in A. T. L.
3. Unpublished letter from Murry to Lucy O'Brien, Humanities Research Centre, Austin, Texas.
4. *Letters of Katherine Mansfield*, p. 407.
5. Ibid., p. 387.
6. Ibid., pp. 366–7.
7. Personal note from Maude Morris to the author.
8. Mantz and Murry, *Life*, p. 114.
9. Ibid., p. 117.

NOTES TO CHAPTER TWENTY-ONE: 'AT THE BAY'

1. Frank O'Connor, 'An Author in Search of a Subject', in *The Lonely Voice* (Cleveland, 1963) p. 140.
2. Marvin Magalaner, *The Fiction of Katherine Mansfield* (Carbondale, Ill., 1971) p. 39.
3. In Katherine Mansfield's juvenilia there is a clear correlation between the heat of the sun and masculine potency. The sun is depicted as a lover in two early poems, 'The Rangitaki Valley' and 'The Awakening River'. 'O mystical marriage of Earth / With the passionate summer sun!' Katherine Mansfield writes in 'The Rangitaki Valley'. In 'The Awakening River', the river 'lies on silver pillows, the sun leans over her. / He warms and warms her, he kisses and kisses her.' The author warns the river, 'Be careful, my beautiful waking one! You will catch on fire.' There is a similar metaphor in the prose fragment, 'Radiana and Guido'. Radiana tells her lover, 'My soul is like a great stretch of sand on which the sun has shone all the long day – it is dried up, parched, hot.' Guido replies, 'It is as though I had a great torch in my heart that leaps up and flames and burns all over my body. . . . Let me pour into you the fire that is consuming me.' As late as 1915, Katherine Mansfield called her brother 'my little sun'; and she named the male protagonist in the 1918 story, 'Sun and Moon', Sun.
4. Magalaner, *The Fiction of Katherine Mansfield*, p. 129.
5. Katherine Mansfield's juvenilia shows the association in her mind between the sea and womanhood, especially the sea-as-mother. In a 1903 poem (MS. papers 119, A. T. L.) she wrote, 'The great sad ocean shall be our mother / We are tired and she will rock us, brother.' In an adolescent prose fragment the heroine is depicted listening to 'a wonderful, agitating sound – the call of her savage, lawless mother – the sea.' In a 1907 vignette, 'By the Sea', the sea is likened to an enticing woman. In two poems written in 1911, 'The Sea Child' and 'The Sea', the sea is portrayed as a threatening female force. The sea is a rejecting mother in 'The Sea Child'; in 'The Sea' the personified ocean alternates between teasingly sadistic offers of love – and rejection.

   The Sea called – I lay on the rocks and said:
   'I am come.'
   She mocked and showed her teeth,
   Stretching out her long green arms.
   'Go away!' she thundered.

NOTES TO CHAPTER TWENTY-TWO: HAUNTED BY DEATH

1. Magalaner, *The Fiction of Katherine Mansfield*, p. 129.
2. Saralyn Daly, *Katherine Mansfield* (New York, 1965) p. 109.
3. *Undiscovered Country: The New Zealand Stories of Katherine Mansfield*, ed. I. A. Gordon (London, 1974).
4. Typescript dated 18 March 1922 in A. T. L.

NOTES TO CHAPTER TWENTY-THREE: POSTSCRIPT

1. *Letters of Katherine Mansfield*, p. 413.
2. All the letters cited from Katherine Mansfield to Ida Baker are taken from *Katherine Mansfield: The Memories of L. M.* (London, 1971).
3. *Letters to John Middleton Murry*, p. 656.
4. *Letters of Katherine Mansfield*, p. 398.
5. Ibid., p. 398.
6. Ibid., p. 503.
7. A. R. Orage, 'Talks with Katherine Mansfield', *Century Magazine*, May 1924, pp. 36–40.

Select Bibliography

I. BY KATHERINE MANSFIELD

In a German Pension (London: Stephen Swift, 1911).
Prelude (Richmond, Surrey: Hogarth Press, 1918).
Je Ne Parle Pas Français (Hampstead: Heron Press, 1920).
Bliss and Other Stories (London: Constable, 1920; New York: Alfred A. Knopf, 1921).
The Garden Party and Other Stories (London: Constable, 1922; New York: Alfred A. Knopf, 1922).
The Dove's Nest and Other Stories, ed. J. M. Murry (London: Constable, 1923; New York: Alfred A. Knopf, 1923).
Poems, ed. J. M. Murry (London: Constable, 1923; New York: Alfred A. Knopf, 1924).
Something Childish and Other Stories, ed. J. M. Murry (London: Constable, 1924). American edn: *The Little Girl* (New York: Alfred A. Knopf, 1924).
The Journal of Katherine Mansfield, ed. J. M. Murry (London: Constable, 1927; New York: Alfred A. Knopf, 1927); Definitive Edition, ed. J. M. Murry (London: Constable, 1954).
The Letters of Katherine Mansfield, ed. J. M. Murry, 2 vols (London: Constable, 1928); 1 vol. (New York: Alfred A. Knopf, 1929).
The Aloe, ed. J. M. Murry (London: Constable, 1930; New York: Alfred A. Knopf, 1930).
Novels and Novelists, ed. J. M. Murry (London: Constable, 1930).
Stories by Katherine Mansfield (New York: Alfred A. Knopf, 1930).
The Scrapbook of Katherine Mansfield, ed J. M. Murry (London: Constable, 1937; New York: Alfred A. Knopf, 1940).
Collected Stories of Katherine Mansfield (London: Constable, 1945).
Katherine Mansfield's Letters to John Middleton Murry, 1913–1922, ed. J. M. Murry (London: Constable, 1951; New York: Alfred A. Knopf, 1951).
'The Unpublished Manuscripts of Katherine Mansfield', transcribed and ed. Margaret Scott in six parts, in *Turnbull Library Record* (Wellington) new ser.:

1. 'Juliet': III, no. 1 (Mar 1970) 4–28.
2. Juvenilia from 1906: III, no. 3 (Nov 1970) 128–36.
3. Juvenilia, *c.* 1907–8, and fragments of the play 'A Ship in the Harbour' (Apr 1917): IV, no. 1 (May 1971) 4–20.
4. Wörishofen fragment, 'Elena and Peter': V, no. 1 (May 1972) 19–25.

5. 'The Laurels', fragment of a play written and acted at Garsington, Christmas 1916: VI, no. 2 (Oct 1973) 4–8.

6. Two 'Maata' fragments (1913): IV, no. 1 (May 1974) 4–14.

'Brave Love' (1915), transcribed by Margaret Scott, in *Landfall* (Christchurch) XXVI, no. 1 (Mar 1972) 3–30.

•

II. SELECTED CRITICISM AND BIOGRAPHY

Alpers, Anthony, *Katherine Mansfield: A Biography* (New York: Alfred A. Knopf, 1954). Now superseded by *The Life of Katherine Mansfield* (London: Jonathan Cape, 1979; New York: Viking Press, 1980).

[Baker, Ida], *Katherine Mansfield: The Memories of L. M.* (London: Michael Joseph, 1971).

Berkman, Sylvia, *Katherine Mansfield: A Critical Study* (New Haven, Conn.: Yale University Press, 1951).

Daly, Saralyn, *Katherine Mansfield* (New York: Twayne, 1965).

Magalaner, Marvin, *The Fiction of Katherine Mansfield* (Carbondale, Ill.: Southern Illinois University Press, 1971).

Mantz, Ruth Elvish, and Murry, J. M., *The Life of Katherine Mansfield* (London: Constable, 1933).

Meyers, Jeffrey, *Katherine Mansfield: A Biography* (London: Hamish Hamilton, 1978).

Morrell, Lady Ottoline, *Ottoline: The Early Memoirs, 1873–1915*, ed. Robert Gathorne Hardy (London: Faber and Faber, 1963).

—— *Ottoline at Garsington, 1915–1918*, ed. Robert Gathorne Hardy (London, Faber and Faber, 1974).

Murry, John Middleton, *Between Two Worlds: An Autobiography* (London: Jonathan Cape, 1935).

Index

Katherine Mansfield's juvenilia, letters, poems and story fragments are listed under Katherine Mansfield. Titles of Katherine Mansfield's individual stories and books are listed separately.